May Sinclair

May Sinclair
Re-Thinking Bodies and Minds

Edited by Rebecca Bowler
and Claire Drewery

EDINBURGH
University Press

Edinburgh University Press is one of the leading university presses in the UK. We publish academic books and journals in our selected subject areas across the humanities and social sciences, combining cutting-edge scholarship with high editorial and production values to produce academic works of lasting importance. For more information visit our website: edinburghuniversitypress.com

© editorial matter and organisation Rebecca Bowler and
  Claire Drewery, 2017
© the chapters their several authors, 2017

Edinburgh University Press Ltd
The Tun – Holyrood Road
12(2f) Jackson's Entry
Edinburgh EH8 8PJ

Typeset in 10.5/13 Adobe Sabon by
Servis Filmsetting Ltd, Stockport, Cheshire

A CIP record for this book is available from the British Library

ISBN 978 1 4744 1575 0 (hardback)
ISBN 978 1 4744 1576 7 (webready PDF)
ISBN 978 1 4744 1577 4 (epub)

The right of Rebecca Bowler and Claire Drewery to be identified as the editors of this work has been asserted in accordance with the Copyright, Designs and Patents Act 1988, and the Copyright and Related Rights Regulations 2003 (SI No. 2498).

Contents

Acknowledgements   vii

    Introduction: May Sinclair's Interdisciplinarity   1
    Rebecca Bowler and Claire Drewery

Part I: The Abstract Intellect

1. 'Dying to Live': Remembering and Forgetting May Sinclair   21
   Suzanne Raitt
2. Learning Greek: The Woman Artist as Autodidact in May Sinclair's *Mary Olivier: A Life*   39
   Elise Thornton
3. Portrait of the Female Character as a Psychoanalytical Case: The Ambiguous Influence of Freud on May Sinclair's Novels   59
   Leslie de Bont
4. Feminism, Freedom and the Hierarchy of Happiness in the Psychological Novels of May Sinclair   79
   Wendy Truran
5. Architecture, Environment and 'Scenic Effect' in May Sinclair's *The Divine Fire*   98
   Terri Mullholland

Part II: Abject Bodies

6. Disembodying Desire: Ontological Fantasy, Libidinal Anxiety and the Erotics of Renunciation in May Sinclair   119
   Faye Pickrem

7 May Sinclair and Physical Culture: Fit Greeks and Flabby
   Victorians   139
   Rebecca Bowler
8 Dolls and Dead Babies: Victorian Motherhood in May
   Sinclair's *Life and Death of Harriett Frean*   156
   Charlotte Beyer
9 Why British Society Had to 'Get a Young Virgin Sacrificed:'
   Sacrificial Destiny in *The Tree of Heaven*   177
   Sanna Melin Schyllert
10 'Odd How the War Changes Us': May Sinclair and
   Women's War Work   194
   Emma Liggins
11 Transgressing Boundaries; Transcending Bodies: Sublimation
   and the Abject Corpus in *Uncanny Stories* and *Tales Told by
   Simpson*   213
   Claire Drewery

Notes on Contributors   232
Index   235

Acknowledgements

The editors would like to convey our thanks and appreciation to all contributors to this volume for their excellent chapters, collegiality and enthusiasm for the project. We extend grateful thanks to May Sinclair Society members for a valuable exchange of ideas and knowledge at our introductory symposium in July 2014, and also for their contributions to our Society website. This book would not have been possible without their input. We are indebted to Suzanne Raitt for co-founding the Society with us and giving an excellent keynote talk at the First Symposium, and also to Charlotte Jones, James Connelly and Colin Tyler of the University of Hull, Christine Battersby, Helen Clifford of the Swaledale Museum at Reeth and David McKnight of the Rare Book and Manuscript Library, University of Pennsylvania. Thanks go to Jackie Jones, Rebecca McKenzie, James Dale and Adela Rauchova of Edinburgh University Press, and also to our peer-reviewers for their constructive, helpful feedback. Very special thanks are also due for the constant support and guidance of our valued colleagues at Sheffield Hallam and Keele Universities: Sue McPherson, Katharine Cox, Matthew Pateman, Ana María Sánchez-Arce, Scott McCracken and Chris Hopkins. Above all, our love and appreciation belong to Joe, Iain and Nathaniel.

Rebecca Bowler and Claire Drewery

Introduction: May Sinclair's Interdisciplinarity

Rebecca Bowler and Claire Drewery

May Sinclair was a bestselling author of her day, but her versatile literary output, including criticism, philosophy, poetry, psychoanalysis, cultural history and experimental fiction, now frequently falls between the established categories of literary modernism. Her novels gained international praise and huge popularity in her lifetime. At the beginning of the twentieth century she was famous as the writer of *The Divine Fire* (1904) which was a bestseller in England and America, selling 200,000 copies in the States. All her subsequent novels sold well, and she began to publish essays on class politics as well as philosophy, feminism, war and the new science of psychoanalysis. She became a much-fêted public intellectual. She championed Imagism and other avant-garde literary movements, and her numerous articles on the Brontë sisters are emblematic of the fin-de-siècle repositioning of these writers as cultural icons (she subsequently wrote a biography of the Brontës, and introductions to every volume of the Everyman editions of their novels). She was a novelist and an influential literary historian, but she was much more than this: she was a philosopher, psychologist, biographer, literary critic and essayist.

The interdisciplinarity of Sinclair's output, whilst ensuring her success as an author, eludes straightforward categorisation and this has arguably contributed to the traditional critical neglect of her writing. The reversal of Sinclair's all-but-omission from critical accounts of modernism began with Theophilus Boll's 1959 biography, *Miss May Sinclair: Novelist*; conceived after a series of meetings between Boll, Sinclair's nephew Harold Sinclair, his wife Muriel, and Sinclair's long-term companion, Florence Bartrop. On a visit to Bartrop at her cottage in Bierton, Boll discovered Sinclair's papers housed within her garage in a collection of cardboard boxes and an iron trunk. The online introduction to the

'May Sinclair Papers' housed in the Kisak Center at the University of Pennsylvania details the finding of these materials, which for two weeks were examined, organised and labelled by Boll. These papers, donated by Boll to the Pennsylvania archives as the '[g]ift of Harold L. Sinclair and Theophilus Boll, 1959 and 1976', comprise:

> personal and professional correspondence; manuscripts, typescripts, and galleys of published and unpublished novels, short stories, critical reviews, and poetry. Sinclair's literary, philosophical, and psychological writings represent the majority of the collection. Also included is a series of workbooks containing Sinclair's work in the planning stages.

The wealth of information uncovered by Boll, together with his resulting biography, enabled the subsequent, gradual revival of critical interest in Sinclair traced by Suzanne Raitt in the opening essay of this collection. The increasing accessibility of Sinclair's works online, the existence of the May Sinclair Society, founded by Raitt alongside Rebecca Bowler and Claire Drewery in July 2013, and a steadily-growing body of secondary work now mean, Raitt observes, that 'academics are more likely to encounter May Sinclair and more likely to be supported in doing research on her. In other words, she is gaining critical legitimacy, and those who work on her can find a community' (Raitt 2016: 23). This collection of essays brings together the most recent research on Sinclair by established scholars on Sinclair, women's writing and modernism, as well as new researchers who bring in fresh ideas from the completion stages of PhD study. The essays are grouped under two sections entitled 'The Abstract Intellect' and 'Abject Bodies', and address various ways in which Sinclair endeavoured to formulate recognisably modernist aesthetic techniques through which subjective, physical and intellectual experience might be represented.

Modernism, Minds and Bodies

May Sinclair's modernism pivots on her engagement in contemporary aesthetic and intellectual discourses in which the privileging of consciousness invariably falls back on material language and the physical body. This is one of the tensions explored by the essays in this volume. In both Sinclair's fiction and non-fiction, modernist reconceptualisations of subjectivity, consciousness and human identity centre upon negotiations between the public and private, the cerebral and the corporeal, and the spiritual and the profane. The interrelations and conflicts between these spheres have been theorised by Raymond Williams in his seminal study *Marxism and Literature*, in which he emphasises the importance of a consideration of consciousness as operating within the context of a physical world permeated by cultural production and 'manifest social elements':

> For consciousness is not only knowledge, just as language is not only indication and naming. It is also what is elsewhere, and in this context necessarily, specialised as 'imagination'. In cultural production (and all consciousness is in this sense produced) the true range is from information and description, or naming and indication, to embodiment and *performance*. (1977: 139)

Both modernism and Marxism also encompass a shift towards early-twentieth-century conceptualisations of the fragmented, divided subject as opposed to a biological, essentialist model of human identity. According to Peter Childs, both reflect an era of crisis entailing a loss of communal identity and the 'bringing together of the human with the machine' (2008: 40):

> [Modernism's] historical and social background includes the emergence of the New Woman, the peak and downturn of the British Empire, unprecedented technological change, the rise of the Labour Party, the appearance of factory-line mass production, war in Africa, Europe and elsewhere. Modernism has, therefore, almost universally been considered as a literature of not just change, but crisis. (2008: 15–16)

The work of thinkers like Marx, Engels and Freud conceivably paved the way for modernist representations of subjectivity which worked against traditional, biological humanism. Neil Badmington claims that such a stance was enabled by Marx and Engels, because they challenged 'the humanist belief in a natural human essence which exists outside history, politics and social relations' (5) and Freud, because he unmasks humanity as 'motivated by desires which escape the rule of consciousness' with Man thereby losing '"his" place at the centre of things'. 'To read Freud', Badmington concludes, 'is to witness the waning of humanism' (6). Michael Bell likewise argues that, as opposed to being tainted with a humanist ideology which 'naturalised' the given social order, a central recognition of the various aesthetic movements comprising modernism was 'the relative status of the human' (1999: 13). Sinclair was intensely interested in the status of the human, and in her reading of Freud, Jung and others she traced her own psychological theories about the dangers of the unfettered or repressed libido, and artistic expression and physical activity as necessary sublimation; plotting through her psychoanalytical thought how the excesses of the body could be channelled towards the higher life of the mind. Bell argues that Freud's interrogation of the process of sublimation showed how 'consciousness may itself act as a sophisticated barrier to recognising the true nature of instinctual desire. And this is not just a personal problem to be diagnosed, it is the necessary basis of civilisation' (1999: 9). Sublimation is the crux of Sinclair's theories in her writings on psychoanalysis and idealism, and recurs in a number of essays in the collection. Marx and Freud's theories enabled the reconceptualisation of human consciousness that was central to the modernist project.

As Tim Armstrong points out in *Modernism, Technology, and the Body*, the relationship between the body (corps) and the text (corpus) are complicated by modernism's privileging of consciousness and the higher mind on the one hand, and its 'desire to *intervene* in the body' on the other. His study seeks to 'trace the unstable movements between body and text which are themselves central to Modernism, and, in particular, the will-to-power involved in those moments where modernist writers seek to link text and body, to resolve that constitutive uncertainty' (1998: 6). This tension between the embodied and human as offset against the mystical higher self of consciousness is one of Sinclair's prevailing themes, and this is frequently parodied in her satirical depictions of the literary marketplace. Sinclair jealously guarded her privacy and was very careful about her literary reputation. She left no diary or journal. In Raitt's biography of Sinclair, she observes that some of Sinclair's extant letters have small sections cut out of them, 'as if whoever was preparing her correspondence for posterity was on the lookout for events or feelings which needed to be excised' (2000: 6). Raitt continues: 'Her resistance to biography did not mean she did not care whether or not she was forgotten: quite the reverse. Her anxiety was that if too much was known about her private life, however uneventful it was, she would be remembered not as a writer, but as a woman' (Raitt 2000: 9). Raitt picks up these threads again in the first chapter of this volume, '"Dying to live": remembering and forgetting May Sinclair'. In this reading, Sinclair is always trying to escape the corporeal world, and specifically the pain of the past:

> For Sinclair, the past was a wound. She feared being unable to escape it, and she feared in turn her own persistence in a form that she could not control. Mystic ecstasy – what she called the 'new mysticism' – was a way of entering a timeless realm in which there was no longer any past to damage her. But she was also fascinated by what could never be left behind – hence her interest in heredity, the unconscious, and the supernatural. (2016: 22)

The ties that bind the artist to this world are necessary to the production of art, and hinder it. The physical body, the social world and the literary marketplace are both material for art and threats against it. As George

Tanqueray says to Jane Holland in *The Creators*: '"People – people – people – we can't have enough of 'em; we can't keep off 'em. The thing is – to keep 'em off us"' (1910: 10). Raitt's chapter is an excellent introduction to current scholarship on Sinclair, the issues surrounding canonisation and the performance of literary reputation in the literary marketplace, and Sinclair's intellectual interest in theories of mind and their relation to the body: her psychology, philosophy and mysticism.

Consciousness and 'the Abstract Intellect'

Until recently, one of Sinclair's best-remembered contributions to the dominant aesthetic paradigms of literary modernism has undoubtedly been her reconceptualisation of the psychological novel as 'stream-of-consciousness' narrative. Her appropriation of this term, its first acknowledged use in a literary context, appeared in her 1918 review of Dorothy Richardson's *Pilgrimage* and subsequently became the *leitmotif* of Sinclair's own experimentations with the psychological novel, featuring most notably in the two works considered her main contributions to the modernist canon: *Mary Olivier: A Life* (1919), and *Life and Death of Harriett Frean* (1922). Richardson herself, however, loathed the label, writing vehemently that in her opinion Sinclair had devised a 'more than lamentably ill-chosen metaphor' which was 'still, in literary criticism, pursuing its foolish way' (1990: 433). Although Sinclair had also earlier acknowledged that the term was problematic – she wrote in her philosophical work *A Defence of Idealism* that 'the unity of consciousness can certainly not be accounted for or explained on the simple theory of consciousness as a stream' (1917: 80) – Richardson's observation was to prove as enduring as it was accurate. The label has not only persisted in critical accounts of modernism; it has remained synonymous with modernist literature ever since.

Modernism is variously conceptualised as either the sustained preoccupation of artists with subjectivity and interiority, or the response of these same artists to the shocks, ruptures and fissures of modernity, with its trains, wars, cafés and motor cars. In reality, it is about the tension between these two things: how can an artist represent the external physical world as it is perceived by a subjective receiving consciousness? Pericles Lewis identifies modernism as representative of crises which manifested 'in questions about a central feature of literature and art: their ability to represent reality' (2007: 1). More recently, Rebecca Bowler's book *Literary Impressionism* has charted the tensions between subjectivity and objectivity, attempts to represent the unrepresentable, and the series of dislocations between the thing perceived and the written object in the modernist fiction of Dorothy Richardson, Ford Madox Ford, H.D. and May Sinclair. Ástráður Eysteinsson and Vivian Liska also draw attention to the falsifications that occur when modernism is conceptualised primarily as 'an art of interiority and subjectivity': 'When taking a closer look, we may begin to suspect that rather than mediating the inner motions of the mind, modernism is attending to the invisible and slippery border between the inner and outer self – a border that also winds its way through language' (2007: 319).

Sinclair was preoccupied throughout her life with precisely this 'invisible and slippery border between the inner and outer self'. She looked inward and explored the processes of her mind, and then she turned outwards and read about the psychological and biological processes that were behind her experiences. As Mary does in *Mary Olivier*, Sinclair reads in order to find objective validation for her subjective impressions of the world.

Sinclair was, for the most part, not formally educated. She spent one year at Cheltenham Ladies' College and was allowed, by favour of the principal Dorothea Beale, to take Greek and other subjects as special 'electives'. The second chapter in this volume, 'Learning Greek: The Woman Artist as Autodidact in May Sinclair's *Mary Olivier: A Life*', by Elise Thornton, describes the educational practices at Cheltenham Ladies' College and Sinclair's education there, as well as sketching out the progress of her own self-education at home: her reading and the assimilation and development of her intellectual ideas. Thornton writes, of *Mary Olivier*:

> One of the main influences guiding Mary is her desire for knowledge, and Sinclair questions the boundaries of acceptable female education in Victorian England by focusing specifically on Mary's interest in Greek studies; a traditionally masculine subject. Sinclair's extensive detailing of Mary's autodidacticism as a young girl, adolescent and mature adult thoroughly examines the barriers preventing women's intellectual growth in the late nineteenth and early twentieth century. (2016: 39)

Mary's adventures in reading are a form of 'intellectual escapism' (2016: 43) from the restraints of her physical domestic environment. Thornton charts the ambivalence Mary feels towards her reading in Greek as a private matter of the mind, and the beginnings of her writing of poetry as a 'woman artist's insecurities about the public reception of her creativity' (2016: 47): Mary, Thornton writes, 'relies on maintaining the divide between her private passion for poetry and her performative, public self' (2016: 54).

The private self that reads and writes poetry is also the self that has mystical visions of reality, and that experiences sublime moments of 'happiness'. The mystical visions Thornton describes in her chapter were formative experiences for Sinclair, and she read widely in psychology, philosophy and the biological, physical and metaphysical sciences in order to find an explanation for them. Psychoanalysis in particular provided some clues as to the nature of these visions and of the workings of her mind, and these theories, gleaned from her reading, inevitably made it into her novels. As Boll points out, 'When the insights of Freud and Jung filtered into the medical and the popular imagination, she [. . .] exasperated the traditionalist critics by assimilating some of those insights into her novels as reasonable confirmations of her own intuitive creativity' (1973: 313). Contemporary reviewers and readers were either admiring of this interweaving of psychoanalytic theory into fiction, and what 'psychological science [. . .] could tell them about human behaviour' (ibid.), or openly hostile to the practice. In a review of *The Romantic* Katherine Mansfield writes: 'It is not possible to doubt the sincerity of Miss Sinclair's intentions. She is a devoted writer of established reputation. What we do deplore is that she has allowed her love of writing to suffer the eclipse of psycho-analysis' (1930: 274).

Leslie de Bont's chapter, 'Portrait of the Female Character as a Psychoanalytical Case: The Ambiguous Influence of Freud on May Sinclair's Novels', examines the prevalent influence of psychoanalytic theory on May Sinclair's writing in *The Creators* and *Mary Olivier*. Sinclair read Freud's works with great interest, and de Bont posits that her subsequent fiction goes so far as to present her characters as Freudian case studies. However, Sinclair was engaging with psychoanalysis more widely and deeply than many modernist writers. She was not only incorporating psychoanalytical ideas into her fiction, she was writing psychoanalytic papers herself. As de Bont notes, these papers show the breadth of her reading and her interest:

> Sinclair's key psychological research papers – 'The Way of Sublimation' (1915), 'Clinical Lectures' (1916) and 'Psychological Types' (1923) – suggest that she favoured a Jungian-based eclectic approach to psychoanalysis rather than Freud's sexual theory, which she also integrated into her two philosophical books, *A Defence of Idealism* (1917) and *The New Idealism* (1922). (2016: 59)

Herein lies another reason why Sinclair's interdisciplinarity makes her so difficult to contextualise and to canonise: she combines psychology and philosophy (and biology, physics, mathematics and mysticism) in her non-fiction texts so as to make each discipline inform the other. There is also a close similarity between the styles of her fictional and non-fictional writing; discernible for example in the clear dialogue between her two works on philosophical idealism and her volume of short fiction entitled *Uncanny Stories*, or philosophical writings and her experiments with the psychological method in *Mary Olivier: A Life*. Wendy Truran's chapter, 'Feminism, Freedom, and the Hierarchy of Happiness in the Psychological Novels of May Sinclair', navigates some of these interdisciplinary boundaries and discusses sublimation (psychology) and Spinozan pantheism (philosophy) as they relate to the concept of 'affect' in *The Three Sisters*, *Mary Olivier: A Life*, and *Life and Death of Harriett Frean*. Truran raises the question:

> Why focus on happiness when many modernist scholars have either characterised literary modernism as anti-emotional or theorised modernist emotions as predominantly negative? Whilst aesthetic modernism viewed emotions and embodied sentiment with deep suspicion, T. S. Eliot's theory of impersonality being but one example, in fact many modernists sought to re-evaluate the place and function of emotion with arts, science and philosophy. (2016: 80)

Happiness in Sinclair's novels is simultaneously embodied and disembodied. As Truran points out, Sinclair 'privileges a cerebral "perfect happiness" above sensual pleasure, yet she also prefers sexual satisfaction over the damaging repression of the libido' (2016: 80).

Unlike Sinclair, who treated the afterlife as a serious area of philosophical study, her contemporary Virginia Woolf was outwardly sceptical of the supernatural and directly critical of the 'ecstatic moods' Sinclair attached closely to the metaphysical philosophy and sublimative values she explored in her work. In a letter to Lady Robert Cecil in April 1909, Woolf recalled meeting with Sinclair, who 'talked very seriously of her "work"; and ecstatic moods in which she swings (like a spider again) half way to Heaven, detached from earth' *(L1* 390). In Woolf's paraphrase of Sinclair's description, the ecstatic moment enables a detachment from the earth and, implicitly, from the body. Her barely concealed scorn here is, however, misleading. Woolf, like many of her fellow modernists, had a strong mystical bent. Julie Kane has pointed out that the work of Woolf is extremely mysticist, despite her 'posture of utter contempt towards her fellow "mystics" prior to writing *The Waves*' (1995: 328). Dismissive even of mysticism in her friends, Woolf wrote of E. M. Forster that he was 'mystic, silly, but with a childs [sic] insight' (Woolf 1978: 204).

In *Mary Olivier*, as Truran points out, there are several types of happiness. The mystical visions that the young Mary sees are inextricably linked to the physical world, and are thus 'embodied happiness'. The happiness she attains towards the end of the novel is, conversely, enabled by a letting go of all material and earthly ties, much as Sinclair describes herself to Woolf as 'detached from earth'. This happiness, which Truran characterises as 'perfect happiness', is one that Savage Keith Rickman seeks in the novel *The Divine Fire*. However, Rickman, unlike Mary, cannot let go of his earthly ties, and the novel plays out, as Terri Mullholland describes, as a 'struggle with environment' in which 'the inner, spiritual life of the mind and the exterior world of commerce' are always at odds (2016: 100). Mullholland's chapter, 'Architecture, Environment, and "Scenic Effect" in May Sinclair's *The Divine Fire*', explores modernity and particularly the modernity of the commercial public space as threatening to both private domesticity and to the inner life of the artist to whom 'perfect', disembodied happiness and genius are co-dependent. Mullholland evokes Benjamin's concept of the phantasmagoria, 'a term derived from magic lantern shows and exhibitions of optical illusions', and observation of modernity under capitalism as a 'dreamworld, from which society must awake into political consciousness' (2016: 99–100). The navigation of the boundaries between body and mind becomes an issue of 'the play between illusion and reality, exterior and interior, and the commercial versus the domestic' (2016: 98).

Sinclair's literary output contains numerous satirical commentaries on the literary marketplace, which is the key focus of *The Divine Fire* (1904), the novel which made her name, and *The Creators: A Comedy* (1909). Michelle Troy notes that the latter novel was, ironically, 'a resounding failure in the literary marketplace' (2004: 51) and Sinclair herself disliked the serialised version of *The Creators*. Troy notes that 'In a letter of 2 August 1909, to American poet Witter Bynner, Sinclair further declares that the drive to meet deadlines has reduced *The Creators* to a "dreadful" and "appalling book"' (2004: 69). In Sinclair's short stories, the volume of *Tales Told by Simpson* in particular, there is an ironic recognition that the 'immortalising' of authors after death by publishers and biographers determines this transitional process into posterity or obscurity. Her stories 'The Pin-Prick', 'The Wrackham Memoirs' and 'Fame' are all ironic commentaries on the theme of the literary marketplace, as discussed in Claire Drewery's chapter; the corruption of capitalism represented by the 'abject' body of the artist's textual corpus.

Physicality and 'the Material Body'

In her essay 'Professions for Women', first delivered as a lecture to the National Society for Women's Service on 21 January 1931, Virginia

Woolf identified two related, gender-specific issues which must be confronted by the woman writer. First was her famous proclamation of the symbolic murder of the phantom 'Angel in the House', whose pretensions to Victorian sacrifice and domestic servitude threatened to 'pluck the heart' out of Woolf's writing. The second was the woman writer's confrontation with the physical body:

> Her imagination had [. . .] sought the pools, the depths, the dark places where the largest fish slumber. And then there was a smash. There was an explosion. There was foam and confusion. The imagination had dashed itself against something hard. The girl was roused from her dream. [. . .] To speak without figure she had thought of something, something about the body, about the passions which it was unfitting for her as a woman to say. (2000: 357)

For Woolf the inhibitions of 'the extreme conventionality of the other sex' prevented the woman writer from 'telling the truth about my own experiences as a body'. This is a problem Woolf doubts any woman writer has solved, because the obstacles 'are still immensely powerful – and yet they are very difficult to define' (2000: 359–60). The fact that Sinclair's novels repeatedly return to sex and sexuality appears to refute this claim. As much as she hankers after a perfect happiness or a disembodied state, she is drawn again and again to stories 'about the body, about the passions which it was unfitting for her as a woman to say'. As George Johnson notes, the sexual natures of Sinclair's characters 'are revealed with a surprising degree of candidness, considering the period in which she wrote' (2006: 116). This point in history is noted for the censorious nature of the society and literary marketplace in which Sinclair lived and worked; a theme Adam Parkes explores in detail in his study of *Modernism and the Theatre of Censorship*. Parkes writes that in his view, 'the development of literary modernism was shaped in significant ways by an ongoing dialogue with a culture of censorship' (Parkes 1996: viii). Sinclair's frank, often explicit representations of sexuality, couched as they are in terms of psychological repression and hysteria, are all the more surprising at a time when literature was often banned outright if censors detected what they saw as an outrage to public decency.

As Herbert Howarth has noted, however, Sinclair 'had courage in literature, which rushed her to the confrontation of sex ahead of other novelists, and courage in life which sent her to the Belgian battlefields with the Red Cross in 1914' (1965: 272). Rachel Potter has pointed out that the *Little Review*'s serialisation of James Joyce's *Ulysses* is an extreme example of what could happen to a literary work if sex and the body were treated too explicitly. In America, the 'Nausicca' episode, 'in which Bloom masturbates while gazing at the teenage Gerty MacDowell' prompted police 'to seize copies of the journal and take the editors to court for publishing obscene literature' (2013: 93). Likewise, in the UK five sections of the book had been published in the *Egoist* before the printer bowed to the constraints of 'the less public judgements of printers, customs officials, the director of public prosecutions, and the Home Office' (ibid.). Whilst blasphemy and politically seditious language were pitfalls for contemporary editors it was, nonetheless, references to sex and the body which saw the banning of books and the ensuing obscenity trials. In the writing of her fiction, Sinclair had to negotiate this threat of censorship, and her ambivalent attitudes towards the constraints imposed are reflected in her depictions of the abstract intellect and material bodies.

Faye Pickrem's chapter, 'Disembodying Desire: Ontological Fantasy, Libidinal Anxiety and the Erotics of Renunciation in May Sinclair', examines Sinclair's writing through an analysis of desire, anxiety and the process of subjectivisation. Pickrem isolates the markers of anxiety that haunt both Sinclair's fiction and theory and argues that these textual tics betray abhorrence, disgust and even contempt for the body with respect to base carnality and the 'unharnessed libido', as well as an insistent need to corral and discipline the libido into what she deems to be a higher, sublimated form:

> In her textual bid for Hegelian wholeness, Sinclair employs philosophical idealism and psychology as tools for 'psycho-synthesis'. Reader and protagonist are discursively 'situated' so as to be 'lured by the vision of that "Sublimation" which is held out before him as the end'. (2016: 120)

There is gap, an absence, and a fissure between mind and body that sublimation of the libido into artistic and creative endeavour only partially solves. Rebecca Bowler's chapter, 'May Sinclair and Physical Culture: Fit Greeks and Flabby Victorians', extends this discussion of the sublimation of the libido to a consideration of physical activity in Sinclair's psychological novel *Mary Olivier: A Life* and her earlier work, *The Combined Maze*. Bowler writes that Sinclair's characters, throughout her fiction, are 'continually negotiating the boundaries between their free and wild pagan selves and their higher ideals; of intellectual or of moral and spiritual beauty'. The tension between mind and body is one that plays itself out in non-artists and non-intellectuals as well:

> In 'primitive man', Sinclair says, much of the libido must have been channelled into 'the energies of battle and hunting and later of agriculture'. She presents a model of sublimation in which the libido, in creative and intellectual people, manifests itself as cultural production, and in less intelligent people manifests as 'concrete' production or as physical activity. In both of these types, sublimation is linked to morality. (2016: 143)

This chapter explores the rise of physical culture at the very beginning of the twentieth century and the way echoes of this modernist emphasis on 'fitness' (physical and moral) echo through Sinclair's oeuvre. The desirable modernist body was one that was fit for purpose; machine-like; in tune with the Vortex.

Women's bodies, however, were not always included in discourses about strength, efficiency and modernity, or if they were, it was in terms of their fallibility and weakness, or their role as mothers of the race. The next three articles, 'Dolls and Dead Babies: Victorian Motherhood in May Sinclair's *Life and Death of Harriett Frean*' by Charlotte Beyer, 'Why British Society Had to "Get a Young Virgin Sacrificed": Sacrificial Destiny in *The Tree of Heaven*' by Sanna Melin Schyllert, and 'Odd How the War Changes Us: May Sinclair and Women's War Work' by Emma Liggins all explore the representation of the female body in Sinclair's fiction.

In Beyer's chapter, representations of mothering, class and maternal affect are brought to the fore. Her chapter argues that Sinclair's *Life and Death of Harriett Frean* engages with the social and cultural dimensions of maternal identity by problematising the lack of maternal power and agency, and by foregrounding the complexities of class and religion in relation to maternal experience. The presentation of the maternal figure in Sinclair's novels is complex, featuring 'the idealisation of the mother-figure and an emphasis on feminine appearance and conduct on the one hand and, on the other, the erasure of motherhood through the hidden and hushed-up practice of baby-farming' (2016: 158). In Schyllert's chapter, women's bodies are erased even more comprehensively. Sinclair believed, and wrote in 'A Defence of Men', that because women are continually required by society and their own moral codes to sacrifice themselves to some higher cause, they attain to spirituality more readily than men. In other words, women have access to the higher realm of disembodied mind because they can, and do, sacrifice their bodies. As Schyllert writes: 'To be required to sacrifice one's sexual desire, or in other words to sublimate one's libido, is a fundamental aspect of being a Sinclair heroine' (2016: 178). The presence of women's bodies on the battlefields of the First World War is equally problematic. As Schyllert writes in her chapter:

> Sinclair's texts written around the time of the war exhibit the opposition between the needs of the community and that of the individual, which is an issue that comes to the fore in times of national crisis. The concept of sacrifice, then, is not only central to Sinclair's work, but evolves with it through the early decades of the twentieth century. (2016: 191)

Liggins extends this discussion to a cultural and historical reading of Sinclair's war fiction and her autobiographical *A Journal of Impressions in Belgium*. At a time when modernist fiction was still trying to find a suitable place and role for the surplus woman, Sinclair offered a significant commentary in her novels on the choices between work, domesticity and politics for her female characters. However, her public endorsement of women's work is at odds with contradictory attitudes to the woman worker in her fiction, who is often repositioned in the boredom of home in the final chapters. The chapter considers male and female reactions to the dangerous figure of the woman in khaki in war fiction, a visual reminder of the incongruity between the old domestic self and the modern type of patriotic female masculinity. Sexual difference appears inescapable at the Front, even as Sinclair considers ways in which it might be transcended through war work.

In the final chapter of the volume, Claire Drewery's 'Transgressing Boundaries; Transcending Bodies: Sublimation and the Abject Corpus in *Uncanny Stories* and *Tales Told by Simpson*', we return to sublimation and to Sinclair's ambivalence about the purity of the higher mind and the taint of the physical. Sinclair's short fiction, Drewery argues, displays 'a continual aesthetic tension between the spiritual form of subjective consciousness frequently associated with the modernist epiphany – in Sinclair's writing represented as spiritual and pure – and physical, corporeal sexuality which, conversely, she depicts as repellent, distorted and grotesque' (2016: 213). Like Faye Pickrem's, this chapter argues that the body is rejected as a site of unsublimated sexuality; but where Pickrem investigates this under the framework of Sinclair's philosophical theories of the Hegelian Absolute, this chapter, which interrogates the links between Sinclair's aesthetic of sublimation and the Joycean epiphany, focuses upon Sinclair's psychoanalytic writings on sublimation: principally in her two 'Clinical Lectures on Symbolism and Sublimation'. The chapter also draws upon the theoretical framework of Kristeva's essay on abjection, *Powers of Horror*, and the Freudian uncanny to explore Sinclair's depiction of abject physical bodies and privileging of the cerebral form of spiritual ecstasy she associates with artistic sublimation.

Critical Context

There are currently few monographs devoted exclusively to May Sinclair. Other than three biographical studies – Theophilus E. M. Boll's *Miss May Sinclair: Novelist* (1973), Hrisey D. Zegger's *May Sinclair*

(1976) and Suzanne Raitt's *May Sinclair: A Modern Victorian* (2000) – the first book-length study devoted exclusively to Sinclair was the 2006 volume *May Sinclair: Moving Towards the Modern* (ed. Kunka and Troy), in which the individual essays address the cultural and literary influences on Sinclair's work and her interest in contemporary discourses surrounding psychoanalysis, feminism, suffragism and the First World War. Since the appearance of this volume more than a decade ago there have been no further full-length studies devoted to May Sinclair. Yet the traditional critical neglect of her work has continued to be redressed in recent years.[1]

This volume's focus on Sinclair's engagement with the contemporary literary, intellectual and philosophical discourses of modernism and their radical reappraisal of subjective identity is an attempt to bring together the divergent disciplines of Sinclair's interdisciplinarity and to make connections between her different intellectual interests and endeavours. Together, the two sections of the book investigate the many fruitful connections between Sinclair's fictional, critical and philosophical output and the structures of epochal change traditionally associated with literary modernism. They focus in particular upon Sinclair's engagement with early-twentieth-century cultural changes in perceptions of the construction and representation of the human subject. There still remains a great deal to say about Sinclair's astonishing body of work – fiction, poetry, philosophy and psychological essays – which can shed further light on her significant and interdisciplinary contribution to literary modernism.

Situating May Sinclair within a modernist context reveals her influence as having been more extensive than her experimentations with the psychological novel or coining of the 'stream-of-consciousness' label might suggest. Her contributions to contemporary intellectual and psychological discourses in both her fiction and non-fictional interdisciplinary writings on idealism, psychoanalysis, sublimation and feminism offer fresh potential for investigating possible influences on the key modernist aesthetics of mysticism, moments of transcendent insight and the radical contemporary shift in the textual representation of subjective experience. Ultimately, the essays and the volume as a whole conclude that Sinclair's work might be reappraised in this context as having made a significant contribution to the radical modernist challenge to traditional assumptions about what it means to be human.

Note

1. A bibliography of works on Sinclair appears on the May Sinclair Society website and is continually updated.

Works Cited

Armstrong, Tim (1998), *Modernism, Technology and the Body: A Cultural Study*, Cambridge: Cambridge University Press.
Badmington, Neil, ed. (2000), *Posthumanism*, London: Routledge.
Bell, Michael (1999), 'The Metaphysics of Modernism', in Michael Levenson (ed.), *The Cambridge Companion to Modernism*, Cambridge: Cambridge University Press, pp. 9–32.
Boll, Theophilus E. M. (1973), *Miss May Sinclair: Novelist: A Biographical and Critical Introduction*, Cranbury, NJ: Associated University Presses.
Bowler, Rebecca (2016), *Literary Impressionism: Vision and Memory in Dorothy Richardson, Ford Madox Ford, H.D., and May Sinclair*, London: Bloomsbury.
Childs, Peter (2008), *Modernism*, 2nd edn, London and New York: Routledge.
Eysteinsson, Ástráður, and Vivian Liska, eds (2007), *Modernism: A Comparative History of Literatures in European Languages*, Amsterdam and Philadelphia: John Benjamins Publishing Co.
Howarth, Herbert (1964), *Notes on Some Figures behind T. S. Eliot*, Boston: Houghton Mifflin.
Johnson, George (2006), *Dynamic Psychology in Modernist British Fiction*, Basingstoke: Palgrave Macmillan.
Kane, Julie (1995), 'Varieties of mystical experience in the writings of Virginia Woolf', *Twentieth Century Literature* 41:4 (Winter), 328–49.
Kunka, Andrew J., and Michele K. Troy, eds (2006), *May Sinclair: Moving Towards the Modern*, Aldershot: Ashgate.
Lewis, Pericles (2007), *The Cambridge Introduction to Modernism*, Cambridge: Cambridge University Press.
Mansfield, Katherine (1930), *Novels and Novelists*, London: Constable and Co., Ltd.
Neff, Rebeccah Kinnamon (1979), '"New Mysticism" in the Writings of May Sinclair and T. S. Eliot', *Twentieth Century Literature* 26, 82–108.
Neff, Rebeccah Kinnamon (1983), 'May Sinclair's *Uncanny Stories* as Metaphysical Quest', *English Literature in Transition* 26:3, 187–91.
Parkes, Adam (1996), *Modernism and the Theater of Censorship*, New York and Oxford: Oxford University Press.
Pound, Ezra (1988), *Pound/The Little Review: The Letters of Ezra Pound to Margaret Anderson: The 'Little' Review Correspondence*, ed. Thomas L. Scott, Melvin J. Friedman and Jackson R. Bryer, New York: New Directions.
Raitt, Suzanne (2000), *May Sinclair: A Modern Victorian*, Oxford: Clarendon Press.

Richardson, Dorothy (1990), 'Novels', in Bonnie Kime Scott (ed.), *The Gender of Modernism: A Critical Anthology*, Bloomington: Indiana University Press, pp. 432–5.
Richardson, Dorothy (1995), *Windows on Modernism: Selected Letters of Dorothy Richardson*, Athens: University of Georgia Press.
Sinclair, May (1904), *The Divine Fire*, London: Archibald Constable and Co.
Sinclair, May (1910), *The Creators: A Comedy*, London: Hutchinson and Co.
Sinclair, May (1912a), 'A Defence of Men', *The Forum* 48 (October 1912), 409–20.
Sinclair, May (1912b), *The Three Brontës*, London: Hutchinson.
Sinclair, May (1913), *The Combined Maze*, New York and London: Harper & Brothers.
Sinclair, May (1914), *The Three Sisters*, London: Hutchinson.
Sinclair, May (1917), *A Defence of Idealism: Some Questions and Conclusions*, London: Macmillan.
Sinclair, May [1919] (1980a), *Mary Olivier: A Life*, intro. Jean Radford, London: Virago.
Sinclair, May (1922), *The New Idealism*, London: Macmillan.
Sinclair, May [1922] (1980b), *Life and Death of Harriett Frean*, intro. Jean Radford, London: Virago.
Sinclair, May (1923), *Uncanny Stories*, London: Hutchinson.
Sinclair, May (1930), *Tales Told by Simpson*, New York: Macmillan.
Sinclair, May (1990a), 'Prufrock and Other Observations: A Criticism', in Bonnie Kime Scott (ed.), *The Gender of Modernism: A Critical Anthology*, Bloomington: Indiana University Press, pp. 448–53.
Sinclair, May (1990b), 'The Reputation of Ezra Pound', in Bonnie Kime Scott (ed.), *The Gender of Modernism: A Critical Anthology*, Bloomington: Indiana University Press, pp. 468–76.
Troy, Michele K. (2004), 'May Sinclair's *The Creators*: High-Cultural Celebrity and a Failed Comedy', *English Literature in Transition (1880–1920)* 47:1, 50–74.
Williams, Raymond (1977), *Marxism and Literature*, Oxford: Oxford University Press.
Woolf, Virginia [1909] (1976), 'To Lady Robert Cecil', 12 April 1909 (letter 480) in Nigel Nicolson and Joanne Trautmann (eds), *The Flight of the Mind: The Collected Letters of Virginia Woolf*, vol. 1 (1888–1912), New York: Harcourt, pp. 389–90.
Woolf, Virginia (1978), *The Diary of Virginia Woolf, vol. 2 (1920–4)*, ed. Anne Olivier Bell, London: The Hogarth Press.
Woolf, Virginia [1931] (2000), 'Professions for Women', in Michèle Barrett (ed.), *A Room of One's Own/Three Guineas*, London: Penguin, pp. 356–61.
Zegger, Hrisey D. (1976), *May Sinclair*, Boston: Twayne.

Online Resources

The May Sinclair Society, https://maysinclairsociety.com (last accessed 21 June 2016).

The May Sinclair Papers, Kislak Center for Special Collections, Rare Books and Manuscripts, University of Pennsylvania, http://dla.library.upenn.edu/dla/ead/detail.html?id=EAD_upenn_rbml_MsColl184 (last accessed 21 June 2016).

Part I
The Abstract Intellect

Chapter 1

'Dying to Live': Remembering and Forgetting May Sinclair
Suzanne Raitt

Virginia Woolf did not think much of May Sinclair. When she had tea with her in 1909, she wrote to Lady Robert Cecil that Sinclair was a 'woman of obtrusive, and medicinal morality' with 'little round eyes bright as steel' (Woolf 1976: 390). But Woolf was famously catty about writers with whom she felt a sense of rivalry, and it was Sinclair, not Woolf, who was the first of the pair to publish an experimental, stream-of-consciousness novel (*Mary Olivier: A Life*, in 1919). The two writers had more in common than Woolf would care to admit. Both were interested in reproducing the texture of the inner world; both were preoccupied with the psychology of women; and both sought to explore the process and experience of memory: the 'present sliding over the depths of the past', as Woolf would put it years later in her memoir (Woolf 1985: 98). In 1917, Sinclair imagined what it might be like if we had no psyche to select and shape what we remember:

> Suppose that we remember, never because we choose, but always because we must [. . .] then our consciousness would be like nothing on earth but an immense fantastic telephone exchange; an exchange where messages, indeed, received and registered and answered themselves, but all at once, and in overwhelming multitudes; an exchange deafened and disorganised; bells ringing incessantly all through its working hours; messages rushing in from all parts of the city and suburbs at once, crossed and recrossed by trunk calls from all parts of the outlying country; casually crossing and recrossing, interrupting and utterly obliterating each other. (Sinclair 1917: 104–5)

Sinclair suggests that not the brain but the psyche brings order to this potential chaos: 'the psyche uses the brain, and the memories which have become the habits of its body and its brain, as its machine, and its vehicle; and [. . .] the secret of its remembering and forgetting is its own' (Sinclair 1917: 105). Sinclair favoured the idea that 'psychical disposition' (Sinclair 1917: 105–6) working through 'an act of will' (Sinclair 1917: 17) could free the consciousness from the burden of the past, but she was not entirely sure that this idea was right. Indeed, she spent much of her career – at least after 1914 – preoccupied with how to manage her relationship to the past. For Sinclair, the past was a wound. She feared being unable to escape it, and she feared in turn her own persistence in a form that she could not control. Mystic ecstasy – what, in *The Defence of Idealism*, she called the 'new mysticism' (Chapter 7) – was a way of entering an other-worldly realm in which the past, dissolved into timelessness, could no longer do any harm. But she was also fascinated by what could never be left behind – hence her interest in heredity, the unconscious and the supernatural. This chapter traces the ambivalence with which Sinclair wrote about remembering, being remembered and being forgotten. Sinclair was both eager to be remembered (though in a form she could control) and also preoccupied with – and frightened of – what it means not to forget.

May Sinclair – like so many others – has a chequered history as far as her literary reputation is concerned. A bestseller in the early decades of the twentieth century, her star waned during the late 1920s and was almost extinguished for many years after her death in 1946. The tide began to turn when in 1959, Theophilus Boll, Professor of English at the University of Pennsylvania, to whom all Sinclair critics owe a great debt, met Harold and Muriel Sinclair – May Sinclair's nephew and his wife – while on a trip to scout out primary sources for a biography of an English modernist woman writer. The Sinclairs directed Boll to their aunt's last home in Aylesbury, where he found the papers that formed the basis for his biography of Sinclair in 1973 (Boll 1961: 4 ff.). There were intermittent articles on Sinclair throughout the 1970s and early 1980s, and Hrisey Zegger's book in the Twayne English Authors series came out in 1976.[1] During the wave of feminist recovery in the early 1980s, Virago Press reissued *Mary Olivier*, *The Life and Death of Harriett Frean* and *The Three Sisters* with introductions by Jean Radford in their Modern Classics series. But by the early 1990s, when I started work on my own biography of Sinclair, those three volumes were no longer in print. A few articles on Sinclair, stimulated perhaps by the continued circulation of the Virago volumes, appeared in the 1990s.[2] My own biography of Sinclair, *May Sinclair: A Modern Victorian*, was published in 2000, and a few of Sinclair's novels were reissued during the subsequent decade. In 2002, New York Review Books published a new edition of *Mary Olivier*; in 2003, Random House republished *Life and Death of Harriett Frean* in their Twentieth-Century Rediscoveries series; and in 2006, the Wordsworth Press issued a volume containing *Uncanny Stories* and 'The

Intercessor'. Michele Troy and Andrew Kunka's edited collection, *May Sinclair: Moving Towards the Modern*, appeared in 2006, and three of Sinclair's stories ('Victim', 'Token', 'Villa Désirée') were anthologised in 2008 and in 2012 as classic examples of the ghostly and the erotic. Most of Sinclair's texts are now available online on Project Gutenberg, Hathitrust Digital Library and/or the Internet Archive; Bibliobazaar and HardPress will supply unedited photographic copies of many of the novels. In July 2013, Rebecca Bowler, Claire Drewery and I founded the May Sinclair Society, which held its inaugural conference in the summer of 2014. Edinburgh University Press will shortly embark on a series of critical editions of Sinclair's works. Add to that the increasing number of critics who have been steadily publishing on Sinclair over the last decade or so, and it looks as if May Sinclair is making a comeback.[3] Even her Rolls-Royce resurfaced recently in Sarasota, Florida ('May Sinclair's Rolls Royce', 2015).

So what does this resurgence – if it is a resurgence, rather than a consolidation of work that has been quietly going on for thirty or forty years – mean? One obvious point is that it is easier to join a conversation than to start one. The existence of the Society and a small but growing body of secondary work means that academics are more likely to encounter May Sinclair and more likely to be supported in doing research on her. In other words, she is gaining critical legitimacy, and those who work on her can find a community. It is easier for academics to acquire her texts, and there are more reference works to fill in biographical and other details. She has always been popular with general readers, when they were able to find her works. I remember my excitement when in 1998, a friend handed me a copy of the *Nation* in which columnist Katha Pollitt mentioned in passing 'the once-celebrated, now totally forgotten novels of May Sinclair, which I love' (Pollitt 1998); in 2002 Pollitt wrote the introduction for the New York Review of Books reissue of *Mary Olivier*. More recently, Jonathan Coe and Charlotte Jones have sung May Sinclair's praises in a British national newspaper.

Critics have begun to speculate about the reasons for her comparative neglect. Philippa Martindale suggests that some women writers 'did not fit the traditional version of high Modernism' (Martindale 2003: 7) and were therefore to some extent unintelligible to the critical establishment; George Johnson notes that 'Sinclair produced a large number of novels, not all of which maintained a high quality, but the same might be said of D. H. Lawrence, who has consistently maintained a place in the canon' (Johnson 2004: 179). James Miracky is more forthright in his denunciation of some of Sinclair's early novels, calling them 'offensively elitist', 'numbingly clichéd', and full of 'passages of lofty prose, heavy-handed symbolism, and idealized characterization' (Miracky 2003: 75, 72). There is also the question of the wide range of Sinclair's interests and a division in her following because of it, some critics (such as Christine Battersby and Elizabeth Mosimann) emphasising her philosophical thought, others (for example, Philippa Martindale and Luke Thurston) looking at her through the lens of psychoanalytic theory and practice, some emphasising her poetry (Jane Dowson) and still others reading her as a feminist modernist. In the patchwork of responses to May Sinclair in the last three or four decades, we see the gradual (though uneven) establishment of a multifaceted critical reputation.

May Sinclair herself, of course, was no stranger to the making and breaking of literary reputations. In the early years of the twentieth century, she involved herself in the development of the Everyman series, founded by J. M. Dent in 1906 with the goal of making classic novels available – usually in single volumes – at affordable prices: 'for a few shillings, the reader may have a whole bookshelf of the immortals' ('History', 2015). Between 1907 and 1914, Sinclair wrote introductions to Everyman editions of six Brontë novels and to Elizabeth Gaskell's *Life of Charlotte Brontë*, and in 1912 she published a biography of the three Brontë sisters, *The Three Brontës*. A year or two later, she made efforts to build the reputations of T. S. Eliot, Ezra Pound, Dorothy Richardson, F. S. Flint, Richard Aldington and H.D., with essays published in the *Little Review*, *The Egoist*, the *English Review*, *The Dial* and the *Fortnightly Review* between 1915 and 1922. In a number of these essays, Sinclair positions herself as the defender of work that is ahead of its time: the 'genius' of *Prufrock, and Other Observations* has produced 'outbursts of silliness' on the part of critics, because Eliot's genius is 'not in any tradition' (Sinclair 1990a: 448, 449); in the essay on H.D., Sinclair defends H.D.'s 'novelty of [. . .] form' (Sinclair 1915: 89) and in the piece on 'The Reputation of Ezra Pound', Sinclair celebrates Pound's 'incorruptible devotion to his craft' (Sinclair 1990c: 469) against accusations of lack of originality and talent.

But she was worried all the same about the future. It is evident in the essays on the Imagists that she disliked it when literature that she valued was misunderstood, dismissed or forgotten. Like any author, she wanted to be read. But her work on the Brontës makes it clear that she did not want to be read for the wrong reasons. She objected to many of the interpretations of the Brontës' lives that were current in 1911, when she was working on *The Three Brontës*, and she explicitly presented her own book as a correction:

> So, because all the best things about the Brontës have been said already, I have had to fall back on the humble day-labour of clearing away some of the rubbish that has gathered round them.
>
> Round Charlotte it has gathered to such an extent that it is difficult to see her plainly through the mass of it. Much has been cleared away; much remains. Mrs Oliphant's dreadful theories are still on record. The excellence of Madame Duclaux's monograph perpetuates her one serious error. Mr Swinburne's *Note* immortalises his. M. Héger was dug up again the other day.
>
> It may be said that I have been calling up ghosts for the mere fun of laying them; and there might be something in it, but that really these ghosts still walk. At any rate many people believe in them, even at this time of day. M. Dimnet believes firmly that poor Mrs Robinson was in love with Branwell Brontë. Some of us still think that Charlotte was in love with M. Héger. They cannot give him up any more than M. Dimnet can give up Mrs Robinson.
>
> Such things would be utterly unimportant but that they tend to obscure the essential quality and greatness of Charlotte Brontë's genius. Because of them she has passed for a woman of one experience and of one book. There is still room for a clean sweep of the rubbish that has been shot here.
>
> In all this, controversy was unavoidable, much as I dislike its ungracious and ungraceful air. If I have been inclined to undervalue certain things – 'the sojourn in Brussels,' for instance – which others have considered of the first importance, it is because I believe that it is always the inner life that counts, and that with the Brontës it supremely counted. (Sinclair 1912: 14–15)

The 'ghosts' with which she had to deal were the spectres of stories about the Brontës' personal lives. When in 1913 four letters from Charlotte Brontë to Constantin Héger were published, Sinclair was incensed: 'we have no business to read what she says', she wrote in an essay in *The Dial* (Sinclair 1913: 344). 'Her case raises a large question of literary ethics, of the public's "right to know", of the biographer's right to publish what was never meant for publication,' she declared. Confronted with this indiscretion, she warned, 'decent average people' would feel 'nothing but the sickness of disgust' (Sinclair 1913: 344, 345). Sinclair also castigated journalists who attempted to publish personal information about her based on informal conversations, writing to Witter Bynner in 1905 after reading a draft of an article he was planning: 'You admit that you have repeated some things told you in confidence! I assure you that if you had intended deliberately to hurt me you cd. not have succeeded better' (Sinclair 1905). The article was never published. She continued to manage her reputation with ruthless efficiency, maintaining a careful reserve in all her published interviews and going through her private papers with a pair of scissors to make sure nothing she wanted to hide would be revealed after her death.

It was not actually the revelation of intimate information or feelings that disgusted her. In the *Dial* essay, she defends – or at least excuses –

the publication of love letters between Robert Browning and Elizabeth Barrett Browning, even though 'publication of even this unique correspondence was regarded by many scrupulous people as more or less an outrage against perfect decency'. However, 'You will not find in them one word which either Robert Browning or his wife could have wished not to have written.' They are 'the expression of a unique and perfect passion', and when he published them, their son was 'in no sense' 'dishonoring his father and mother' (Sinclair 1913: 344).

But Charlotte Brontë's letters to Héger tell a very different story, and this, I think, is key to understanding Sinclair's horror of publicity and her fear of the past. Sinclair notes that what is revealed in Brontë's letters is not her love, but her anguish at the fact that her feelings were not returned. 'They are not the expression of a perfect love, acknowledged and crowned. They are the pitiful, almost abject cry of a passion – secret, unacknowledged, incomplete, such passion, as, with all its innocence, abhors publicity' (Sinclair 1913: 344). The problem for May Sinclair is not the exposure of the intimate language of love, but the exposure of the language of pain – and perhaps especially the language of rejection. In her fiction, when the past does erupt into the present – as it does, by definition, in her ghost stories – it frequently reveals the ways in which the living have damaged the dead, as if past wounds cannot be laid to rest. The supernatural tales depict a nightmare world in which the pain of loss persists unaffected by the passage of time. The uncanny tales are about people who cannot forget; and – as I shall argue later – the only experience Sinclair could imagine that would erase the past and the personal absolutely was the experience of a mystical ecstasy that abandoned time, need and desire absolutely.

Of the seven 'uncanny' stories in the volume Sinclair published in 1923, four are centrally concerned with the pain of rejection. In 'The Token', Cicely, the sister of the narrator, returns as a ghost after her death in the hope that the husband she adores will finally admit that he loves her, reappearing with 'a look of supplication, such supplication as I had seen on my sister's face in her lifetime, when she could do nothing with him and implored me to intercede' (Sinclair 2006: 53). Rosamond, in 'The Nature of the Evidence', repeatedly thwarts her husband's sexual union with his new wife and finally seduces him into sex with her own ghost, which peculiar form of infidelity understandably enough destroys his second marriage. The ghost's intervention reduces the beautiful, though lascivious, second wife to writhing on the floor and pleading: 'Oh, don't, don't push me away!' (Sinclair 2006: 121). In 'The Victim', Steven Acroyd kills the employer who subsequently haunts him, because he believes he dissuaded the woman he loves from marrying him. In 'If the Dead Knew' (and of course they always do), Wilfrid Hollyer causes his mother's death by wishing for it so that he can get married, and is then haunted by the ghost of the mother, who seems to have overheard him complaining about her overbearing ways to his new wife. 'The Intercessor', published in the *English Review* in 1911 and included in the 2006 reissue of *Uncanny Stories*, similarly contains the ghost of a child who returns because her mother has rejected her.

In almost all the supernatural stories, ghosts return at moments of trauma (often either sexual or oedipal) to remind the living of an anguish that refuses to remain in the past and threatens to overwhelm the present. These dead cannot be forgotten, however much the living might wish to do so. After his mother's death, Wilfrid Hollyer 'felt so safe. His mother couldn't hear him' (Sinclair 2006: 134). But of course, unforgotten, she can. The supernatural stories – for all their careful resolutions (Hollyer's ghostly mother appeased by his longing for her, Cicely in 'The Token' finally convinced that her husband loved her all along, Rosamond in 'The Nature of the Evidence' sated by her posthumous sex act, and so on) – paint a dark picture of a world in which pain can spill through the boundaries of space and time. This is the nightmarish side of a world in which time has no sequence, and the past returns to hurt us.

In some of these ghosts, the physical form of their living original is almost obliterated by the material shape of their suffering. The ghost of Effy in 'The Intercessor' looks barely human: 'Its face was so small, so shrunken and so bleached, that at first its actual features were indistinct to him. What *was* distinct, was the look it had; a look not to be imagined or defined, and thinkable only as a cry, an agony, made visible' (Sinclair 2006: 188). Similarly, the ghost of Wilfrid Hollyer's rejected mother in 'If the Dead Knew' is only just recognisable:

> Its face was an insubstantial framework for its mouth and eyes, and for the tears that fell in two shining tracks between. It was less a form than a visible emotion, an anguish. [...] No fleshly eyes could have expressed such an intensity of suffering, of unfathomable grief. He thought: the pain of a discarnate spirit might be infinitely sharper than any earthly pain. It might be inexhaustible. (Sinclair 2006: 137–8)

In a brilliant reading, Luke Thurston suggests that 'The Intercessor' reworks Freud in exploring traumas that engage with something outside and beyond signification and subjectivity: 'What is thus indicated, what lies at the ruined site beyond memory, can be neither re-presented or forgotten: it thus has an *incessant* status, returning in an endless loop at odds with the logic of narrative closure that governs the textual mesh around it' (Thurston 2012: 123). At their most poignant and intense, then, Sinclair's ghosts are phantasms not of the living people whose survivors they are, but of a pain that overwhelms the constraints of time. What lives on is not the person, but their anguish. The living may have forgotten – though at least in 'The Intercessor', they too are haunted by memories – but the agony of the dead persists and seeks out the living for some kind of redemption or resolution.

There are other forms of obsession in these stories as well. In 'Where Their Fire Is Not Quenched', the future traps Harriott Leigh even more surely than the past: what she became during her life folds back on itself and projects the past into the future apparently without any end. After her death, Harriott cannot escape a lover she despised, Oscar Wade, who has predeceased her. Everywhere she goes leads back to significant places from her past, and in each of those places, Oscar is waiting for her. 'The strange quality of her state was this, that it had no time. [. . .] So now she thought: If I could only go back and get to the place where it hadn't happened' (Sinclair 2006: 39). But because there is no time, there is no place 'where it hadn't happened'. Oscar explains to Harriott: '"You think the past affects the future. Has it never struck you that the future may affect the past? In your innocence there was the beginning of your sin. You *were* what you *were to be*"' (Sinclair 2006: 44). When Harriott asks him how long their state of enforced togetherness will last, Oscar cannot tell her. '"I don't know whether *this* is one moment of eternity, or the eternity of one moment"' (Sinclair 2006: 44). Paul March-Russell reads this story as a comment on female sexual hypocrisy: 'Harriott is fated to spend the rest of eternity with Oscar not only because she has denied him [to her priest on her deathbed], but because she has also repressed what he represents: sexual desire rather than romantic love' (March-Russell 2006: 17). I read the story in a slightly different way – even if there is a trace of Sinclair's 'medicinal morality' in the treatment of Harriott's tawdry desire (Woolf 1976: 390). Harriott's fantasy of an escape from her own history – and the nightmare recognition that such a possibility may not exist – is echoed in numerous other Sinclair texts. A place where there is no time might seem at first to offer an obvious solution to the problem of individual history, but in this story, the timelessness of the realm beyond death traps Harriott in a past that has lost its internal boundaries. If the future shapes the past, the past lies partly in the future and is continually re-encountered. There is no possibility of escape, because there is nowhere where the past is not. The only thing now that can be forgotten is the structure of time itself: Harriott 'remembered dimly that there had once been a thing called time, but she had forgotten altogether what it was like' (Sinclair 2006: 39).

As some Sinclair critics have noted, the strange temporality of the posthumous world of 'Where Their Fire Is Not Quenched' – in which past, present and future are all blended together – is highly reminiscent of early psychoanalytic descriptions of the unconscious. May Sinclair's interest in imagining worlds in which time was disrupted was clearly connected at once to her work as an idealist philosopher (Kant even appears in 'The Finding of the Absolute' [Sinclair 2006: 169–74]); to her early interest in psychoanalytic theory and practice; to her unorthodox spirituality; and to her mysticism (see Battersby 2002: 117; Finn 2007: 198). Sinclair attempted to develop a language and a philosophy that synthesised all these different traditions and disciplines. In *A Defence of Idealism* (1917), in a passage on the unconscious, Sinclair notes that what we have forgotten is never really lost: 'if we are to keep the image of consciousness as a "stream" we had better say that [our memories] sink to the bottom and stay there until some eddy in the deep stirs them up again' (Sinclair 1917: 291). Like ghosts, forgotten memories wait somewhere in a place that is neither the past nor the present, until they can find a way in. Mystic experience too is linked in *A Defence of Idealism* to the unconscious. Sinclair explicitly links mysticism to a 'state of dissociation' (Sinclair 1917: 291), the same word she uses to describe the state which underlies 'all mental maladies' (Sinclair 1917: 290). Mystical experience, she notes, is 'a very dangerous state' (Sinclair 1917: 291). When a mystic enters a state of mystical ecstasy, she or he enters the same psychic space – 'the country of abnormal consciousness' – as she or he would enter if she were developing a neurosis or a psychosis: 'The country of abnormal consciousness stretches forwards as well as backwards, and belongs every bit as much to our future as to our past' (Sinclair 1917: 292). In mystical states or while dreaming, the psyche experiences the multiple times of 'abnormal consciousness', that realm in our psyche which is inhabited by the things we have forgotten or which have yet to come about.

> In his abnormal state the mystic has before him the entire range of the 'Unconscious' and 'Subconscious': [. . .] his psyche hovers between its old forgotten playground of the past and its unknown playground of the future. It may be the prey and the victim of powers, of instincts, and of memories, which once served its development, and which have dropped from it by disuse; or it may be the experimenter with undeveloped powers of which it is by no means the master. (Sinclair 1917: 292–3)

In mystical states, the soul transcends itself, inhabiting its own future as well as its own present. The past is the enemy of this partial emancipation. 'Normal consciousness', if it is to advance at all, must temporarily break with 'the past that it suppresses but is powerless to destroy'

(Sinclair 1917: 292). But it is all too easy for the psyche in a state of mystical self-transcendence to go back 'down that well-trodden path by which it came. It can go a short way, or even a fairly long way and yet return. But if it goes *too* far it is lost; it is hopelessly estranged from itself and from the life of the normal living; it is (not to mince matters) mad' (Sinclair 1917: 293). In order for the psyche in a state of dissociation – whether mystical or neurotic – to remain sane, it must move forward into the undeveloped future and avoid being pulled back into the past, which it can temporarily forget, but never erase. This realm in which the future and past are both equally present is linked in Sinclair's philosophy to both the Freudian unconscious and the mystical experiences about which she wrote so often and so powerfully.

But for Sinclair, mysticism, unlike madness, could take the self out of the body and thus out of past traumas and into the future. Sinclair had abandoned her faith in God while still in her teens, but she continued to believe in the possibility of transcendence and to invoke religious language whenever she wrote about mystical experience. If, she wrote, 'everyday, present consciousness' 'is to advance at all beyond its normal state, it can only do so by a process of detachment or dissociation; by that letting go and forgetting of the actual, by that renunciation and self-surrender, that dying to live which is the secret of the mystic life' (Sinclair 1917: 292). As the psyche grows, the 'Will-to-live, the Desire to have life' 'grows with it, [. . .] into a consuming passion; it passes beyond physical bounds; and the Love of Life becomes the Love of God' (Sinclair 1917: 274). Spalding in 'The Finding of the Absolute' is ecstatic as he contemplates the world through the prism of 'cubic time':

> The whole universe stood up on end round him, doubling all its future back upon all its past. [. . .] He saw the vast planes of time intersecting each other, like the planes of a sphere [. . .] He passed from God's immanent to his transcendent life, into the Absolute. For one moment he thought that this was death; the next his whole being swelled and went on swelling in an unspeakable, an unthinkable bliss. (Sinclair 2006: 175–6)

In 'cubic time', his wife's adultery is forgotten: 'He had now no memory of [her] adultery or of his own' (Sinclair 2006: 176). Mary Olivier too learns to forget the pain of remorse and regret by surrendering 'all the things that entangle and confuse [the will]': 'When you lay still with your eyes shut and made the darkness come on, wave after wave, blotting out your body and the world, blotting out everything but your self and your will, that was a dying to live; a real dying, a real life' (Sinclair 1980a: 377). Real dying – mystical dying – involves forgetting the self and the world; false dying – like that which creates ghosts – traps the psyche in its own pain and forces it to continually re-experience the suffering of its life.

There is a danger, of course, in 'real dying'. The process of self-erasure, with its promise of emancipation from the troubles of the psyche and of the world, also threatens to destroy the self completely. A number of critics have noted that there is something ambiguous and poignant about the ending of *Mary Olivier*. Mary seems to celebrate having lost everything: 'For twenty-three years something had come between her and reality. She could see what it was now. She had gone through life wanting things, wanting people, clinging to the thought of them, not able to keep off them and let them go' (Sinclair 1980a: 378). Losing everything allows her to see reality – 'this ultimate passion' (379) – though she allows herself to doubt: 'Supposing there's nothing in it, nothing at all? That's the risk you take' (Sinclair 1980a: 379). Christine Battersby describes the end of the novel as 'an open-ended conclusion – one that raises as a possibility the *dangers* of perverting Spinozism into a philosophy of renunciation, as opposed to a philosophy of affirmation' (Battersby 2002: 119); Howard Finn notes that the epiphany at the end is 'a "letting-go" of worldly happiness that can be read as a displaced form of letting go of worldly trauma, one denial substituting itself for another, and a stoical resignation is played out as the precarious ecstasy of self-realization' (Finn 2007: 198); Penny Brown worries that Mary's 'inner freedom [. . .] founded on solitude, withdrawal, passivity and self-denial' is 'an intensification, if anything, of the state which an unquestioning acceptance of the traditional female role would have produced' (Brown 1992: 35). Faye Pickrem, in an insightful reading, argues that the mystical 'sublimation' described so painstakingly in Sinclair's novels allows her characters to evade carnality in what Pickrem suggests is a form of erotic displacement, a 'visceral response to an anxiety regarding desire': 'Instead of sexual consummation, an erotics of renunciation is instituted and reified, through which carnal desire is eliminated from the body and re-cathected onto a metonym of desire: nature, immanence, the Absolute' (Pickrem 2015: 5, 11). Perhaps escaping pain by escaping the world is simply another tragic form of self-suppression, as if obsession with the past can be countered only by denying both the body and the self with which it is identified.

A similar sad fate might have awaited May Sinclair herself, as she struggled to be both remembered and forgotten by the readers of the future of whom she was at times so mistrustful. As she carefully covered her traces, she ran the risk of making it impossible for us to remember her, except through the texts she published. And this of course is what she wanted. But – and perhaps this is a sad fact – it is much more difficult to establish a reputation for a writer that is based on their works alone. There are countless authors whom May Sinclair revered who have sunk almost without a trace, except for the published texts they left behind: Beatrice Harraden, Evelyn Sharp and Gwendoline Keats, to name just a few. As Claire Drewery has noted: 'The potential for articulating a literary "voice" and surviving within the canon is inextricably posited against death's shadowy "other": silence, marginalization and oblivion' (Drewery 2011: 65). The implication is that survival is always haunted by its opposite. In the Freudian psyche, forgetting and remembering are similarly intertwined: memories move traumatically between the unconscious and the unconscious, so that remembering something – just like forgetting it – is always tenuous and contingent. Even the idea of a timeless and redemptive mysticism is inextricable from the idea of a past that can never be escaped or erased. As Howard Finn notes (above), at the end of *Mary Olivier*, pain is avoided, but so is joy. We are reminded of Harriett Frean dismissing her maid because it is agony for her to watch the tenderness with which Maggie breastfeeds her baby (Sinclair 1980b: 137). If there is no time, there is no past to remember, but there is also no future to bring redemption and resolution. Sinclair's vision of an ecstatic, mystic timelessness is born out of pessimism about the possibilities of recovery within time. She rejects the idea that one might move forward into a new world in which the past can be remembered in a way that no longer hurts, but heals.

So what is the role of literary criticism in bridging the gap between authors of the past and the present – in historical 'recovery'? It is readers, of course, who are primarily responsible for restoring forgotten texts to consciousness, but critics – and publishers – are readers too. In more than one of Sinclair's ghost stories, there is an 'intercessor' who stands between the world of the dead and the world of the living, and allows the dead in: 'The Intercessor', for example, or 'The Token'. In 'The Intercessor', Garvin sees the ghost of Effy when no-one else can, because he is not afraid of her. Falshaw tells Garvin: 'they doan't coom to those that are afeard of 'em' (Sinclair 2006: 196), and even when Effy climbs into bed with him and presses her little body against his, Garvin can still 'swear to his own state of mind – he was *not* afraid' (Sinclair 2006: 189). Instead, he feels protective of the child, noticing that it is 'responsive to his pity and accessible to his succour' (Sinclair 2006: 191). As the title makes clear, Garvin intercedes between Effy and the Falshaws: Effy 'could only get at her mother through Garvin, who had no fear' (Sinclair 2006: 210). Garvin's conversations with Mrs Falshaw, and his presence by the bed in which Mrs Falshaw is cradling her stillborn child, make possible Mrs Falshaw's final acceptance of Effy: 'Her arms pressed the impalpable creature, as it were flesh to flesh; and Garvin knew that Effy's passion was appeased' (Sinclair 2006: 216). In 'The Token', the narrator is the only character who can see Cicely's ghost, and the ghost turns on her 'a look of supplication' (Sinclair 2006: 53). The narrator describes the ghost to its husband, and eventually makes possible the redemptive embrace between a groaning Donald and the ghost, which collapses in a 'flicker of light' (Sinclair 2006: 56). Both intercessors help the dead extract expressions of love from the living, and Effy's ghost is replaced by a little shrine in her memory: 'an enlarged photograph' above 'a shelf with her things – a cup she used to drink out of – some tiny animals – a doll' (Sinclair 2006: 216). The child who has been ruthlessly rejected and suppressed is finally brought out of the unconscious into the world of conscious remembrance.

It is too fanciful to say that critics of May Sinclair are intercessors like Garvin or Cicely's sister-in-law, healing the wounds of the dead and the forgotten. Indeed, as we saw, May Sinclair was very suspicious of critics, even though she herself was one of our number. But it is also clearly the case that editing and publishing out-of-print texts, writing books, publishing articles and organising conferences are ways of protecting someone's reputation from oblivion – ways of mediating between the past and the present, between the living and the dead. As May Sinclair did for the Brontës, it is our responsibility and privilege communally to shape the reputations of the writers on whom we work, and to release them into a future in which we do not know what they will become. The dead can have their own kind of timelessness, if only we living are willing to embrace them.

Notes

1. See, for example, Boll 1970a, 1970b; Gillespie 1978; Kaplan 1971; Neff 1980; Padmanabhan 1982; Robb 1973.
2. See, for example, Kemp 1990; Phillips 1996; Stark 1992.
3. See, for example, Battersby 2002; Dellamora 2006; Dowson 2002; Drewery 2011; Forster 2008; Johnson 2004, 2006; Miracky 2003; Pease 2012; Pykett 2000; Seed 2001; Thurston 2012; Wallace 2000, 2004; Cheryl Wilson 2003; Leigh Wilson 2003.

Works Cited

Battersby, Christine (2002), '"In the Shadow of His Language": May Sinclair's Portrait of the Artist as Daughter', *New Comparison: A Journal of Comparative and General Literary Studies* 33:4, 102–20.
Boll, Theophilus E. M. (1961), 'On the May Sinclair Collection', *Library Chronicle of the University of Pennsylvania* 27:1, 1–15, https://archive.org/stream/librarychronicle27univ/librarychronicle27univ_djvu.txt (last accessed 21 June 2016).
Boll, Theophilus E. M. (1962), 'May Sinclair and the Medico-Psychological Clinic of London', *Proceedings of the American Philosophical Society* 27:3, 310–26.
Boll, Theophilus E. M. (1970a), 'The Mystery of Charlotte Mew and May Sinclair: An Inquiry', *Bulletin of the New York Public Library* 74:9, 445–53.
Boll, Theophilus E. M. (1970b), 'May Sinclair: A Check-List', *Bulletin of the New York Public Library* 74:9, 454–67.
Boll, Theophilus E. M. (1973), *Miss May Sinclair: Novelist: A Biographical and Critical Introduction*, Cranbury, NJ: Associated Presses.
Brown, Penny (1992), *The Poison at the Source: The Female Novel of Self-Development in the Early Twentieth Century*, London: Palgrave Macmillan.
Coe, Jonathan (2007), 'My Literary Love Affair', *The Guardian*, 6 October 2007, http://www.theguardian.com/books/2007/oct/06/fiction.jonathancoe (last accessed 21 June 2016).
Dellamora, Richard (2006), 'Female Adolescence in May Sinclair's *Mary Olivier* and the Construction of a Dialectic between Victorian and Modern', *Nineteenth Century Studies* 20, 171–82.
Dowson, Jane (2002), *Women, Modernism and British Poetry 1910–39: Resisting Femininity*, Burlington, VT: Ashgate.
Drewery, Claire (2011), *Modernist Short Fiction by Women: The Liminal in Katherine Mansfield, Dorothy Richardson, May Sinclair and Virginia Woolf*, Burlington, VT and Farnham: Ashgate.
Finn, Howard (2007), 'Writing Lives: Dorothy Richardson, May Sinclair, Gertrude Stein', in Morag Shiach and Suzanne Hobson (eds), *The Cambridge Companion to the Modernist Novel*, Cambridge: Cambridge University Press, pp. 191–205.
Forster, Laurel (2008), 'Women and War Zones: May Sinclair's Personal Negotiation with the First World War', in Teresa Gómez Reus, Aránzazu Usandizaga and Janet Wolff (eds), *Inside Out: Women Negotiating, Subverting, Appropriating Public and Private Space*, Amsterdam: Rodopi, pp. 229–48.
Gillespie, Diane F. (1978), 'May Sinclair and the Stream of Consciousness: Metaphors and Metaphysics', *English Literature in Transition (1880–1920)* 21:2, 134–42, http://muse.jhu.edu/journals/english_literature_in_transition/v021/21.2.gillespie.html (last accessed 22 June 2016).
Gillespie, Diane F. (1985), '"The Muddle of the Middle": May Sinclair on Women', *Tulsa Studies in Women's Literature* 4:2, 235–51, http://www.jstor.org/stable/463698?pq-origsite=summon&seq=1#page_scan_tab_contents (last accessed 22 June 2016).

'The History', *Everyman's Library*, http://www.randomhouse.com/knopf/clas sics/about.html (last accessed 22 June 2016).

Johnson, George M. (2004), 'May Sinclair: From Psychological Analyst to Anachronistic Modernist', *Journal of Evolutionary Psychology* 25: 3–4, 179–89.

Johnson, George M. (2006), *Dynamic Psychology in Modernist British Fiction*, London: Palgrave Macmillan.

Jones, Charlotte (2013), 'May Sinclair: The Readable Modernist', *The Guardian*, 1 August 2013, http://www.theguardian.com/books/booksblog/2013/aug/01/may-sinclair-readable-modernist (last accessed 22 June 2016).

Kaplan, Sydney (1971), '"Featureless Freedom" or Ironic Submission: Dorothy Richardson and May Sinclair', *College English* 32:8, 914–17, http://www.jstor.org/stable/375630?pq-origsite=summon&seq=1#page_scan_tab_contents (last accessed 22 June 2016).

Kemp, Sandra (1990), '"But how Describe a World seen without a Self?": Feminism, Fiction and Modernism', *Critical Quarterly* 32:1, 99–118.

Kunka, Andrew J., and Michele K. Troy, eds (2006), *May Sinclair: Moving Towards the Modern*, Burlington, VT: Ashgate.

March-Russell, Paul (2006), 'Introduction', in May Sinclair, *Uncanny Stories*, Ware: Wordsworth Editions, pp. 7–21.

Martindale, Philippa (2003), 'The ceasing from the sorrow of divided life; May Sinclair's women, texts and contexts (1910–1923)', PhD dissertation, Durham University, http://etheses.dur.ac.uk/3691/ (last accessed 22 June 2016).

'May Sinclair's Rolls Royce' (2015), *May Sinclair Society*, http://maysinclairsociety.com/2015/03/28/may-sinclairs-rolls-royce/ (last accessed 22 June 2016).

Miracky, James J. (2003), *Regenerating the Novel: Gender and Genre in Woolf, Forster, Sinclair, and Lawrence*, New York: Routledge.

Mosimann, Elizabeth Ann (2003), 'Reading a Modernist Absolute: Philosophy and Psychology in May Sinclair', PhD dissertation, Temple University, http://search.proquest.com/mlaib/docview/54111135/ADD020035BF84006PQ/1?accountid=15053 (last accessed 22 June 2016).

Neff, Rebecca Kinnamon (1980), '"New Mysticism" in the Writings of May Sinclair and T. S. Eliot', *Twentieth Century Literature* 26.1, 82–108, http://www.jstor.org/stable/441242?pq-origsite=summon&seq=1#page_scan_tab_contents (last accessed 22 June 2016).

Neff, Rebecca Kinnamon (1983), 'May Sinclair's Uncanny Stories as Metaphysical Quest', *English Literature in Transition (1880–1920)* 26:3, 187–91, http://muse.jhu.edu/journals/english_literature_in_transition/v026/26.3.neff.html, (last accessed 22 June 2016).

Padmanabhan, P. S. (1982), 'The Irritant and the Pearl: "Jones's Karma" and the Poetry and Drama of T. S. Eliot', *Canadian Review of Comparative Literature/Revue Canadienne de Littérature Comparée* 9:2, 188–99, http://ejournals.library.ualberta.ca/index.php/crcl/issue/view/229 (last accessed 22 June 2016).

Pease, Allison (2012), *Modernism, Feminism and the Culture of Boredom*, Cambridge: Cambridge University Press, http://lib.myilibrary.com/ProductDetail.aspx?id=392281 (last accessed 22 June 2016).

Phillips, Terry (1996), 'Battling with the Angel: May Sinclair's Powerful

Mothers', in Sarah Sceats and Gail Cunningham (eds), *Image and Power: Women in Fiction in the Twentieth Century*, New York: Longman, pp. 128–38.

Pickrem, Faye (2015), 'Disembodying Desire: Ontological Fantasy, Libidinal Anxiety and the Erotics of Renunciation in May Sinclair', typescript.

Pollitt, Katha (1998), 'Subject To Debate', *The Nation* 267:6, 9.

Pykett, Lyn (2000), 'Writing Around Modernism: May Sinclair and Rebecca West', in Lynne Hapgood and Nancy L. Paxton (eds), *Outside Modernism: In Pursuit of the English Novel, 1900–1930*, New York: Macmillan/St Martin's, pp. 103–22.

Raitt, Suzanne (2000), *May Sinclair: A Modern Victorian*, Oxford: Clarendon/Oxford University Press.

Robb, Kenneth A. (1973), 'May Sinclair: An Annotated Bibliography of Writings about Her', *English Literature in Transition (1880–1920)* 16:3, 177–231, http://muse.jhu.edu/journals/english_literature_in_transition/v016/16.3.robb.html (last accessed 22 June 2016).

Scott, Bonnie Kime, ed. (1990), *The Gender of Modernism: A Critical Anthology*, Bloomington: Indiana University Press.

Seed, David (2001), '"Psychical" Cases: Transformations of the Supernatural in Virginia Woolf and May Sinclair', in Andrew Smith and Jeff Wallace (eds), *Gothic Modernisms*, New York: Palgrave, pp. 44–61.

Sinclair, May (1905), Letter to Witter Bynner, 11 December 1905, bMS Am 1891 (766), Houghton Library, Harvard University.

Sinclair, May (1907), 'Introduction', in Emily Brontë, *Wuthering Heights*, London: Dent, pp. vii–xiii.

Sinclair, May (1908a), 'Introduction', in Charlotte Brontë, *Jane Eyre*, London: Dent, pp. vii–xvii.

Sinclair, May (1908b), 'Introduction', in Charlotte Brontë, *Shirley*, London: Dent, vii–xv.

Sinclair, May (1909a), 'Introduction', in Elizabeth Gaskell, *The Life of Charlotte Brontë*, London, pp. vii–xxii.

Sinclair, May (1909b), 'Introduction', in Charlotte Brontë, *Villette*, London: Dent, pp. vii–xv.

Sinclair, May (1910), 'Introduction', in Charlotte Brontë, *The Professor*, London: Dent, 1910, pp. vii–xi.

Sinclair, May (1911), 'The Intercessor', in Sinclair [1923b] 2006, pp. 177–216.

Sinclair, May (1912), *The Three Brontës*, London: Hutchinson.

Sinclair, May (1913), 'The New Brontë Letters', *The Dial* 55:657, 343–6.

Sinclair, May (1914), 'Introduction', in Anne Brontë, *The Tenant of Wildfell Hall*, London: Dent, pp. vii–xiii.

Sinclair, May [1914] (1982), *The Three Sisters*, intro. Jean Radford, London: Virago.

Sinclair, May (1915), 'Two Notes. I. On H.D. II. On Imagism', *The Egoist* 2:6, 88–9, http://library.brown.edu/pdfs/1306936865671879.pdf (last accessed 22 June 2016).

Sinclair, May (1917), *A Defence of Idealism: Some Questions and Conclusions*, London: Macmillan, https://archive.org/details/adefenceidealis02sincgoog (last accessed 22 June 2016).

Sinclair, May [1917] (1990a), '"Prufrock: and Other Observations": A

Criticism', *The Little Review* 4:8, 8–14, reprinted in Scott (1990), pp. 448–53.
Sinclair, May [1918] (1990b), 'The Novels of Dorothy Richardson', *The Egoist* 5:4, 57–9, reprinted in Scott (1990), pp. 442–8.
Sinclair, May [1919] (1980a), *Mary Olivier: A Life*, intro. Jean Radford, London: Virago.
Sinclair, May [1919] (2002), *Mary Olivier: A Life*, intro. Katha Pollitt, New York: New York Review of Books.
Sinclair, May [1920] (1990c), 'The Reputation of Ezra Pound', *English Review* 30:1, 326–35, reprinted in Scott (1990), pp. 468–76.
Sinclair, May (1921a), 'The Poems of F. S. Flint', *English Review* 32:1, 6–18, http://babel.hathitrust.org/cgi/pt?id=njp.32101077260733;view=1up;seq=7 (last accessed 4 June 2015).
Sinclair, May (1921b), 'The Poems of Richard Aldington', *English Review*, 32:1, 397–410, http://babel.hathitrust.org/cgi/pt?id=njp.32101077260733;view=1up;seq=12 (last accessed 4 June 2015).
Sinclair, May [1922] (1980b), *Life and Death of Harriett Frean*, intro. Jean Radford, London: Virago.
Sinclair, May [1922] (2003), *Life and Death of Harriett Frean*, intro. Francine Prose, New York: Modern Library/Penguin Random House.
Sinclair, May (1922), 'The Poems of H.D.', *The Dial* 72:12, 203–7; longer version reprinted in *Fortnightly Review* 121:723 (1927), 329–40, reprinted in Scott (1990), pp. 453–67.
Sinclair, May [1922] (2008a), 'The Victim', reprinted in Mike Ashley (ed.), *Unforgettable Ghost Stories by Women Writers*, New York: Dover, pp. 73–95.
Sinclair, May [1923] (2008b), 'The Token', reprinted in Richard Dalby (ed.), *The Virago Book of Ghost Stories,* London: Virago-Little, Brown, pp. 196–208.
Sinclair, May [1923] (2006), *Uncanny Stories*, intro. Paul March-Russell, Ware: Wordsworth Editions.
Sinclair, May [1926] (2012), 'The Villa Désirée', in A. Susan Williams (ed.), *The Penguin Book of Erotic Stories by Women*, 2nd edn, London: Penguin.
Stark, Susanne (1992), 'Overcoming Butlerian Obstacles: May Sinclair and the Problem of Biological Determinism', *Women's Studies: An Interdisciplinary Journal* 21.3, 265–83, http://web.b.ebscohost.com/ehost/pdfviewer/pdfviewer?vid=4&sid=f9777f4b-31e4-49ee-b695-81d0899a4b0f%40sessionmgr198&hid=124 (last accessed 25 May 2014).
Thurston, Luke (2012), *Literary Ghosts from the Victorians to Modernism: the Haunting Interval*, New York: Routledge.
Wallace, Diana (2000), *Sisters and Rivals in British Women's Fiction, 1914–39*, New York: St Martin's.
Wallace, Diana (2004), 'Uncanny Stories: The Ghost Story as Female Gothic', *Gothic Studies* 6:1, 57–68, http://web.b.ebscohost.com/ehost/pdfviewer/pdfviewer?vid=7&sid=f9777f4b-31e4-49ee-b695-81d0899a4b0f%40sessionmgr198&hid=124 (last accessed 19 May 2014).
Wilson, Cheryl A. (2003), 'The Victorian Woman Reader in May Sinclair's *Mary Olivier*: Self-Stimulation, Intellectual Freedom, and Escape', *English Literature in Transition (1880–1920)* 46:4, 365–81, http://web.b.ebscohost.

com/ehost/pdfviewer/pdfviewer?vid=10&sid=f9777f4b-31e4-49ee-b695-81d0899a4b0f%40sessionmgr198&hid=124 (last accessed 4 June 2015).

Wilson, Leigh (2003), '"She in Her 'Armour' and He in His Coat of Nerves": May Sinclair and the Re-writing of Chivalry', in Ann Heilman (ed.), *Feminist Forerunners: New Womanism and Feminism in the Early Twentieth Century*, London: Pandora, pp. 179–88.

Woolf, Virginia [1909] (1976), 'To Lady Robert Cecil', 12 April 1909 (letter 480) in Nigel Nicolson and Joanne Trautmann (eds), *The Flight of the Mind: The Collected Letters of Virginia Woolf*, vol. 1 (1888–1912), New York: Harcourt, pp. 389–90.

Woolf, Virginia [1930–40] (1985), 'A Sketch of the Past', in Jeanne Schulkind (ed.), *Moments of Being: A Collection of Autobiographical Writing*, 2nd edn, New York: Harcourt, pp. 61–159.

Zegger, Hrisey D. (1976), *May Sinclair*, Boston: Twayne.

Chapter 2

Learning Greek: The Woman Artist as Autodidact in May Sinclair's *Mary Olivier: A Life*

Elise Thornton

May Sinclair's reimagining of the late-Victorian poet in *Mary Olivier: A Life* examines the obstacles facing the artist-heroine in her quest for intellectual freedom, self-definition and artistic autonomy at the turn of the century. One of the main influences guiding Mary is her desire for knowledge, and Sinclair questions the boundaries of acceptable female education in Victorian England by focusing specifically on Mary's interest in Greek studies, a traditionally masculine subject. Sinclair's extensive detailing of Mary's autodidactism as a young girl, adolescent and mature adult thoroughly examines the barriers preventing women's intellectual growth in the late nineteenth and early twentieth century, and Mary's struggle for an equal educational experience to men prefigures much of Virginia Woolf's non-fiction writing on women's education and professionalisation. Sinclair draws upon her own experiences of autodidactism and formal education at Cheltenham Ladies' College in her *Künstlerroman*, and she explores how education influences not only the development of the woman artist, but how it impacts upon Mary's own understanding of her creative potential.[1]

Sinclair portrays the portrait of the artist narrative from the protagonist's early infancy and returns to the nineteenth-century realist tradition of developmental *Bildung* – wherein the idea of training and preparation are considered necessary for the hero/ine. While this might superficially suggest the text revisits the more traditional themes associated with the *Bildungsromane* of her male predecessors, who often align the male protagonist's self-formation within formal schooling and the public domain, Sinclair instead identifies the woman artist's struggle for creative fulfilment with the autodidact and locates much of Mary's intellectual and artistic development in the private sphere. This chapter examines how Mary challenges many of the period's patriarchal standards concerning women's right to an education and the consequences this has on her artistic development.

Women's Education in the Nineteenth Century

In Woolf's essay 'Two Women' (1927), she argues that young women taught in the nineteenth century were given a 'negative education, [one] which decree[d] not what you may do but what you may not do, that cramped and stifled' their intellectual aspirations (419). The ideologies of separate spheres placed women in a subordinate role to men, thereby making them 'relative' rather than 'autonomous beings', and any formal education they received reflected this second-class status (Purvis 1991: 2).[2] Raised to become the idealised 'ladylike homemaker', middle- and upper-class girls were not expected to take up any kind of paid labour and their education often accentuated 'ornamental knowledge' that would attract, but not threaten, a potential suitor (6, 63). Psychiatrist Henry Maudsley in 'Sex in Mind and Education' (1874) maintained that a rigorous curriculum taught to adolescent girls 'could produce permanent injury', or possible sterility, leading to severe psychological consequences such as mental instability and breakdowns (Showalter 1987: 124). Girls who took these alleged reproductive and psychological risks and engaged in some form of education were usually taught at home or private day schools. While boys were often sent off to funded grammar schools or expensive private boarding institutions to learn a variety of subjects like Latin, Greek, mathematics and science, girls experienced a very different education (Walford 1993b: 12, 14).

What was taught at home varied according to a family's financial status and the majority of nineteenth-century girls' day schools based their curriculum on rote learning; pupils often undertook courses like English history, reading, grammar, arithmetic and geography (Purvis 1991: 70–1). As the girls advanced in their lessons, they were also expected to master more feminine accomplishments which, depending on their class status, included needlework, piano lessons and some modern languages such as French and German. In addition to the discrepancies in subject matter, the cost of tuition differed greatly at girls' and boys' schools and, while thousands of pounds could be spent on a boy's secondary and university tuition, girls were given less, if any, financial allowance by their family and received a mostly 'unpaid-for education' (Woolf 2000: 203). The 'relative poverty of women's colleges and [society's] resistance to women's education' was openly criticised during the twentieth century in such texts as Woolf's *A Room of One's*

Own (1929) and *Three Guineas* (1938) (Jones and Snaith 2010: 39). Nevertheless, this obvious sex-division was validated by the separate spheres ideology, as boys were groomed for the 'professional and public world' while women were prepared for a private life centred on domestic and familial duties (Purvis 1991: 65).

Private ladies' colleges like the North London Collegiate School and Cheltenham Ladies' College began to appear in the mid-nineteenth century. Elizabeth Raikes reproduces the Cheltenham Ladies' College founders' manifesto in her biography *Dorothea Beale of Cheltenham* (1908):

> The founders [...] were anxious to make it clear that their aim was to develop in the pupils character and fitness for the duties of later life [...] 'an education based upon religious principles which, preserving the modesty and gentleness of the female character, should so far cultivate [a girl's] intellectual powers as fit for the discharge of those responsible duties which devolve upon her as a wife, mother, mistress and friend, the natural companion and helpmeet for man. (87)

Raikes' introductory language about the founders' apprehension suggests that prejudice against women's education was still very much an immediate presence at the college. The school's declaration that it would uphold the Victorian ideals of femininity, teach appropriate courses for the female mind and reinforce its students' expected domestic roles is an obvious attempt to diminish any potentially damaging criticism directed towards the new girls' college.

The college struggled in its first few years and it was not until the election of Dorothea Beale as principal in 1858 that its financial status and student enrolment numbers finally improved. Beale was an advocate for improving women's education, although 'remodelling rather than revolution was her aim' (109). She wished to include more advanced courses in the college's core syllabus, like science and mathematics, but delayed adding such male-oriented courses until her position was more established within the school and community (Kamm 1958: 56). If a girl presented herself as a self-disciplined student, Beale would allow her 'to pursue special studies' like geometry, Latin and Greek (Beale 1866: 11). By offering these modules as electives, she saved the college from additional disapproval and granted serious female students the chance to participate in more advanced studies. Crucially, though, despite Beale's introduction of more demanding courses, the principal did not deviate from the founders' original intent, as she constantly reiterated in her writing, that educated girls could 'provide "healthy intellectual companionship"' to their husbands (Beale, Soulsby and Francis 1898: 5).

Beale believed that 'the foundation, the main and leading elements of instruction, should be the same' in women's institutions as in men's, although she argued women should not compete intellectually with men for fear of causing unwanted rivalry between the sexes (Great Britain 1869: 6). In her writing, she argues that this can be avoided by maintaining sex segregation in schools and that female students should undergo different examinations. This suggestion that women's intellectual aspirations should be founded on similar principles to men's, yet diverge in relation to evaluation, was rooted in the belief that women's colleges were meant to prepare students how to accept and 'perform that subordinate part in the world' (Beale 1865: 1). Beale believes that 'moral training is the end' and 'education the means' when instructing girls, and 'the habits of obedience to duty' and 'self-restraint' must be encouraged at women's colleges (13–14). She further argues that these specific teaching methods stress 'the true woman's ornament of a meek and quiet spirit' rather than fuelling a masculine, competitive temper (14). Her description of the ideal middle-class, female education promotes Victorian principles of the cult of domesticity and reinforces the masculinist ideology of separate spheres and women's subservient position to men in all matters of society.

Beale recognised that not all of her students shared her opinions and she states in her published writing that a woman should not feel ashamed if she decided to further her studies, although the principal is quick to say that any student with domestic or marital duties awaiting them at home should not disregard them in her pursuance of certificates and degrees (Beale 1869: xxxiii). Most students at Cheltenham did not need to seek employment upon leaving school, and Beale often encouraged her pupils to improve their intellectual capacity 'within the context of family life' and the 'wider community' rather than the professional realm (Beaumont 2007: 4; Flint 2002: 120). Despite her advocacy for improving women's education, Beale was a 'model' for her students 'in being feminine rather than feminist' (Boll 1973: 32). Sinclair encountered this conservative form of instruction while at Cheltenham, and she would later transcribe her experiences in her *Künstlerroman*.

Born into a 'mercantile middle class' family in 1863, Mary Amelia St Clair was the youngest of six children and the only surviving daughter of William and Amelia Sinclair, and Suzanne Raitt points out in her biography of the author that Sinclair did not encounter the 'masculine injustice' of the Victorian period until she was denied the same educational opportunities as her brothers (2000: 19). Sinclair yearned to undergo the same tutelage as her brothers, and her mother's obvious favouritism towards her sons forced Sinclair to find some form of retreat from this maternal rejection by 'educating herself in languages, the classics and philosophy' (24). As she would later write about Charlotte Brontë, Sinclair's own exhaustive and diverse reading would inherently influence and create 'a style exclusively and inimitably her own' (Sinclair 1908: viii). By the time she was eighteen, Sinclair 'had taught herself German, Greek, and French, and read the works by Shakespeare, Aristophanes, Euripedes, Shelley, Plato, Hume, and Kant' (Raitt 2000: 24).

Sinclair enrolled at Cheltenham in 1881. She attended the college for only a year and did not revise for any of the external university examinations recently opened to women. Her relationship with the formidable principal was initially antagonistic when Sinclair refused to write an essay assigned by Beale about God, but the principal accepted Sinclair's demand for independent thought and took it upon herself to personally guide Sinclair in her studies (25). Beale allowed Sinclair to take on elective subjects, such as Greek and 'the study of Western and Eastern philosophies', in the hope they would 'strengthen her wavering faith' (25). She further encouraged Sinclair to 'develop [her] intellectual autonomy' through the written word and submit original work to the college's journal, the *Cheltenham Ladies' College Magazine*, which published many of her early philosophical essays, poetry and Greek translations (27). Sinclair undoubtedly appreciated the support she received from the principal, but Raitt maintains the author was not always in agreement with Beale's techniques and expectations as a teacher, for she 'demanded an extraordinary amount of effort and self-discipline' from her students even after their departure from the college (27). Nevertheless, Beale remained a valuable friend and, following her mentor's advice, Sinclair spent the remainder of the nineteenth century trying to 'develop her own philosophy of mind' through essays, poetry and fiction (31).

Sinclair's year at Cheltenham played a major role in her development as a writer and assured her that the 'intellectual life' was the one place she could find 'solitude and comfort' amidst her many family tragedies and growing alienation from her mother (30). Sinclair's intellectual escapism, like so many women of the period, occurred mostly within the private sphere, and she makes it a dominant theme in her semi-autobiographical *Künstlerroman*. Mary's autodidacticism heavily influences her development as an artist as she attempts to recreate an equivalent education to her brothers' instruction, and this chapter explores how Mary's specific demand to master Greek redefines the nineteenth-century presentation of the woman reader and artist-heroine.

Greek and the Woman Writer

The figure of the Victorian woman reader has been a widely discussed subject in nineteenth- and twentieth-century literary studies, and much of the analysis tends to analyse how this figure either succumbs to the negative stereotypes of the 'idle, ignorant, young novel-reader' or achieves some form of autonomy through her negotiation of patriarchal power with her transgressive modes of reading (Brantlinger 1998: 28). Sinclair introduces an alternative depiction of the woman reader in *Mary Olivier: A Life*, as Mary is forced to challenge the authority of her mother. Victorian and Edwardian attitudes concerning acceptable reading habits upheld books that developed one's 'private and moral life' and denounced any gratuitous and arbitrary reading 'as morally debilitating' (Flint 2002: 48). In this vein, Caroline Olivier repeatedly criticises Mary's autodidacticism and tries to thwart her intellectual growth throughout the novel.

Latin and Greek were the core subjects taught to boys, as they 'instilled [the] masculinist values' of Victorian patriarchy and introduced them to 'a privileged and priestly language' usually denied to women (Gilbert and Gubar 1988: 243). As required courses at men's colleges and universities, the study of Latin and Greek 'was inseparable from a masculinising of culture', and women's exclusion from learning the classics 'automatically debarred them from the habits of mind which dominated mainstream culture' (Dusinberre 1997: 48). Famed Greek scholar and teacher W. H. D. Rouse thought the inclusion of classics courses at women's colleges was 'a radical change', and he argued the underlying purpose of women's education should remain as a means to impart 'an intelligent and sympathetic interest in life' rather than 'to turn out finished scholars' (1898: 67).[3] Beale agreed with Rouse and allowed some diligent students to undertake Greek as a personal 'favour' and reward for their serious studies; however, she maintains that no student at the college 'ha[d] a right to demand' being taught Greek (Great Britain 1869: 209). It is this specific mandate which Sinclair challenges in her *Künstlerroman* as Mary repeatedly confronts her mother for this male privilege. The woman artist's aim to 'master' Greek is a common issue found in the writing of Sinclair's predecessors, who often undermined men's control over the language through their female protagonist's 'perverse and subversive meditations on Greek' (Gilbert and Gubar 1988: 244). Sinclair avoids this combative narrative tactic and, much like Woolf's own connection with the language, she depicts Mary's ideal relationship with Greek as one which is based upon a desire for 'intimacy', 'familiarity' and just a little bit of 'magic' (Fowler 1999: 217, 219).

Woolf's essay, 'On Not Knowing Greek' (1925), epitomises the nineteenth- and twentieth-century woman writer's complicated relationship with the language and examines many of the same issues raised in Sinclair's *Künstlerroman*. The narrator's tone in the beginning of the essay resonates with exasperation as she admits it is 'vain and foolish to talk of knowing Greek' when one's inadequate education prevents one from learning the basic fundamentals of the language, such as 'how the words sounded, or where precisely [one] ought to laugh, or how the actors acted' (Woolf 1925: 38). In spite of her ignorance, the narrator admits she cannot escape the longing she feels for the language and she finds it mystifying that she 'should wish to know Greek, try to know Greek, feel for ever drawn back to Greek, and be for ever making up some congruous notion of the meaning of Greek' (38). While Woolf states the obvious in regards to women's exclusion from the same educational experiences as men, she contends that not knowing Greek is more about being denied access to the past and translating different cultures, understanding the body, performance and pleasure rather than just a gap in one's education. The narrator's continuous repetition of the word 'Greek' further signifies her wish for a better comprehension of these concepts, which have a tendency to escape her grasp, and it is this elusive quality which causes her to romanticise the language and culture throughout the remainder of the essay. Woolf is not lamenting her deficiency in understanding the grammar and formal characteristics of Greek, for what she really wishes to understand is 'the real meaning of' the language and culture – the humour, the drama, and truth – which is lost in the 'ambiguity' of the unknown Greek words and remains unrepresented in its various English interpretations (39, 44). She wishes to get lost in the 'wild and apparently irrelevant utterances' of Greek and to explore the deeper meanings of the words, which she believes are found 'just on the far side of language', for it is during such 'moments of astonishing excitement and stress' that one is able to produce 'in a rapid flight of the mind' a visual and emotional significance of the work (45, 44). Woolf believes the uneducated reader in Greek is unable to achieve this impressionistic and emotive connection to Greek and is thus forced to undergo a restricted reading experience with English translations.

Before the inclusion of structured language courses at women's colleges near the turn of the century, women were barred from learning the language in a formal classroom environment, and they were subsequently reliant on English translations of the classics. Woolf's narrator critiques the male Oxbridge scholar who merely spells out the words and mangles the 'symmetry' of the Greek text (43). She lists Percy Bysshe

Shelley's rendition of Plato's 'The Banquet' (1818) as an example which represents the negative consequences of reading in translation:

> Every ounce of fat has been pared off, leaving the flesh firm. Then, spare and bare as it is, no language can move more quickly, dancing, shaking, all alive, but controlled. Then there are the words themselves which, in so many instances, we have made expressive to us of our own emotions. (49)

Her description of Greek as a naturally uninhibited language, now restricted in its English interpretation, suggests that the translation process obscures the original meaning and underlying tone of the text. Furthermore, Woolf's characterisation of the Greek words as 'dancing' and 'shaking' across the page alludes to a sense of pleasure and sexualisation in the language that is now repressed in Shelley's more 'controlled' English version. Being denied the option of forming an original interpretation of the passage leads Woolf to declare that the original 'Greek is the only expression' which allows for an unrestricted reading experience, and she maintains that Shelley's translation epitomises how the translator can only give 'a vague equivalent' of the original as his edition 'is full of echoes and associations' that are lost forever to an uneducated reader in Greek (49). Sinclair actively avoids this limiting reading experience in her *Künstlerroman* as Mary takes it upon herself to not only learn Greek for her own intellectual development and inclusion in this patriarchal institution, but to additionally improve her own understanding of her creative potential as a poet.

Sinclair introduces Mary's wish to learn Greek near the end of the 'Childhood' section of the novel. While sitting at a piano with her older brother Mark, Mary recites various lines from Milton's 'Lycidas' (1637) and Pope's translation of the *Illiad* (1715–20), and it is during this impromptu performance that she reflects upon the pleasure she finds in words and how 'there was nothing she liked so much as making these lines' (Sinclair 2002: 77). It is only after noticing Pope's 'lines had to rhyme' that Mary first mentions her growing interest in Greek:

> 'Silent he wandered by the sounding sea,' was good, but the Greek line that Mark showed her went 'Be d'akeon para thina poluphloisboio thalasses'; that was better.
> 'Don't you think so Mark?'
> 'Clever Minx. Much better.'
> 'Mark – if God knew how happy I am writing poetry he'd make the earth open and swallow me up.' (77)

This scene is also the first time Mary vocalises her ambition to write poetry, and her overly dramatic fears about the consequences of such an aspiration communicate the woman artist's insecurities about the public reception of her creativity. Nevertheless, the scene's progression from Mary's general reflection about her pleasure in reading poetry, to her first declaration about wanting to write it, is inherently shaped by her fascination with Greek. Woolf argues in 'The Feminine Note in Fiction' (1905) that the woman writer's 'study of the Greek and Latin classics may give her that sterner view of literature which will make an artist of her' (16). I argue that Mary's confrontation with Greek throughout the novel not only improves her artistry but also transforms her troubled perception of her creativity.

At this point in the narrative Mary has only just embarked on her Greek lessons as she reads Mark's hand-me-down *Greek Accidence* and Smith's *Classical Dictionary* before her piano lessons with Miss Sippett. Mary's understanding of the language is basic and she is unable to read Homer without Mark's assistance. Sinclair's phonetic transliteration of the Greek line in the above passage reflects Mary's illiteracy and inexperience with the language, and the words signify nothing more than gibberish. In spite of her ignorance, Mary still considers Homer's original to be the supreme version, and her offhand reflections suggest Pope's poetic style and use of rhyme are the English translation's biggest fault. While Mary's thoughts about Pope's use of rhymed verse appear only fleetingly, this brief observation foreshadows Mary's later adoption of Sinclair's own views on how the 'unrhymed cadence' of *vers libre* can transform and improve the formal structure of translations and poetry (Sinclair 1921: 11). Mary additionally recognises early on in her self-education that there is a commanding presence surrounding the language, and she subsequently 'leave[s] the Accidence open where Miss Sippett could see it and realise she was not a stupid little girl' (Sinclair 2002: 78). Greek quickly becomes a symbol of intellectual authority for Mary, and Sinclair's juxtaposition of her artist-heroine's autodidactism with the piano lessons further signifies the transgressive undertones associated with Mary's resistance to a traditional feminine education and her active decision to trespass on male intellectual terrain.

Mary's preference for a more masculine form of instruction quickly becomes obvious and Mrs Olivier is unable to ignore her daughter's enthusiasm for the language:

> There was something queer about learning Greek. Mamma did not actually forbid it; but she said it must not be done in lesson time or sewing time, or when people could see you doing it, lest they should think you were showing off. You could see that she didn't believe you *could* learn Greek and that she wouldn't like it if you did. But when lessons were over she let you read Shakespeare or Pope's *Iliad* aloud to her while she sewed. (78)

Mrs Olivier's suspicions about the potentially dangerous influences Greek might have on her daughter are located in her fear of a 'potential gender-role transgression' as Mary wishes to master this masculine tradition of knowledge (Wilson 2003: 372). It was expected that a daughter's reading material would be chosen and supervised by her mother with the utmost care (Flint 2002: 23): Mary's refusal to allow her mother complete control over her recreational reading and self-education is a considerably defiant act for the period. Mrs Olivier's complicated response to her daughter's Greek interests convolutes the rebellious nature of Mary's studies because, as it is a language, it is not considered morally debased reading material, but learning Greek is time-consuming and interferes with Mary's domestic responsibilities. This is what Mrs Olivier most objects to as she, at first, tries to positively reinforce Mary's domestic duties within the home: 'I like to see you behaving like a little girl, instead of tearing about and trying to do what boys do' (Sinclair 2002: 70). Even though Mrs Olivier does not forbid her daughter to learn Greek, she can dictate when and where Mary is allowed to read it. Her request that Mary read only approved texts in the drawing room not only inhibits her daughter's private reading time, but also promotes a false impression of domestic accord in the household as mother and daughter only communicate successfully when discussing the works of acceptable English writers.

By the time Mary is an adolescent she has not really advanced in her Greek studies as her mother's once ambiguous attitude towards the language has now evolved into pure contempt. Mary's longing for the language remains unchanged and she constantly reflects on what little Greek she does know. Poetry acts, once again, as a catalyst for her Greek contemplations as she attempts to visualise how lines made from such images as 'the white dust' and 'the wind in the green corn, of the five trees' would make 'the most beautiful poems in the world' (125). She imagines that these more emotional images slowly 'begin to move before her' as they eventually transform into 'a moving white pattern of sound', although, when she tries to 'catch' the essence of this white pattern in her writing, it almost always 'broke up and flowed away' (125).

Mary blames her inability to create a cohesive pattern on reading 'too much Byron', and it is during these reflections on the relationship between image and sound patterns in the poetry of the Romantics that she focuses on those specific 'patterns of sound' which 'haunt and excite' her the most (125). Rather than drawing upon the formal characteristics of the English poetry she has access to, it is the 'hard and still' sound patterns of the elusive Greek words which dominate her thoughts (125). Mary's relationship with Greek sound patterns is defined by a sense of absence and melancholy that echoes Woolf's aching tone in her essay, and Mary mentally discloses to the reader that 'there were bits of patterns, snapt off, throbbing wounds of sound that couldn't heal', such as, those '[l]ines out of Mark's Homer' now lost to her (125). Mary's aural impressions of these hieroglyphs as fragmented utterances and festering wounds is a far cry from the images of 'white dust' she associates with image patterns found in Romantic poetry as the Greek words, perhaps, reflect her disappointment at being unable to capture these particular sound patterns. Because Mary's comprehension of Greek is still quite limited, she can only really focus on the sounds of the words rather than their underlying meanings and connotations in relation to an entire work. Her focus on the fixed nature of these words as 'hard and still' further signifies the phallic undertones associated with the masculinist language, and additionally reinforces her earlier subconscious critique of Pope's decision to use rhyming lines in his translation. In contrast to her earlier illustration of the phonetic sounds Mary recites to Mark, Sinclair places an extract of untranslated Greek in the text to further emphasise the impenetrability of the words. Her insertion of the original Greek passage, without any formal attempt at translation by Mary, isolates the quotation from the rest of the scene and consequently forces any reader uneducated in Greek to experience the same illiteracy as Mary.[4] Rowena Fowler discusses the effects the untranslated language has on the 'Greekless reader', and she maintains that 'it appears as abstract visual pattern' that is 'unassimilable to the surrounding text' (1999: 224). In this vein, the Greek passage represents the intertwined image and sound pattern Mary tries to achieve in her original poetry although, because she can't comprehend its meaning, the untranslated passage becomes a textual signifier of her unfulfilled potential as a student and poet.

Mary has the resources and the intellectual capacity to master Greek – her biggest obstacle is not the language itself, but her mother. Mrs Olivier subscribes to the ideology that girls are expected 'to learn for the sake of the lesson and not for pleasure's sake' (Sinclair 2002: 74). When Mary tries to persuade Mrs Olivier to give her Mark's books, she rebukes her daughter and declares, 'Just because Mark learnt Greek, you think *you* must try. I thought you'd grown out of all that tiresome affectation' (126). The two women argue over the schoolbooks and because Mrs Olivier finally insults Mary's ambition as nothing more than a superficial, 'silly vanity', Mary finally challenges her mother with the simple declaration: 'You are afraid' (126, 127).

Cheryl A. Wilson's comprehensive analysis of the argument discusses why Mrs Olivier questions Mary's underlying incentive to learn Greek, reluctance to submit to God's will and inability to fulfil her domestic duties (2003: 372–3). Wilson's examination of Mrs Olivier's hostile reaction to Mary's self-education and how it negatively affects her daughter's own perception of her private reading practices is compelling, but Wilson does not explore why Mary is so drawn to the language or how she overcomes her mother's verbal assaults and regains control of her Greek lessons. Throughout the confrontation, Sinclair presents both Mary's spoken and unspoken responses to her mother's argument. Mary initially tries to reason with her mother but, once Mrs Olivier insults her daughter's ambitions, she finally snaps: 'This flash of queerness was accompanied by a sense of irreparable disaster. Everything had changed; she heard herself speaking, speaking steadily, with the voice of a changed and unfamiliar person' (Sinclair 2002: 126–7). When Mrs Oliver questions the point of learning Greek, Mary remains silent:

> She knew the sound patterns were beautiful, and that was all she knew. Beauty. Beauty could be hurt and frightened away from you. If she talked about it now she would expose it to outrage. Though she knew that she must appear to her mother to be stubborn and stupid, even sinful, she put her stubbornness, her stupidity, her sinfulness, between it and her mother to defend it. (127)

One reason for Mary's silence is that she has not been given the chance to develop her knowledge of Greek, and she feels it is an injustice to the language to communicate her evolving, and incomplete, theories about aesthetics, images and sounds to her mother's already hardened opinions. Primarily, though, Mary's mental lamentations about the possible loss of Greek, and her need to protect the one positive outlet in her life, are associated with how her autodidactism allows her to transcend her mother's psychological oppression as well as the repressive limitations of nineteenth-century British society. It is specifically Mary's desire to know Greek which helps her psychologically, and emotionally, distance herself from the life of feminine domesticity as the Victorian Angel in the House that her mother actively endorses.

Mary finally realises that in order to preserve the beauty, innocence and pleasure she associates with Greek, art and poetry, she needs to protect her thoughts, her 'real, secret self', from her mother (374). Mary finally defies the decorum of a dutiful daughter with her one spoken declaration that Mark joined the army to escape her mother's controlling ways. Mrs Olivier breaks down and gives Mary the Greek books, warning her that she will regret her action and, almost immediately, Mary does: '[s]he hated everything that separated her and made her different from her mother and Mark' (129). While she is unwilling to break away from her mother at this moment in the narrative, she later becomes aware that 'to be happy with her either you or she had to be broken, to be helpless and little like a child' (194).

The final division occurs when Mary realises that her mother lied to her about why she was sent home from a girls' boarding school:

> Suddenly she felt hard and strong and grown-up in her sad wisdom. Her mother didn't love her. She never had loved her. Nothing she could ever do would make her love her. Miracles didn't happen [...] Her childhood had died with a little gasp. (145)[5]

As in the earlier argument between Mary and her mother, Sinclair creates an atmosphere of finality as Mary enters the disenchanted realm of adulthood, where she finally does what she pleases and continues her self-education regardless of her mother's opinion. Mary embraces this newfound intellectual freedom and she toils at her studies – which primarily focus on philosophy, psychology and Greek – although she remains conflicted about her transgression and still struggles to overcome her fear that her desire to write and publish her translations and poems is a 'monstrous thought' and 'deadly sin' (313, 234).

Mary does confront these fears near the end of Book Four, 'Maturity', when she spends three years translating Euripides' *Bacchæ* and writing poetry:

> You could do it after you had read Walt Whitman. If you gave up the superstition of singing; the little tunes of rhyme. If you left off that eternal jingling and listened, you could hear what it ought to be.
> Something between talking and singing. If you wrote verse that could be chanted: that could be whispered, shouted, screamed as they moved. Agave and her Maenads. Verse that would go with a throbbing beat, excited, exciting; beyond rhyme. That would be the nearest to Greek verse. (326)

Mary's interpretation of Euripides foreshadows the style of translation Woolf demands in 'On Not Knowing Greek'. Mary's wish to finally break the residual rhyming patterns found in previous English translations like Pope's *Iliad* is finally implemented in her translation of Euripides' drama, and her suggestion that the words should be spoken, not sung, reflects back to her earlier belief that Greek words are meant to be hard and still. Mary maintains that the established motif of rhyming verse becomes yet another form of concealment which prevents the Greekless reader from capturing the correct sound patterns and meaning of the original text.

Furthermore, Mary's contention that Whitman's poetry establishes a verse pattern that modern translations should adhere to reiterates Sinclair's own views that contemporary poetry should 'escape tradition', 'clear the mind of cant, the cant of iambics', 'cast off the tinkling golden fetters of rhyme' (Sinclair 1906: 326). Sinclair's own belief that rhyming verse has mechanised poetry into submission as a 'stale literature' is echoed in Mary's theories about the problems of translation (Sinclair 1921: 9). Moreover, her artist-heroine's request for a more pulsating, 'throbbing beat' in English translations alludes to the sexual and dangerous undertones associated with such rhythmic release found in the original Greek. This is further underpinned by her allusion to such mythological figures as Maenads/Bacchantes, who were often presented in Greek art and literature as madwomen capable of mutilating and eating both wild animals and humans ('maenads'; Hedreen 1994: 49). Such moments of insanity were only temporary, and Albert Henrichs argues that 'the cultic reality of maenadism was more subdued and less exotic' (1978: 123). He maintains that both married and unmarried women's 'escape from house and home' to participate in various rituals was often a short-lived emancipation from their 'restricted role in Greek society' (122). Mary's allusion to Hellenistic maenadism does draw attention to the wild and ecstatic nature associated with their rituals, although what she also suggests is that the poetic and translation process should emulate these sensations through unconventional rhyming patterns and *vers libre* – liberating the translation from the static conventions of traditional English verse. While Sinclair does not include an example of Mary's revolutionary translation of the *Bacchæ*, Mary's narrative voice and original poetry do assume these hard and still sound patterns.

The reader is not introduced to samples of Mary's original poetry until much later in the novel, and even then these are only short samples. Sinclair does present Mary's artistic consciousness through her experimentation with style, narration and point of view. Sinclair utilises both the stream-of-consciousness narrative and free indirect thought, and the narrative voice often assumes Mary's developing poetic vision and takes on her burgeoning Imagist style:

> Stone walls. A wild country, caught in the net of the stone walls.
> Stone wall following the planes of the land, running straight along the valleys, switchbacking up and down the slopes. Humped-up, grey spines of the green mounds.
>
>   Stone walls, piled loosely, with the brute skill of earth-men, building centuries ago. They bulged, they toppled, yet they stood firm, holding the wild country in their mesh, knitting the grey villages to the grey farms, and the farms to the grey byres. Where you thought the net had ended it flung out a grey rope over the purple back of Renton, the green shoulder of Greffington [...]
>   When you had got through the gate you were free. (Sinclair 2002: 178)

Mary's reflections about the structure and composition of the 'stone walls' and 'wild countryside' reflect the Imagist's desire for 'direct contact with reality', wherein 'there is nothing between you and the object' (Sinclair 1915: 88). Natan Zach argues in his essay 'Imagism and Vorticism' (1976) that the Imagist movement 'is perhaps best viewed as a doctrine of *hardness*' which shapes the concrete image, 'style, rhythm and emotion' of a poem (1991: 238). Mary's preference for the hard and still sound patterns in Greek verse shapes her Imagist aesthetics and is reproduced in her thoughts and writing.[6] Mary's impressions are succinct and straightforward as she employs the emergent trend of *vers libre* to present the '"rough" (i.e. irregular) contours of "things"' (238); for example, the material composition of the stone walls and the '[h]umped-up, grey spines' of the rolling hills.

Rather than imitating the mechanised cadence of 'orthodox iambics', alliteration and assonance associated with Romanticism and Victorian poetry, the pace of Mary's stream of consciousness appears to be shaped by the particular object she is currently focused upon (Sinclair 1921: 6). When describing the walls, for example, Mary's description is concise and to the point as she reflects upon the dense materiality of the cold, hard stone: '[t]hey bulged, they toppled, yet they stood firm' (Sinclair 2002: 175). The tempo shifts and expands once she switches her gaze to the vast countryside spread out before her and, like the curved slope of the '[h]umped-up hills', the rhythm of Mary's thoughts rise and fall like a wave – 'switchbacking up and down' – before returning to the terse diction associated with the 'stone walls' trapping both her and the 'wild country' (175).

The Imagists refrained from using traditional rhyme and metre in their work, but their poetry did not lack rhythm and in the 'Preface to *Some Imagists Poets*' (1915) the editors argue that that the Imagist should 'create new rhythms – as the expression of new moods – and not to copy old rhythms, which merely echo old moods' (Jones 1972: 135). Sinclair agreed, and in her defence of the movement she maintains that, like Greek, Imagist poetry '*proves* the power of the clean, naked sensuous image to carry the emotion without rhyming – *not*, I think, without rhythm; the best Imagist poems have a very subtle and beautiful rhythm' which she recreates in her representation of Mary's stream of consciousness (1915: 88). It is the juxtaposition of these two contrasting images of restriction and freedom, and their distinctly different sound patterns, that prevents Mary's poetic voice from succumbing to the rhythm patterns, moods and expressions associated with nineteenth-century poetry.

While Mary's stream of consciousness successfully presents the hard and still image and the sound patterns of the stone walls and Greffington countryside, Sinclair still manages to create an emotional connection between Mary and these images as her thoughts develop into a much more comprehensive realisation about the reality of her restricted existence. Her prolonged focus on the town's barricades and the metaphorical net they cast over its inhabitants reflects Mary's psychological repression in nineteenth-century society and, rather than feeling secure within the towering stone walls, the clipped, staccato phrases of her thoughts reveal a sense of oppression embedded within the town's framework as the net of society continuously extends. It is only once she crosses the threshold of the last gate, which leads to the wild country, that her stream of consciousness starts to unfold in a more relaxed, impressionistic style:

> Inlets of green grass forked into purple heather. Green streamed through purple, lapped against purple, lay on purple in pools and splashes.
> Burnt patches. Tongues of heather, twisted and pointed, picked clean by fire, flickering grey over black-earth. Towards evening the black and grey ran together like ink and water, stilled into purple, the black purple of grapes. (Sinclair 2002: 178)

Free from 'the net of the walls', Mary's thoughts become more creative and she begins to play with the various images found in nature as if she were mentally composing a poem (178). Even though the Imagists said 'good-bye to the mere symbol', they still welcomed the metaphor in their poetry if it could be used in more interesting ways, 'to convey a more striking image', and Mary's metaphor of the burnt heather as vibrating tongues presents a more sensual impression of the wild countryside than was previously seen behind the stone walls (Sinclair 1921: 7). Mary's stream of consciousness transforms the pastoral setting into Imagist prose, and this scene undoubtedly reveals her artistry and potential as a poet and is a significant example of Sinclair's experiments with the presentation of narrative voice.

Throughout the majority of the novel, Sinclair's artist-heroine fears the public perception of her artistry, and she relies on maintaining the divide between her private passion for poetry and her performative, public self. She believes keeping her writing a secret protects her from the judgemental attitudes of her family and society. It is not until Book Five of the novel, 'Middle-Age', that Mary's extensive knowledge of Greek finally allows her the chance to enter the public domain as secretary to a renowned classics scholar, Richard Nicholson. As the work relationship develops from collegiality into friendship and finally romance, Mary eventually finds the courage to let him read her translation of the *Bacchæ*.

In contrast to her mother's reactions to her self-education, Richard seems genuinely interested in Mary's divergent path and approves of her interpretation of Euripides: '"Yes. Yes. It *is* the way to do it. The only way... You see, that's what my Euripides book's about. The very thing I've been trying to ram down people's throats, for years. And all this time you were doing it – down here – all by yourself – for fun"' (338). Nicholson's agreement with Mary's theories about rhyme and translation offers her some validation for her intellectual isolation all these years and he pushes her to publish, but he wants the reading public to be aware that she 'is a poet translating; not the other way on' (339). It is through Richard's support that Mary finally transcends her previous anxieties about the public reception of her artistry. This support allows her to contemplate the possibility of life as a poet and embrace the potential of living an independent life away from her mother.

Throughout *Mary Olivier: A Life*, Sinclair contests Beale's argument that there is 'no comparison between the mental abilities of boys and girls' as Mary surpasses her brothers in their Greek studies and proves that women can compete with men in the intellectual and artistic sphere (1866: 1). Sinclair situates this battle for intellectual autonomy as a visceral and physical fight as Mary's mental struggles and sacrifices are repeatedly depicted throughout the novel. Christine Battersby maintains the *Künstlerroman* is a '"A Portrait of the Artist as a Middle-Aged Woman"' and fails to truly fulfil the attributes of the genre (119). I argue Sinclair presents an honest portrayal of the woman artist's difficult struggle to achieve intellectual and artistic fulfilment at the turn of the century, and I believe her complicated relationship with the language is one of the driving forces behind her eventual creative fulfilment and professionalisation as a female poet.

Notes

1. The *Künstlerroman* is a subgenre of the *Bildungsroman* and is concerned specifically with the hero/ine's artistic development and participation in the creative process.
2. This chapter focuses specifically on the education of middle-class women in England.
3. Not all women's colleges followed Rouse's suggestion. The Ladies' Department at King's College London offered more advanced Greek courses. Woolf was enrolled there from 1897 to 1901, and her Greek classes were 'prescribed for the final pass BA exams of the University of London' (Jones and Snaith 2010: 15).
4. Virago's 2002 edition of *Mary Olivier* remains true to the original publication and does not include any footnotes or translations of Greek extracts inserted throughout the novel.

5. Mary attends the Clevehead School for a fleeting, unrepresented period. Sinclair's brief description of the fictional college suggests it is modelled upon Cheltenham as Mary is taught Greek 'with the old arithmetic master' based on Beale (146).
6. The connection between Greek and Imagism appears repeatedly in the prefaces, essays and letters of the movement's members. In a letter to Harriet Monroe, the founder and editor of *Poetry: A Magazine of Verse*, Ezra Pound maintains that modern poetry reproduces the style of Greeks: 'Objective – no slither; direct – no excessive use of adjectives, no metaphors that won't permit examination. It's straight talk, straight as the Greeks!' (Jones 1972: 17).

Works Cited

Battersby, Christine (2002), '"In the Shadow of His Language": May Sinclair's Portrait of the Artist as Daughter', *New Comparison: A Journal of Comparative and General Literary Studies* 33:4, 102–20.
Beale, Dorothea (1866), 'On the Education of Girls', paper read at the Social Science Congress, October 1865, and reprinted from the *Transactions*, London: Bell & Daldy.
Beale, Dorothea (1869), 'Preface' in Great Britain Royal Commission on Education, *Reports issued by the Schools' Inquiry Commission, on the Education of Girls*, London: David Nutt, p. xxxvi.
Beale, Dorothea, Lucy H. M. Soulsby and Jane Francis Dove (1898), *Work and Play in Girls' Schools*, London: Longmans & Co.
Beaumont, Jacqueline (2007), 'Dorothea Beale (1831–1906)', *Oxford Dictionary of National Biography*, Oxford: Oxford University Press, http://www.oxforddnb.com/view/article/30655 (last accessed 22 June 2016).
Bradbury, Malcolm, and James McFarlane, eds (1991), *Modernism: A Guide to European Literature, 1890–1930*, London: Penguin Books.
Brantlinger, Patrick (1998), *The Reading Lesson: The Threat of Mass Literacy in Nineteenth-Century British Fiction*, Bloomington and Indianapolis: Indiana University Press.
Brontë, Charlotte [1847] (1908), *Jane Eyre*, London: J. M. Dent & Co; New York: E. P. Dutton & Co.
Dusinberre, Juliet (1997), *Virginia Woolf's Renaissance: Woman Reader or Common Reader?*, London: Macmillan.
Flint, Kate (2002), *The Woman Reader, 1837–1914* (1993), Oxford: Clarendon Press.
Fowler, Rowena (1999), 'Moments and Metamorphoses: Virginia Woolf's Greece', *Comparative Literature* 51:3, 217–42.
Gilbert, Sandra, and Susan Gubar (1988), *No Man's Land: The Place of the Woman Writer in the Twentieth Century – Volume I: The War of the Worlds*, New Haven, CT and London: Yale University Press.
Great Britain Royal Commission on Education (1869), *Reports issued by the Schools' Inquiry Commission, on the Education of Girls*, London: David Nutt.

Hedreen, Guy (1994), 'Silens, Nymphs, and Maenads', *The Journal of Hellenic Studies* 114, 47–89.
Heinrichs, Albert (1978), 'Greek Maenadism from Olympia to Messalina', *Harvard Studies in Classical Philology* 82, 121–60.
Jones, Christine Kenyon, and Anna Snaith (2010), '"Tilting at Universities": Woolf At King's College London', *Woolf Studies Annual* 16, 1–44.
Jones, Peter, ed. (1972), *Imagist Poetry*, London: Penguin.
Kamm, Josephine (1958), *How Different from Us: A Biography of Miss Buss & Miss Beale*, London: The Bodley Head.
Kunka, Andrew J., and Michele K. Troy, eds (2006), *May Sinclair: Moving Toward the Modern*, Hampshire and Burlington: Ashgate Publishing Ltd.
Pound, Ezra [1913] (1978), 'A Few Don'ts By an Imagiste', in P. Jones (ed.), *Imagist Poetry*, London: Penguin, pp. 130–4.
'Preface to *Some Imagist Poets 1915*' (1978), in P. Jones (ed.), *Imagist Poetry*, London: Penguin, pp. 134–5.
Purvis, June (1991), *A History of Women's Education in England*, Milton Keynes and Philadelphia: Open University Press.
Raikes, Elizabeth [1908] (1909), *Dorothea Beale of Cheltenham*, 3rd edn, London: Archibald Constable and Company Ltd.
Raitt, Suzanne (2000), *May Sinclair: A Modern Victorian*, Oxford: Clarendon Press.
Rouse, W. H. (1898), 'Classical Studies', in Dorothea Beale, Lucy H. M. Soulsby and Jane Francis Dove (eds), *Work and Play in Girls' Schools*, London: Longmans & Co, pp. 67–93.
Showalter, Elaine (1982), *The Female Malady: Women, Madness and English Culture, 1830–1980* (1985), London: Virago Press Ltd.
Sinclair, May (1906), 'Three American Poets of Today: Edward Arlington Robinson, William Vaughan Moody and Ridgely Torrence', *Atlantic Monthly* 98 (September 1906), 325–35.
Sinclair, May (1908), 'Introduction', in Charlotte Brontë, *Jane Eyre*, London: J. M. Dent & Co; New York: E. P. Dutton & Co, pp. vii–xviii.
Sinclair, May (1915), 'Two Notes', *The Egoist* 2:6 (1 June 1915), 88–9.
Sinclair, May [1919] (2002), *Mary Olivier: A Life*, London: Virago Press.
Sinclair, May (1921), 'The Poems of F. S. Flint', *English Review* 32 (January 1921), 6–18.
Walford, Geoffrey, ed. (1993a), *The Private Schooling of Girls: Past and Present*, London: Woburn Press.
Walford, Geoffrey (1993b), 'Girls' Private Schooling: Past and Present,' in Walford, *The Private Schooling of Girls: Past and Present*, London: Woburn Press, pp. 9–32.
Wilson, Cheryl A. (2003), 'The Victorian Woman Reader in May Sinclair's *Mary Olivier*: Self-Stimulation, Intellectual Freedom, and Escape', *English Literature in Transition, 1880–1920* 46:4, 365–81.
Woolf, Virginia (1886–2011), *Essays of Virginia Woolf*, 6 vols, ed. Andrew McNeillie and Stuart N. Clarke, London: The Hogarth Press.
Woolf, Virginia (1905) 'The Feminine Note in Fiction', in Andrew McNeillie and Stuart N. Clarke (eds), *Essays of Virginia Woolf: Volume One, 1904–1912*, London: The Hogarth Press, pp. 15–17.

Woolf, Virginia (1925), 'On Not Knowing Greek', in Andrew McNeillie and Stuart N. Clarke (eds), *Essays of Virginia Woolf: Volume Four, 1925–1928*, London: The Hogarth Press, pp. 38–53.
Woolf, Virginia (1927), 'Two Women', in Andrew McNeillie and Stuart N. Clarke (eds), *Essays of Virginia Woolf: Volume Four, 1925–1928*, London: The Hogarth Press, pp. 419–26.
Woolf, Virginia [1938] (2000), *Three Guineas*, London: Penguin Classics.
Zach, Natan (1991), 'Imagism and Vorticism,' in *Modernism: A Guide to European Literature, 1890–1930* (1976), London: Penguin Books, pp. 228–42.

Chapter 3

Portrait of the Female Character as a Psychoanalytical Case: The Ambiguous Influence of Freud on May Sinclair's Novels

Leslie de Bont

> The case represents a problem or event that has animated some kind of judgment. Any enigma could do – a symptom, [. . .] a situation, [. . .] or any irritating obstacle to clarity. (Berlant 2007: 1)

When May Sinclair started to write fiction and read psychoanalytical papers in the 1890s, case histories were emerging as a crucial medium that helped Sigmund Freud and the other founding fathers of psychoanalysis circulate the new and singular questions raised by their most puzzling patients (Martindale 2003: 5; Bortoli 1998: 146). The case quickly became a valuable tool in psychoanalytical epistemology; it enabled the first psychoanalysts to develop their discipline, challenge existing theories and set up new therapeutic approaches. But the case study is also a textual object that relies on *deixis*, dialogues, narratives and analyses, in ways that are similar to fictional writing. Because of their structure and undeniable appeal, Freud's case histories have actually often been compared to fictional texts: Michel de Certeau shows that Freud's texts have little to do with contemporary scientific papers precisely because of their return to narrativity (de Certeau 1981: 23), while Freud himself asks his reader not to consider his texts as mere *'romans à clefs'* (Freud 1970: 3). Conversely, commentators have also compared Sinclair's fiction to Freud's case histories (Cooper 1912; Lubbock 1923; Radford 1980); a perspective I would like to explore in this chapter.

Sinclair's key psychological research papers – 'The Way of Sublimation' (1915), 'Clinical Lectures' (1916) and 'Psychological Types' (1923) – suggest that she favoured a Jungian-based eclectic approach to psychoanalysis rather than Freud's sexual theory, which she also integrated into her two philosophical books, *A Defence of Idealism* (1917) and *The New Idealism* (1922).[1] Yet Freud's influence remained central to her fiction and non-fiction, and more particularly to her textual strategies and character depictions. This chapter thus argues that Sinclair's idiosyncratic integration of Freudian psychoanalysis has produced some of her most innovative experimentations with feminine modernist fiction. Following Freud's case studies, Sinclair's novels represent female characters as particular cases, psychoanalytical experiments, open questions or enigmas, rather than illustrations or generic demonstrations, and thus invite readers to probe into the female protagonist's psychic apparatus and investigate her specific subjectivity, as well as her contradictory desires and aspirations.

Sinclair's modernism focuses on portraying the psychological singularity and 'misfit femininity' of her heroines, and on showing their maladaptation to public discourses, available research or social groups and the norm (Wilson 2000: 49). Her fiction systematically conveys neglected feminine issues that actually challenged Freudian theories, just as Freud's cases challenged the psychological and medical discourses of his time. Sinclair's stylistic explorations (such as the shifts in pronouns or the emphasis on her characters' names as a means to show their irreducible individual singularity), her subject matters (such as the lesser-known questions of femininity, ranging from the sensuality of breastfeeding to the specificities of ageing in female characters), and her methodology (through the direct references to psychoanalysis, the constant questioning of the stabilised textual references or the appeal to the reader's psychoanalytical skills) have indeed a lot in common with Freud's psychoanalytical case-based research.

In order to address Freud's complex and ambiguous influence on May Sinclair's fiction, this chapter will analyse the textual proximity between Freud's case histories and Sinclair's feminist and clinical portrayal of two of her female characters: Jane Holland (*The Creators*, 1910) and Mary Olivier (*Mary Olivier: A Life*, 1919). Sinclair's representation of psychoanalytical time will then be examined as yet another example of her open-ended adaptation of Freud's case-based theories. Contrary to what her two neo-idealist essays might have led us to assume, her *Bildungsromane* do not follow an idealist temporality leading towards closure. Rather, and perhaps truer to Freud's 1937 article 'Analysis Terminable and Interminable', which emphasises the many ways in which the unconscious escapes linearity, they rely on a complex use of temporality that stresses the difference in individual patterns and focuses on individual time-frames rather than on the individual's relation to universal temporal landmarks. Lastly, a study of dreams and self-analysis in *Mary Olivier* will show that the novel's informed references to Freud's theories on dreams and symbols echo modernist experimentations with metafiction, through the specific aesthetics of scientific uncertainty.

Textual Proximity: A Feminist Portrait of the Heroine as a Clinical Case

Sinclair's use of the word 'case' is always significant. One of the most interesting occurrences can be found in the story 'Portrait of my Uncle' (1917) from the collection *Tales Told by Simpson*, in which Uncle Simpson becomes blind after a fight with his wife:

> Filson explained it all scientifically on some theory of the Subconscious. It seems that Freud, or Jung, or Morton Prince, or one of those johnnies, had a case exactly like my uncle's. He said my uncle could not see, and did not see, because he did not want to see. His blindness was the expression of a strong subconscious wish never to see his wife again, a wish which, of course, his conscious self had very properly suppressed. On the one side it was a laudable effort at self-preservation [. . .]; on the other side, of course, it was just a morbid obsession. (37–8)

The use of the word 'case', despite its ironic context, shows how the uncle's situation is both a clear illustration of the 'theory of the Subconscious', and a rather enigmatic question.[2] The entire story actually provides the reader with a clinical anamnesis of uncle Simpson's disorder and will bring out links between his complex feelings for his wife, his health – besides blindness, he'll suffer from 'some obscure heart trouble' (40) – and a painting, the portrait of the title, which represents the couple as a unit. This works as a symbolic key, and clearly weaves art and case-studies together: a perspective that is reinforced when Sinclair depicts female artists.

Diseases and mysterious afflictions are often indicators of the complexity of Sinclair's female characters. In *The Creators*, Jane Holland is examined by two doctors, Henry Brodrick and Owen Prothero, who make conflicting diagnoses. She is referred to as 'a marvel and a mystery' (253) and her genius is represented through a whole array of denominations, including the pronouns *he* and *it*, and curious phrases such as 'the thing', showing the potentially worrying inhumanity of her very existence, as well as being a likely reference to Freud's choice of a neutral pronoun *id*, or *Es* in the original German, for describing 'the dark, inaccessible part of our personality' (Freud 1933: 73). Her genius is also called 'a great Neurosis' (360) by Dr Brodrick. This choice of term refers to modern psychological sciences, yet the content of his discourse echoes Cesare Lombroso's theories of genius as degeneration and Henry Maudsley's *Sex in Mind and in*

Education, in which he warns women against the side-effects of education, among which stand sterility and giving birth to degenerate or weak children (Lombroso 1891: 4 and Maudsley 1894: 6). The latter scenario is what happens to Jane, but the novel provides an alternative explanation: that of existing antecedents in the Brodrick family. In a word, Jane's genius challenges Dr Brodrick's normative discourse:

> 'I shouldn't be surprised,' said [Dr Brodrick], 'if some time or other she was to have a bad nervous break-down.' [. . .]
> 'My dear Henry, you wouldn't be surprised if everybody had a bad nervous break-down. [. . .]'
> Henry said he *did* expect it in women of Miss Holland's physique, who habitually over-drive their brains beyond the power of their body. He became excessively professional as he delivered himself on this head. It was his subject. He was permitted to enlarge upon it from time to time. [. . .]
> 'I have had her,' said he, 'under very close observation.'
> 'So have I,' said Hugh. 'You forget that she is an exceptional woman.'
> 'On the contrary, I think her so very exceptional as to be quite abnormal. Geniuses generally are.' (Sinclair 2009c: 263)

The contrast between the objectification of Jane ('*It* was *his* subject. He was permitted') and the intensity of her symptoms ('over-drive', 'beyond', 'exceptional', etc.) is striking and points to the more obvious contradictions in Henry's speech (see the proximity of the terms 'abnormal' and 'generally'). Through its distanced narrative voice, the text suggests that if all geniuses are abnormal, then the norms need to be redefined. In other words, if Jane does not fit Henry's chartered medical discourses, perhaps it is because his discourse, rather than her behaviour, is excessive. This is also at stake in the ironic use of the term 'excessively': excess, which Henry attributes to all geniuses, is here associated with the ('excessively professional') doctor, and not to his patient. By contrast, Prothero's diagnosis is much more articulate:

> There were *cases*, he declared, where disease was a higher sort of health. 'Take,' he said, 'a genius with a pronounced neurosis. *His* body may be a precious poor medium for all ordinary purposes. But he couldn't have a more delicate, more lyrical, more perfectly adjusted instrument for *his* purposes than the nervous system you call diseased.' (420; emphasis added)

One of the key words in this short extract is of course 'cases', which is in keeping with Prothero's many contextual nuances, hypotheses and open questions. In that respect, Prothero's discourse resembles Jane's and shows how Sinclair's heroines challenge the stasis of medical ideology; how they need to have medical discourses adapted to their situations and not the other way around:

Jane had been ill. [. . .] Dr. Henry had been profoundly interested *in her case*. So had his sister, Mrs Heron, and Mr John Brodrick and Mrs John, and Sophy Levine and Gertrude Collett, and Winny and Eddy Heron. Since the day when they had first received her, the Brodricks had established a regular cult of Jane Holland. [. . .] She knew that Brodrick's family had begun by regarding her as part of Brodrick's property, the most eligible, the most valuable part. (244; emphasis added)

Philippa Martindale offers an enlightening comparison of the ideological background that underlies Prothero's and Brodrick's discourse:

> In *The Creators* two doctors with opposing medical views offer very contrasting opinions on the nature of genius. The traditional, patriarchal Dr Henry Brodrick follows Lombroso's conclusions: genius is a malady, a neurosis. [. . .] An examination of Prothero's interpretation shows that it is entirely in line with the contemporary debate surrounding the psychological aetiology of genius. William James refers to the fully integrated self when he reviewed the current literature on the subject in his article 'Degeneration and Genius' (1895). (2003: 62–4)

The discrepancy is also clearly perceptible in their methodology. When Prothero focuses on the patient ('his body', 'his purpose', etc.) and emphasises his distance from general discourses ('the [. . .] system *you* call diseased'), Brodrick's use of the word 'case' is nothing but makeshift. What Brodrick underlines is not Jane's fruitful singularity, but rather, its consequences to his family. Unlike Brodrick's self-centred approach, Prothero adapts his knowledge as well as the form and content of his discourse to his patient, and thus appears as a much more modern physician, who abides by the key tenets of the earliest psychoanalytical case-based research. Another example of case-based portrayal can be found in the 1901 story 'Superseded', in which ageing is given a casuistic treatment, showing that the feminine psychology of old age is little addressed, and thus necessitates new tools, such as bibliotherapy ('Superseded', George Johnson argues, is 'the first instance of bibliotherapy in fiction' as 'Dr. Cautley prescribes a course of light literature' as part of a 'forward thinking talking cure' [Johnson 2006: 122–4]). Other shorter texts, such as *The Romantic* (which is very close to a case analysed by Alfred Adler that Sinclair comments upon in her 1915 unpublished essay 'The Way of Sublimation': 37–8), also bear resemblances to case histories in a similar way.

This is perhaps where May Sinclair's writing most greatly differs from other modernist authors, whose depiction of the echoes that resonate between fragmented and diverse experiences greatly differs from Sinclair's focus on exceptional or particular experiences. She depicts the singularity of her characters, showing how they do not fit public discourses and available research.

Besides their depiction of the feminine issues related to old age, Sinclair's novels often seem to focus on the specific questions raised by femininity (Liggins 2014: 117–62). One of Sinclair's central themes is what we call today the attachment theory, after John Bowlby's and Mary Ainsworth's studies, 'The Nature of the Child's Tie to His Mother' (1958) and *Attachment and Loss* (1969), which set out to describe and analyse a child's tie with his or her primary caregiver and its consequence on the child's life and development.[3] Yet, before any theoretical development on the subject, several of Sinclair's novels depict the evolutions, and sometimes the disorders, of the attachment relation between a child and her mother with a nearly clinical approach. Sinclair's fictional representation of attachment owes a lot to her reading of Jung's analysis of the fantasies of the return to the mother in 'The Way of Sublimation', in which she studies both the strength of attachment and the necessity to go beyond it; 'the child must win or remain forever immature' (Sinclair 1915: 39) is one of the key issues in Mary's *Bildung* (apprenticeship). In other words, Sinclair's conception stands halfway between Freud and Jung's psychoanalytical approach on the one hand, which includes the Oedipus complex or possibly Jung's Elektra complex, and Bowlby's developmental approach on the other (Jung 1915: 69–70 and Bowlby 1969: xxvi). This combination is precisely at stake in the opening pages of *Mary Olivier*, which rely on the sensuality of infancy as well as on the complexity of the mother-daughter link:

> She screamed. Mamma took her to her big bed. Mamma's breast: a smooth, cool, round thing that hung to your hands and slipped from them when they tried to hold it. You could feel the little ridges of the stiff nipple as your finger pushed it back into the breast. (4)

The alternation of pronouns shows the necessity to both cancel and create some distance, whenever there is an intense and ambiguous situation; while showing the complexity of the mother-child relation, a subject which was still missing in public discourses. Indeed, by providing fictional, and dense, examples of the Oedipus complex, Sinclair shows the inadequacy of Freud's texts and not only anticipates later developments by Bowlby on the impact of attachment throughout life, but also by Klein on the age of the onset of such a complex, and by other female psychoanalysts on the role of the pre-symbolic, as Humm and Martindale have convincingly argued (Humm 1995: 74 and Martindale 2003: 24).

In her non-fiction, Sinclair makes numerous comments about the absence of feminine specificities in theoretical and public discourses. Her novels seem to fill such gaps and represent many feminine events such as the physical pain of menstruation (*Mary Olivier*), the emotional aspect of ageing ('Superseded'), a mother's distress at her newborn's cries or ambivalence towards breastfeeding (*The Tysons* and *The Creators*). Such an approach is again very close to the case-based investigation of psychoanalysis, in which the main goals were to examine 'exceptional facts' and 'to call for an introduction of new frameworks [. . .] that allow us to redefine norms and exceptions' (Passeron and Revel 2005: 10).[4]

Indeed, if the novel has been considered as a protest against the masculine point of view of psychoanalysis by Humm and Martindale among others (Humm 1995: 74 and Martindale 2003: 24), we can also investigate *Mary Olivier* as exploratory fiction, drawing from the way Freud's case histories had explored uncharted situations. However, Sinclair's fiction creates even more complex situations than those considered by Freud or Jung, since in the case of Mary, the tyrannical mother soon becomes a widow, and thus embodies both paternal law and maternal tenderness. The combination is anxiety-provoking; another prospect that would be investigated by Melanie Klein some ten years later (Klein 1929: 217). Sinclair turns her fiction into a dialogic material that incorporates a psychoanalytical exploration into the aesthetic representation of her character's *Bildung* and even anticipates later researches on the specificities of the female experience which are related to her specific interest in early feminism.

Sinclair's fiction also enters a larger dialogue with her work on psychoanalysis and enriches her own research questions. The much-discussed final page of the *Bildungsroman Mary Olivier* is a very ambiguous application of Sinclair's theories of ultimate consciousness (1917: 379) and sublimation (1915: 9). Mary lies on her bed; she has returned, alone, to her dead mother's home and has rejected Richard's marriage proposal. She is overwhelmed with open-ended questions and potentially worrying ecstasies.

> Supposing there isn't anything in it? Supposing – Supposing –
> Last night I began thinking about it again. I stripped my soul; I opened all the windows and let my ice-cold thoughts in on the poor thing; it stood shivering between certainty and uncertainty. I tried to doubt away this ultimate passion, and it turned my doubt into its own exquisite sting, the very thrill of the adventure.
> Supposing there's nothing in it, nothing at all?
> That's the risk you take.
> There isn't any risk. This time it was clear, clear as the black pattern the sycamore makes on the sky. If it never came again I should remember. (379–80)

What is first remarkable about this ending is that it is a place of anaphoric repetition, indicating a deep questioning, but also a shift from nothingness ('nothing in it, nothing at all') to clarity ('clear, clear'). Mary has evolved but remains a near oxymoron; '*clear* as the *black* pattern', or an enigma that defies the theories that should have framed her development. Through Mary's path towards knowledge, the text does convey an aesthetic of the particular case, more than an actual attempt at illustrating any theory, or any literary genre. The intense physical dimension of the scene ('the very thrill of the adventure'/'exquisite sting') and the lexis, which is reminiscent of Sinclair's writings on idealism and ultimate reality, the 'ultimate passion', could also signal that Mary has indeed sublimated her libido. However, the scene does not correspond to any of the six ways that Sinclair identifies in her essays on the subject: besides the four ways of sublimation (religion, art, scientific research and 'concrete activities', 85) that Sinclair analyses in 'The Way of Sublimation', she refers to love and heroic behaviour as ways of sublimation in *A Defence of Idealism* (379). In *Mary Olivier*, what is at stake is not traditional religion, since Mary spent most of the novel criticising her mother's Anglicanism, but it could be a personal, mystical version of religion, that has the potential to be combined to both her scientific and philosophical research and her poetry in free verse: 'How do I know my writing isn't like my playing? This is different. There's nothing else. If it's taken from me, I shan't want to go on living' (313) and 'Reality breaking through, if only in flashes coming and going altogether and forgotten – why had you to wait so long before you could remember it and be aware of it before; she had only thought about and about it, about Substance, the Thing-in-itself, Reality, God' (378). Indeed, if sublimation is indeed at stake in this scene, it is Mary's idiosyncratic and interactive combination of religion, research and art: a perspective that Sinclair overlooks in her essays.

This final scene also evokes other Sinclairian endings: those of *The Tysons* (1898), *The Creators* (1910) and *Life and Death of Harriett Frean* (1922), for instance, all depict the heroine lying on a bed while reintroducing, however differently, a sense of uncertainty. Marianne Hirsch sees these inconclusive endings as a deliberate 'strategy of oscillation and contradiction' that aims at creating an alternative model of fictional exploration (Hirsch 1989: 93).[5] Such a perspective is central to Sinclair's fiction and psychoanalytical research, which both argue for a dynamic conception of psychological development in which the self disappears and reappears according to its own pattern. The end of *Mary Olivier*: 'Let everything go except yourself. But you felt your self going. Going and coming back' (378) can thus be read as a fictional echo of Sinclair's remark in *A Defence of Idealism* that 'the self may have identity and lose it, and recover it and lose it again' (316). Through this aesthetics of perpetual change and open analysis, we could also see Sinclair's novel as a pre-theorisation of what Elaine Showalter says about the absence of epilogue in Freud's female case narratives (Showalter 1997: 95), and in anticipation of his 1937 article 'Analysis Terminable and Interminable'. Indeed, except for 'Little Hans', none of Freud's psychoanalytical case narratives reach any sense of closure: the analysis stopped, either because of the patient's refusal to continue or because the patient moved away and never returned to Freud.

Since Sinclair's *Bildungsromane* do not follow a neo-idealist temporality leading towards closure or completion, they also call for new aesthetic discourses. They provide us with a complex representation of temporality that is deeply influenced, once again, by Freud's theories, epistemology and case-based methodology, but also announce several psychoanalytical and psychological time-frames that were yet to be outlined.

Temporal Ruptures and Psychoanalytical Time

The many links between Sinclair's fiction and several of Melanie Klein's seminal concepts have been underlined by Philippa Martindale (2003), Kuno Shin (2006) and George Johnson (2006). Sinclair's fiction also anticipates Klein's work on positions, instead of the notion of 'stages', used by Sigmund Freud and C. G. Jung, which offers a freer, or more adaptive depiction of psychological pattern, temporality and structure, as they lay a greater emphasis on an individual's specific relation to time.[6] For Klein, the potential atemporality of positions does not necessarily presume any normative time-frame; on the contrary, it allows various overlapping, resurfacing, regressions and forward leaps. Klein's seminal work on positions also implies that a child's development is not a series of general phases but a unique combination of micro-patterns, which she clearly shows in 'Love, Guilt, and Reparation' as she investigates the possible simultaneity of contradictory feelings and experiences without ever referring to particular stages:

> Both the repressed emotions of love and hate – repressed because of the conflict about hating a loved person – can find fuller expression in more or less socially accepted directions. Children ally themselves in various ways and develop certain rules as to how far they can go in their expressions of hatred or dislike of others. (Klein 1937: 328)

This discrepancy between linear time (e.g. a given age or phase) and personal psychological structures can be found in the mismatch between the five book titles in *Mary Olivier* and their actual dates or contents. For instance, Book Two, 'Childhood', is to begin in 1869, yet the first paragraph already announces New Year's Eve and the year 1870, showing from the very beginning the inadequacy of titles and labels. Similarly, 'maturity' is reached long before the fourth book, as the novel contrasts temporal landmarks with both the heroine's psychological development and her subjective experience of time so as to show her specific hesitations and contradictions:

> Eighteen ninety-eight. Eighteen ninety-nine. Nineteen hundred. Thirty-five – thirty-six – thirty-seven. Three years. Her mind kept on stretching, it held three years in one span like one year. The large rhythm of time appeased and exalted her. (335)

The echo with Bergson's conception of subjective time is first and foremost linguistic. The use of the verb 'stretching' seems like a direct reference to the metaphor of the elastic band that Bergson uses when introducing the concept of *durée* in *La Pensée créatrice* (1907) and *La Pensée et le mouvant* (1934), in which he asks his readers to imagine an elastic band being stretched; a metaphor he uses as a way to show how stretching, like time, is both multiple and indivisible (184–5). Bergson's *durée* also enables Sinclair to show how the self attempts to resist incorporation into social time, i.e. representing Mary's peculiar experience of time is yet another means of suggesting that she is a particular case, whose specificities do not quite fit with the general time-frame: such temporal discrepancy shows that her *Bildung* is being developed at its own pace and according to its own specific temporality. It also functions as a means of emphasising the inadequacy of social time, and, by extension, of the social organisation of Victorian society, a key theme in almost all of her published writing. There is, for instance, a similar discrepancy between the moment when characters such as Molly Tyson or Jane Holland give birth and the point when they do feel that they have become mothers.

Sinclair's novels also show the complexity and singularity of individual memory. Indeed, her integration of psychoanalytical time to the diegesis also follows and adapts Freud's earliest concepts, such as screen-memories:

> The concept of a 'screen memory' as one which owes its value as a memory not to its own content but to the relation existing between that content and some other, that has been suppressed [. . .] There are people whose earliest childhood memories are concerned with everyday and indifferent events [. . .]

but which are recollected (*too* clearly, one is inclined to say in every detail). (Freud 1899: 306)

Because of its retroactive narration, *Mary Olivier* is filled with screen memories. The concept is best exemplified in the opening pages of the novel, which display a seemingly indifferent scene of the daily life of Mary as an infant, who is first watching her father and is then being breastfed:

> The man stood in the room by the washstand, scratching his long thigh. He was turned slantwise from the nightlight on the washstand so that it showed his yellowish skin under the lifted shirt. The white half-face hung by itself on the darkness. When he left off scratching and moved towards the cot she screamed. Mamma took her to her big bed. Mamma's breast. (3–4)

A closer look suggests that the scene is everything but indifferent. First, the juxtaposition between Mary's look at her father's and then her mother's body seems to directly echo Freud's comment on how 'the essential elements of an experience are represented in memory by the inessential elements of the same experience' (Freud 1899: 307). The sharp contrast between Mary's fear of her father and the pleasure she experiences when she is in contact with her mother, made perceptible in the depiction of the playfulness of breastfeeding, indicates that the memory is indeed crucial. The clear focus on breastfeeding, as the starting point of a broader reflection on attachment some thirty years before Bowlby's studies on the subject, and on the pre-oedipal description of Mary's relation with her father is ground-breaking, as it paves the way for a new representation of individual identity that does not go through any metaphorical mediation.

Another temporal variation of the Sinclairian representation of the psyche is influenced by Freud's concept of afterwardsness, or *Nachträglichkeit* in the original German, which creates an alternative network of repressed events and memories. When detailing the case of Emma in *Project for a Scientific Psychology*, Freud makes the following observation: 'a memory is repressed which has only become a trauma *after the event* [*nachträglich*]' (Freud 1895: 435). This is what is at stake in the following example, which resorts to *Nachträglichkeit* as Mary overhears, without fully understanding it, a conversation between her mother and Jenny, the maid, about her brother Roddy:

> Something she didn't notice at the time and remembered afterwards when Roddy was well again. Jenny saying to Mamma, 'If it had to be one of them it had ought to have been Miss Mary.'
> And Mamma saying to Jenny, 'It wouldn't have mattered so much if it had been the girl.' (67)

The phrase 'remembered afterward' directly points at Mary's incapacity to process the information she heard then. Interestingly, her memory of the event relates to the depiction of her fear, not explicitly stated, of being unloved by her mother: 'You knew *when* she loved you. You could almost count the times' (68). Indeed, the entire episode revolves around Mary's feeling of illegitimacy and shows how afterwardsness had preserved her from such a blunt realisation. If we follow the hypothesis according to which the narrative voice is the adult Mary, then this delayed awareness process also strongly suggests that time must pass for Mary's memory to work constructively and allow her to access self-analysis.[7]

Afterwardsness is also at stake in the very structure of *Mary Olivier*. The key elements, props, symbols and psychoanalytical issues contained in the following scene are going to be replayed and repeated in various contexts, suggesting that Mary's mind had not initially been able to process them thoroughly:

> Mark and Dank and Roddy watched them over the banisters.
> Aunt Charlotte put her hand deep down in her pocket and brought out a little parcel wrapped in white paper. She whispered:
> 'If I give you something to keep, will you promise not to show it to anybody and not to tell?'
> Mary promised.
> Inside the paper wrapper there was a match-box, and inside the match-box there was a china doll no bigger than your finger. It had blue eyes and black hair and no clothes on. Aunt Charlotte held it in her hand and smiled at it.
> 'That's Aunt Charlotte's little baby,' she said. 'I'm going to be married and I shan't want it any more.'
> 'There – take it, and cover it up, quick!' (37)

After Charlotte gives Mary the doll, Mary has two dreams in which most settings, props, action, and atmosphere are reworked and rearranged. In the first dream, right after this scene, Charlotte is naked and gives her another doll. In the second dream, many pages later, Charlotte stands in the exact same place and also gives Mary a secret gift, showing how Mary's unconscious mind needs time in order to fully grasp what is wrong with, or rather different about, Charlotte. We can also underline how the presence of Mary's three brothers brings to the scene another type of temporality: social time. The brothers, who watch Mary from 'over the banisters', symbolically remind us of the male authority to which Mary and Charlotte are subjected (37).

Interestingly, these events also intervene in another episode in which Mary's mother offers her daughter 'new clothes for [her] new dolly':

> Mamma unfolded them.
> 'New clothes,' she said, 'for your new dolly.'
> 'Oh – oh – oh – I love you so much that I can't bear it; you little holy Mamma!'
> Mamma said, 'I'm not holy, and I won't be called holy. I want deeds, not words. If you love me you'll learn your lessons properly.' (69–70)

This passage stands in sharp contrast with the previous episode. The mother's behaviour first seems to repair the conflict that Charlotte's abnormal behaviour has instilled. Yet the scene is also striking for its introduction of Mrs Olivier's orchestrated repression, as the mother's body movements and authoritative discourse appear like a staged response to Mary's furtive encounter with Charlotte. It progressively becomes apparent that the seminal scene with Charlotte contains a symbolical network that spreads throughout the text; it will even contaminate Mary's dreams and phobias, which she will have to address in order to complete her *Bildung*.

Bildungstraüme, Self-analysis and Metafiction

In its adaptation of psychoanalytical temporality, Sinclairian fiction also integrates a time for analysis and self-analysis, for readers and characters alike. All these temporalities do not converge towards plot resolution; instead, the novel merges the open-ended structure of psychoanalytical case histories into the teleology of the *Bildungsroman*.

Dreams, in Mary Olivier, follow Freud's theories: they displace, condense and rework the textual material which is then confronted to yet another layer of temporality.[8] Indeed, Mary's dreams seem to function as a direct echo to the principle laid out by Freud in 'The Wolf Man', according to which a child's oneiric production is the result of an unassimilated impression (356). This is what is at stake in the following passage, to which Jean Radford referred when she argued that *Mary Olivier* can be read as a modernist rereading of Freud's 'Little Hans' (Radford 1980: xi). In 'Little Hans', Freud emphasises the oedipal relation between Hans and his mother as well as his phobia of horses, which, for Freud, symbolises Hans's fear of his father's sexual organ. Threatening horses do indeed play an interesting role in *Mary Olivier*:

> If she dreamed about any of them it was always Mamma. She had left her in the house by herself and she had got out of her room to the stair-head. Or they were in London at the crossing by the Bank and Mamma was frightened. She had to get her through the thick of the traffic. The horses pushed at

Mamma and you tried to hold back their noses, but she sank down and slid away from you sideways under the wheel.

Or she would come into this room and find her in it. At first she would be glad to see that Mamma was still there; then she would be unhappy and afraid. [. . .] When she woke up she was glad that the dream had been nothing but a dream.

But that meant that you were glad Mamma was not there. The dream showed you what you were hiding from yourself. Supposing the dead knew? Supposing Mamma knew, and Mark knew that you were glad – (374)

Mary's dream strongly resembles Freud's case history: in Sinclair's novel, the frightening horses nearly kill Mamma, which seems to make Mary 'glad'. Yet the symmetry stops here, because first, in the dream, it is not Mary who is afraid of horses: it is Mamma herself, hinting perhaps at a possible cause for her repressive and repressed conduct. Second, in Jung's *Psychology of the Unconscious* horses are symbolically associated with anxiety and motherhood. Their introduction here hints at the anxiety of the mother-daughter relations rather than at any phallic symbolism (Jung 1916: 308–9). A psychoanalytical reading of the passage might argue that when Mary tries to distance her mother from the horses' noses, she is rejecting the idea of her mother's sexuality so as to maintain the illusory, idealised representation or fantasy of the supposedly pure and innocent 'holy Mamma'. The association of sexuality and threat, 'the horses pushed at Mamma', also remind us that, despite Mary's progress – she has broken one of the book's greatest taboos in questioning her mother about their relationship (335) – many things are still left unsaid in Mary's own experience of sexuality.

The temporality and structure of the dream-episode follow Freud's theories on the patterns of oneiric productions. The dream announces future developments, since Mary appears as a protective figure for her mother, subsequently refusing to follow Richard and remaining with her mother. But the dream is also turned to the past as it relies on a network of altered repetitions: details, such as the 'stair-head' (an echo to the 'banister' in a previous scene with Charlotte), the traffic, or even the horses, have all already been encountered in earlier contexts, and gain here new signification true to Sinclair's loose adaptation of Freud's afterwardsness theory.

Lastly, because of the parallel, nearly anaphoric use of 'she', stressing the mother's incomprehensible behaviour, as well as Mary's estrangement from her ('She had left her in the house by herself and she had got out of her room [. . .] but she sank down and slid away from you'), one can note the mother's agency in her own disappearance, which can retrospectively be read as a prediction of her imminent death, thereby constituting yet another hint for both Mary and the readers. Mary pictures herself as being under the scrutiny of Mamma and Mark. As opposed to the previous scene, in which Mary was observed by her three brothers 'over the banisters', having Mark and Mamma as potential external observers prying on her most intimate thoughts and on her unconscious mechanisms works as a triggering factor for self-reflection. Yet Mark and Mamma are not there, but the readers have followed Mary's path through life from the start while being given access to many analytical tools and materials. Thus a very peculiar form of metafictional transference is actually taking place in this particular scene, as Mary ponders how an observer might feel about the expression of her unconscious desires. Such an open-ended question, raised once again by one of her many aposiopeses, functions as a means of redefining the reader's experience into the hybrid piece of writing that is Sinclair's novel.

Through her dream Mary is making a big step forward: she starts to analyse herself, and evolves from patient or case to budding self-analyst. Yet, in the novel, dreams are not only *Bildungstraüme* (formative dreams) since they participate in Mary's development, they also appeal to the readers, who are meant to connect symbols and details with the heroine's life. In this way, the novel works as a *Bildungslesen* or *Bildungsanalyse* (reading or analysing apprenticeship), as it also relies on the reader's psychoanalytical reading skills.

Mary's *Bildung* extends beyond the diegesis: her dreams call for a psychoanalytical reception that is quite reminiscent of Freud's approach to his patients' dreams in his case narratives:

> That night she dreamed that she saw Aunt Charlotte standing at the foot of the kitchen stairs taking off her clothes and wrapping them in white paper [. . .]
>
> When you opened the stair cupboard door to catch the opossum, you found a white china doll lying in it, no bigger than your finger. That was Aunt Charlotte.
>
> In the dream there was no break between the end and the beginning. But when she remembered it afterwards it split into two pieces with a dark gap between. She knew she had only dreamed about the cupboard; but Aunt Charlotte at the foot of the stairs was so clear and solid that she thought she had really seen her.
>
> Mamma had told Aunt Bella all about it when they talked together that day, in the drawing-room. She knew because she could still see them sitting, bent forward with their heads touching, Aunt Bella in the big arm-chair by the hearth-rug, and Mamma on the parrot chair. (37)

Interestingly, Mary only retains a partial and disorganised memory of this dream, but this extract contains several of the key taboos of the novel. The tiny china doll is a clear echo of Charlotte's maternal desires, while the opossum refers to Mary's recent, and embarrassing, misuse of the word; in a previous scene, Mary used the word 'opossum' instead of the word opinion (34), thus when, in the present dream, she opens a cupboard that should have contained an opossum captive, this is a probable reference to her attempt at developing her own opinions.

Because of the specifically psychoanalytical material, the reader's analytical skills are appealed to in a very peculiar way. Not only should Mary make the best of her oneiric productions, but so should we, as the peculiar mention of her mother's 'parrot chair' in the fourth paragraph suggests. The association between the mother and the bird is indeed echoed in the text, as Mrs Olivier constantly repeats the words of others, either betraying secrets or merely voicing other characters' ideas. The use of the animal as a symbol in the paragraph that follows this dream sequence functions as a hint that dream analysis should be carried out one step further. As such, the dream thus works as a metafictional *Bildungstraum*, a formative dream that aims at developing Mary's and the readers' psychoanalytical reading of the entire textual material; which might also be seen as a metonymic echo to Sinclair's psychoanalytical fictionalisation.

Freud's influence on Sinclair is thus dialogic and ambiguous. Sinclair keeps some of his theories on temporality, dreams and consciousness, while she chooses to overlook others on the unconscious or on female sexuality and adapts some of his texts, lexis, concepts and methods to the complexity of fictional writing, thereby reinforcing her idiosyncratic and exploratory approach to fiction. Even if they are partly inspired by the scientific *Zeitgeist* of her time – more, perhaps, than the artistic experimentations – Sinclair's very particular representations of the exceptionality of her heroines require specific tools to help us assess the originality of her aesthetics; just like her heroines who called for new psychoanalytical discourses and still appear as dense and 'interminable' as the theoretical frameworks that Sinclair's texts sought to challenge.

Notes

1. Such eclecticism is also central to the praxis of the Medico-Psychological Clinic of London (to which Sinclair contributed): see Boll 1962; Raitt 2004; Martindale 2003. However, one should note that Sinclair's theory of consciousness ('Primary and Secondary Consciousness', 1923) is very similar to Freud's primary and secondary functions of consciousness ('Project for a Scientific Psychology', 1895: 386).
2. Sinclair uses the term 'Subconscious', which Freud rejected after his 1893 'Preliminary Communication', and which was then mainly used by Pierre

Janet. Interestingly, Sinclair has no real theory of the Unconscious ('The terms Unconscious and Unconsciousness stand for any or all of those psychic or psychophysical states of which we are not conscious' (Sinclair 1917: 4)) and seems to have preferred a hybrid system in which her specific concept of Libido (which drew on Jung's theories, rather than on Freud's) played a central role. We can read this attempt at distancing the text from a strictly Freudian influence as being both a deliberate reference to Sinclair's idiosyncratic psychology and an additional layer of irony, emphasising the characters' distrust in psychoanalysis.
3. Freud does not mention attachment, and only refers to the 'tender current' of the sexual drive. Similarly, Victorian psychologies do not study attachment, as Jenny Bourne Taylor and Sally Shuttleworth's *Embodied Selves: An Anthology of Psychological Texts (1830–1890)* indicate. John Bowlby is a key figure in early developmental psychology. His approach differs from Freudian psychoanalysis: 'my object appeared a limited one, namely, to discuss the theoretical implications of some observations of how young children respond to temporary loss of mother [. . .] My furrows had been started from a corner diametrically opposite to the one at which Freud had entered' (Bowlby 1969: xxvi).
4. The translation is mine.
5. This is also Philippa Martindale's thesis in (Martindale 2003: 100), in which she refers to Julia Kristeva's 'Women's Time' (Kristeva 1981: 13–17 and 23–4) to read Jane Holland and Nina Lempriere's escape from paternalistic temporality.
6. 'In my analyses of children, especially of children between the ages of three and six, I have come to a number of conclusions [. . .] that the Oedipus complex comes into operation earlier than is usually supposed' (Klein 1928: 69).
7. This is also in tune with Caruth's trauma theory, which raises the question of the deferred representation of trauma: '[The] traumatic experience is an experience that is not fully assimilated as it occurs. [. . .] Such a question [. . .] must be asked in a language that is somehow literary: a language that defies our understanding' (Caruth 1994: 15).
8. Yet, dreams are also a context for challenging Freud's authority: '[My] dream appears to break all the rules laid down by Freud for the conduct of the dreams. There was an utter absence in it of the characteristic myth, symbols, or image' (Sinclair 1915: 14–15).

Works Cited

Bergson, Henri [1934] (2008), *La Pensée et le mouvant*, Paris: PUF.
Berlant, Lauren (2007), 'On the Case', *Critical Inquiry* 33 (Summer 2007), 663–72.
Boll, Theophilus (1962), 'May Sinclair and the Medico-Psychological Clinic of London', *Proceedings of the American Philosophical Society* 106:4, 310–26.
Bortoli, Lucia (1998), 'May Sinclair's Modernist Experience: A Political Revision of Female Subjectivity and Autobiographical Writing', PhD dissertation, University of Notre-Dame (Notre-Dame, IN).

Bourne, Taylor, and Sally Shuttleworth (1998), *Embodied Selves: An Anthology of Psychological Texts 1830–1890*, Oxford: Clarendon Press.
Bowlby, John (1958), 'The Nature of the Child's Tie to His Mother', *International Journal of Psychoanalysis* 39, 350–71.
Bowlby, John [1969] (1982), *Attachment and Loss, Vol. 1: Attachment*, New York: Basic Books.
Brooks, Peter (1984), 'Freud's Masterplot' and 'Fictions of the Wolf Man', *Reading for the Plot*, Cambridge, MA: Harvard University Press.
Caruth, Cathy (1996), *Unclaimed Experience: Trauma, Narrative, and History*, Baltimore: Johns Hopkins University Press.
Cohn, Dorrit (2000), *The Distinction of Fiction*, Baltimore: Johns Hopkins University Press.
Cooper, Frederic (1915), 'Some Novelists of the Month', *Bookman* 40, 556.
De Certeau, Michel [1981] (1986), 'The Freudian Novel: History and Literature', *Humanities and Society* 4, 121–44.
Forster, Laurel (2000), 'The Life of the Mind: Psychic Explorations in the Work of May Sinclair', PhD dissertation, University of Sussex.
Freud, Sigmund [1895] (1950), 'Project for a scientific psychology' in *The Origins of Psychoanalysis*, translated by Eric Mosbacher and James Strachey, London: Imago Publishing.
Freud, Sigmund [1899] (1961), 'On Screen Memory', in *The Standard Edition of the Complete Works by Sigmund Freud*, vol. 3, London: The Hogarth Press.
Freud, Sigmund [1901–18] (1970), *Cinq psychanalyses*, Vendôme: Quadrige/PUF.
Freud, Sigmund [1933] (1990), *New Introductory Lectures on Psychoanalysis*, in *The Complete Works of Sigmund Freud – Standard Edition*, New York: Norton.
Freud, Sigmund (1937), 'Analysis Terminable and Interminable', *International Journal of Psychoanalysis* 18, 373–405.
Hirsch, Mariane (1989), *The Mother/Daughter Plot*, Bloomington: Indiana University Press.
Humm, Maggie (1995), 'Psychoanalytical Criticism on May Sinclair and Doris Lessing', in Humm, *Practising Feminist Criticism: An Introduction*, New York: Prentice Hall, Harvester Wheatsheaf.
Johnson, George (2004), 'May Sinclair: From Psychological Analyst to Anachronistic Modernist?', *Journal of Evolutionary Psychology* 25, 1–8.
Johnson, George (2006), *Dynamic Psychology in Modernist British Fiction*, New York: Palgrave Macmillan.
Jung, Carl Gustav [1912] (1916), *Psychology of the Unconscious: A Study of the Transformations and Symbolisms of the Libido*, New York: Moffat Yard and Company.
Jung, Carl Gustav (1915), *The Theory of Psychoanalysis*, New York: Nervous and Mental Disease Publishing.
Klein, Melanie [1928] (1986), 'Early Stages of the Oedipus Conflict', in Juliet Mitchell (ed.), *The Selected Melanie Klein*, New York: The Free Press.
Klein, Melanie (1929), 'Infantile Anxiety Situations Reflected in a Work of Art and in the Creative Impulse', *International Journal of Psycho-Analysis* 10, 436–43.

Klein, Melanie [1937] (1975), 'Love, Guilt, and Reparation' in Klein, *Love, Guilt, and Reparation, and Other Works 1921–1945*, New York: The Free Press.
Klein, Melanie (1952), 'Some Theoretical Conclusions regarding the Emotional Life of the Infant', *Developments in Psycho-analysis*, London: The Hogarth Press.
Kristeva, Julia [1979] (1981), 'Women's Time', *Signs* 7:1, 13–35.
Laget, Anne (1995), *Freud et le temps*, Lyon: PUL.
Laplanche, Jean, and Jean-Bertrand Pontalis [1967] (2002), *Vocabulaire de la psychanalyse*, Vendôme: PUF/Quadrige.
Liggins, Emma (2014), 'Daughters, Aunts, and Outdated Victorianism', in Liggins, *Odd Women? Spinsters, Lesbians and Widows in British Women's Fiction, 1850s–1930s*, Manchester: Manchester University Press, pp. 117–62.
Lombroso, Cesare (1891), *The Man of Genius*, London: Scott.
Lubbock, Percy (1923), 'Uncanny Stories', *Times Literary Supplement*, 6 September 1923, 586.
Marcus, Steven (1975), 'Freud and Dora: Story, History, Case History', *Representations*, New York: Random House.
Martindale, Philippa (2003), 'The ceasing from the sorrow of divided life; May Sinclair's women, texts and contexts (1910–1923)', PhD dissertation, Durham University, http://etheses.dur.ac.uk/3691/ (last accessed 22 June 2016).
Martindale, Philippa (2004), '"Against All Hushing And Stamping Down": The Medico-Psychological Clinic of London and the Novelist May Sinclair', *Psychoanalytical History* 62, 177–200.
Martindale, Philippa (2006), 'Suffrage and The Three Brontës', in Andrew J. Kunka and Michelle K. Troy (eds), *May Sinclair: Moving Towards the Modern*, Aldershot: Ashgate, pp. 179–96.
Maudsley, Henry (1894), *Sex in Mind and in Education*, Syracuse, NY: Bandeen Publishers.
Passeron, Jean-Claude, and Jacques Revel (2005), 'Penser par cas: raisonner à partir de singularités', in Passeron and Revel, *Penser par cas*, Paris: Éditions de l'EHESS, pp. 9–44.
Radford, Jean (1980), 'Introduction', in May Sinclair, *Mary Olivier: A Life*, London: Virago Modern Classics, pp. i–xx.
Raitt, Suzanne (2004), 'Early British Psychoanalysis and the Medico-Psychological Clinic', *History Workshop Journal* 58, 63–85.
Shin, Kuno (2006), 'Humiliating Modernism: Literature Shame and the Public in the Novels of May Sinclair, Wyndham Lewis and Virginia Woolf', PhD dissertation, University of York.
Showalter, Elaine (1982), *A Literature of Their Own: From Charlotte Brontë to Doris Lessing*, London: Virago.
Showalter, Elaine (1997), *Hystories: Hysterical Epidemics and Modern Media*, New York: Columbia University Press.
Sinclair, May [1898] (2009a), *The Tysons: Mr and Mrs Nevill Tyson*, Whitefish, MT: Kessinger Publishing.
Sinclair, May [1901] (2009b), 'Superseded', in *Two Sides of a Question* (1901), Whitefish, MT: Kessinger Publishing.

Sinclair, May [1910] (2009c), *The Creators: A Comedy*, London: Forgotten Books.
Sinclair, May (1912), *The Three Brontës*, London: Hutchinson.
Sinclair, May (c. 1915), 'The Way of Sublimation', May Sinclair Collection, Rare Book and Manuscript Library, University of Pennsylvania, Box 23.
Sinclair, May (1916a), 'Clinical Lecture on Symbolism and Sublimation – I', *The Medical Press and Circular* 153, 118–22.
Sinclair, May (1916b), 'Clinical Lecture on Symbolism and Sublimation – II', *The Medical Press and Circular* 153, 142–5.
Sinclair, May (1917), *A Defence of Idealism: Some Questions and Conclusions*, London: Macmillan, https://archive.org/details/adefenceidealis02sincgoog (last accessed 22 June 2016).
Sinclair, May [1919] (1980), *Mary Olivier: A Life*, London: Virago Modern Classics.
Sinclair, May [1920] (2006), *The Romantic*, Charleston, SC: BiblioBazaar.
Sinclair, May [1922] (2000), *Life and Death of Harriett Frean*, London: Virago Modern Classics.
Sinclair, May [1922] (2010), *The New Idealism*, Charleston, SC: Bibliolife.
Sinclair, May (1923), 'Psychological Types', *The English Review* 36, 436–9.
Sinclair, May (1930), *Tales Told by Simpson*, London: Hutchinson.
Stonebridge, Lyndsey (2004), 'Psychoanalysis and Literature', in Laura Marcus and Peter Nicholls (eds), *The Cambridge History of Twentieth-Century English Literature*, Cambridge: Cambridge University Press.
Wilson, Leigh (2000), '"It was as if she had said. . .": May Sinclair and Reading Narratives of Cure', PhD dissertation, University of Westminster.

Chapter 4

Feminism, Freedom and the Hierarchy of Happiness in the Psychological Novels of May Sinclair
Wendy Truran

> <u>Women</u> if you want to realise yourselves – you are on the eve of a devastating psychological upheaval – all your pet illusions must be unmasked [. . .] Leave off looking to men to find out what you are <u>not</u> – seek within yourselves to find out what you <u>are</u> [. . .] To obtain results you must make sacrifices & the first & greatest sacrifice you have to make is of your '<u>virtue</u>'.
> Mina Loy, 'Feminist Manifesto', 1914

The Self, psychological upheaval, refusal of an androcentric point of view, revelation, sacrifice: Mina Loy's 'Feminist Manifesto' is strikingly resonant with May Sinclair's concerns in her psychological novels. Loy advocates for the 'Absolute Demolition' of gender relations, and both writers claim that a radical shift in consciousness is necessary to make genuine progress towards emancipation rather than simply enfranchisement. Loy and Sinclair demand that women cultivate an 'intelligent curiosity and courage in meeting and resisting the pressure of life' (Loy 1996: 156). For Sinclair, 'resisting the pressure of life' means forging intellectual, emotional and spiritual freedom via self-awareness and individual will. By reading across Sinclair's three psychological novels – *The Three Sisters* (1914), *Mary Olivier: A Life* (1919), and *Life and Death of Harriett Frean* (1922) – it is possible to trace an important form of Sinclair's contribution to her contemporary feminism: affective militancy. Sinclair confronts readers with a depiction of the insidious affective hold the institutions of marriage, family and romance have over women. She establishes three different stages of happiness which she ranks, creating a *hierarchy of happiness* which she then uses to contradict conventional notions of femininity. Connecting Sinclair's feminist position to her position on emotions locates Sinclair within modernist debates on psychology, consciousness and the nature and origin of emotion. These began with Darwin's theory of emotions but came to prominence via the James-Lange theory of the nature of emotions (1894). Sinclair explicitly positions herself against James's Pragmatism in her *Defence of Idealism* (1917) but also implicitly rejects his materialist, physiological basis for emotions. She ultimately concludes that in the pursuit of intellectual and emotional freedom, women are forced to cultivate disembodied, solitary, spiritual happiness in order to resist the constraints of socially prescribed forms of happiness. In other words, Sinclair posits that an extreme form of affective freedom is necessary for women, in order to resist oppression and to access the consolation of the only happiness she believes to be 'perfect': an otherworldly one.

Why focus on happiness when many modernist scholars have either characterised literary modernism as anti-emotional or theorised modernist emotions as predominantly negative? Whilst aesthetic modernism viewed emotions and embodied sentiment with deep suspicion, T. S. Eliot's theory of impersonality being but one example, in fact many modernists sought to re-evaluate the place and function of emotion within arts, science and philosophy. Sinclair's work should be thought of as integral to an understanding of modernist emotion, both within her own cultural moment and within the emerging scholarship of modernism and affect. As a philosopher as well as a novelist, Sinclair's intellectual reach into discourses concerning consciousness, embodiment and psychical and emotional realities places her work in a unique position to reveal modernism's use of, and deep ambivalence towards, emotion and affect. Sinclair herself stated that 'What really matters is a state of mind, the interest or ecstasy with which we close with life. It can't be explained' (Sinclair in Kime Scott 1990: 446). Sinclair was not alone in theorising happiness; her philosophical interlocutor Bertrand Russell also engaged with the problem of happiness and published a collection of lectures which he titled 'How to Be Free and Happy' (1924) and a book entitled *Conquest of Happiness* (1930). Stated as a question, 'how to be free and happy?' might be considered a prototypical modernist question, especially relevant to a historical moment coming to terms with the First World War, disturbing technological and scientific innovations and a loss of religious certainty. All produced anxiety and disillusionment much more than happiness. Despite this, Sinclair permeates her protagonists' lives with intense episodes of rapture, joy and happiness, and understanding the function of these affects is central to an understanding of her novels. By calling Sinclair's episodes of happiness a 'hierarchy' a value judgement is implied; the judgement is Sinclair's own. She privileges a cerebral 'perfect happiness' above sensual pleasure, yet she also prefers sexual satisfaction over the damaging repression of the libido. In the case of Sinclair's psychological fiction it is useful to think of hierarchy in terms of a process; as the unfolding of a form of a youthful consciousness moving through stages of psychic-spiritual development as it matures. Happiness, for Sinclair, becomes a political problem encompassing the psychical challenge of living at a moment of historical, political and cultural transformation.

Affect Theory and the Promise of Happiness

In her influential book *The Promise of Happiness,* Sara Ahmed exposes the discursive imperative to find certain things happy. Certain objects come to offer the promise of happiness more than others – the 'domestic bliss' of heterosexual marriage, for example, or the latest consumer product – and this promise of happiness is 'how we are directed towards certain things' (Ahmed 2010: 2). She theorises that happiness reinforces normative values and that certain forms of happiness become synonymous with being good: 'happiness is used to redescribe social norms as social goods' (Ahmed 2010: 2). Rather than assuming that happiness is simply a possession of happy people, Ahmed asks what forms of personhood are made valuable by certain claims to happiness: 'Attributions of happiness might be how social norms and ideals become affective, as if relative proximity to those norms and ideals creates happiness' (Ahmed 2010: 11). Ahmed suggests social rules of affective behaviour serve as scripts; 'happiness scripts' provide 'a set of instructions for what women and men must do in order to be happy, whereby happiness is what follows being natural or good' (Ahmed 2010: 59). The particular happiness script we see in all three of Sinclair's texts is that of the dutiful daughter. Sinclair depicts the family unit as the key source of the social conditioning attached to happiness. Yet Sinclair's protagonists also refuse socially sanctioned objects of happiness such as marriage and childbearing, which often results in their being labeled unvirtuous. In other words, to be happy in the proper way is to be obedient and good, and to be happy in the 'improper' way is to be deviant and bad. By creating protagonists who are 'differently happy', Sinclair offers her critique of the coercion behind 'proper' forms of happiness. Sinclair's fiction therefore anticipates Ahmed's claim that those who orientate themselves towards happiness differently 'disturb the fantasy that happiness can only be found in certain places' (Ahmed 2010: 66).

A *Hierarchy of Happiness*: Inherited, Embodied and Perfect Happiness

Rather than contentment of mind, happiness for Sinclair is an intense state of heightened awareness, often involving pleasure, but just as often including an element of pain. A young Mary Olivier, for example, experiences arresting happiness that is painful when she realises the beauty of nature for the first time: 'Suddenly, without any reason, she was so happy that she could hardly bear it' (Sinclair 2002: 58). Happiness for Sinclair can be contingent and sudden, which emphasises the 'hap' in happiness, and it brings with it a sense of emotional escape. The positive psychologist Mihály Csíkszentmihályi connects happiness and freedom: 'optimal experiences add up to a sense of mastery – or perhaps better, a sense of participation in determining the content of life' (in Ahmed 2010: 11). Sinclair creates characters that demand this kind of mastery and self-determination in order to be happy, and thereby exemplify Sinclair's unique form of affective militancy.

The Three Sisters offered, in Sinclair's time, a scandalously frank treatment of the sensual desires and sexual frustrations of women. In fact, *The Three Sisters* allows the reader to see each form of happiness: *inherited*, *embodied* and *perfect*, as each sister is emblematic of a different mode of determining their life and happiness. *Mary Olivier*, on the other hand, gives the clearest and most extended consideration of Sinclair's idealist form of *perfect happiness*. Mary escapes the nets of *inherited* and *embodied happiness*, in order to find joy in a spiritual union with God. Finally, the failure of all three forms of happiness is captured in *Life and Death of Harriett Frean* (1922); this surgically lean *Bildungsroman* imagines the consequences of a Mary Olivier-like figure had she not developed an inner life.

The objects that offer the promise of happiness, as Ahmed suggests, are often passed on by parents, education, and moral and social institutions; the first stage of happiness is therefore entitled *inherited happiness*. In *A Defence of Idealism* Sinclair explores heredity and suggests that through unconscious memory 'the individual is one with the race psychically as well as physically' (Sinclair 1917: 5). She emphasises the necessity of adding to the sum total of experience of the human race, and as such she thinks that to acquiesce to other people's ideas of happiness is a betrayal of the self that also has consequences for society. Mary Olivier, for example, recognises that the inherited attitudes and affective transmissions passed down through the Sinclair family for generations are meant to control her: 'If it was even *my* conscience. But it's Mamma's. And her conscience was Grandmamma's. And Grandmamma's—' (Sinclair 2002: 297). Sinclair also considers the inherited dangers within the body. All affects and emotions are registered upon the body: to have feelings is to feel them somatically. Historically, women have been associated with the body rather than the intellect, emotions rather than reason. Sinclair is concerned that *emotion*, being moved, is dangerous in part because it confines women to the narrative of mental and physical inferiority to which they have traditionally been constrained. Many of Sinclair's moments of intense *embodied happiness* occur when characters are young and intellectually immature. Mary's life is mostly sensorial and sensational at this point in her life, and happiness comes from physical activity and bodily pleasures. When Mary, as a baby, is comforted by her mother, the narrator describes Mary's sensuous pleasure in her mother's body and breast. The smell of her mother's face, the warmth of her body, the touch and sight of her mother's breast, moves Mary from distress to calm: 'Her sobs shook in her throat and ceased suddenly' (Sinclair 2002: 6). The need for sensual comfort is complicated when Sinclair considers adult sexuality; on the one hand, sexual happiness is depicted as luxuriating in sensuality, as in the case of Mary Carteret being a 'tranquil sensualist' (Sinclair 1985: 319). On the other hand, repressed sexual energy can be damaging and lead to mental illness, as in the case of Ally Carteret of *The Three Sisters*, or Aunt Charlotte in *Mary Olivier*. For some individuals, Sinclair points out, such embodied happiness is a necessary aspect of sanity. Mina Loy's feminist manifesto concurs, stating that 'there is nothing impure in sex – except in the mental attitude to it' (Loy 1996: 156). *Embodied happiness* as sexual expression and the comforts of marriage are not, Sinclair suggests, an evil in themselves but only in the characterisation of them as dirty.

Perfect, from the Latin, *perfectus*, suggests completion or full development; thus, by calling Mary Olivier's final happiness at the close of the novel *perfect*, Sinclair is gesturing to her highest form of happiness. *Perfect happiness*, Sinclair suggests, offers the possibility for Mary to be fulfilled, to be affectively free, but this requires a disassociation from embodiment. *Perfect happiness* is a kind of emotional balancing act: a withdrawal from 'ungovernable want', an escape from frustrated desires into the peace of a fully developed relationship with a consciousness greater than one's own (Sinclair 2002: 262). In *A Defence of Idealism* Sinclair suggests the 'perfect, intimate immediacy of feeling' might offer 'different kinds of certainty' about the existence of the Absolute Reality behind everyday existence (Sinclair 1917: 337–8). Even at her most abstracted, Sinclair relies upon affects and emotions within her fiction to make her protagonists' spiritual experience feel real to them, and the reader. Thus there is a tension at the heart of *perfect happiness*; it is an idealist's paradox between the sensual and the real. The body is both something dangerous, susceptible to emotions and the influence of which must be minimised, whilst at the same time being absolutely necessary for the registering of the affective evidence of the encounter with the Absolute.

The Three Sisters: Three Stages of Happiness

The Three Sisters follows the fortunes of the Carteret sisters, Mary, Gwenda and Ally, over the course of nine years. Their father, James Carteret, is a small-minded provincial vicar who insists on the ritual of ten o'clock prayers: 'he gloried in them as an expression of his power' and as a 'form of coercion' (Sinclair 1985: 133). Vicar Carteret dictates the rhythm of his daughters' lives, constraining their choices and physical freedom, attempting to force his conception of happiness upon them. He considers himself filled with 'wisdom and patience', when he is in fact a petty tyrant who oppresses his daughters because he is an 'enforced, reluctant celibate' (Sinclair 1985: 136). The drama of this family saga is created when each sister falls in love with the one eligible bachelor in the village: Dr Steven Rowcliffe. As each sister waits, bored, for the 'release' of prayers and bed, they silently reflect on their attraction to Rowcliffe and how they might gain his attention. At this moment, each sister reveals a different approach to a different form of happiness.

Mary, the oldest sister, is 'sweet and good' and exemplifies *inherited happiness* (Sinclair 1985: 74). In Mary's case her object of happiness is to embody the Victorian ideal of 'the Angel in the House'.[1] Silent, subservient and seemingly selfless, Mary relies on traditional notions of femininity in order to attract Rowcliffe: '"On Wednesday I will go into the village and see all my sick people. Then I shall see him. And he will see me. He will see that I am kind and sweet and womanly." She thought, "That is the sort of woman that a man wants". *But she did not know what she was thinking*' (Sinclair 1985: 10; emphasis added). Mary has strongly internalised an ideal constructed for her by her father and the patriarchal biopowers he represents: religion, aggressive masculine sexuality, the control of economic and physical comforts. Unable to admit her own desires, Mary represses them so that she can retain her self-regard as a pure and innocent angel. As Suzanne Raitt states, Sinclair posited that unsatisfied sexual appetites can induce women 'to betray their loved ones, and encourage them to manipulate men into a state of dulled dependency' (Raitt 2000: 140). Mary manipulates

Rowcliffe into marrying her after he is heartbroken by Gwenda's rejection. Mary then has to work to break his will and replace it with 'dulled dependency' upon her. Sinclair condemns this as a crime against both of their souls which results in mental and emotional illness for them both: 'For the first five years it had been hard work for Mary. It had meant, for her body, an ignominious waiting and watching for the moment when its appeal would be irresistible, for her soul a complete subservience to her husband's moods, and for her mind perpetual attention to his comfort . . . But in the sixth year they had begun to tell. [. . .] She had him, bound to her bed and to her fireside' (Sinclair 1985: 374–5). Mary does violence to herself and others in order to act out the script of *inherited happiness*. Mary is not moved, she does not develop. Just as she did not know what she was thinking when she first saw Rowcliffe, so years later she still does not understand her motivations: 'She would have thought you mad if you had told her so [. . .] But to Mary his sorrow and her tenderness were a voluptuous joy' (Sinclair 1985: 374). Sinclair criticises Mary, but more strongly criticises a society that limits women's opportunities to thrive so that women like Mary must manipulate men in order to have security and happiness. In her depiction of the other sisters, Sinclair offers an alternative, more modern, means by which to achieve happiness and avoid this villainy.

Ally, with her sexual needs and her defiant gesture of having a sexually fulfilling affair outside of marriage, represents *embodied happiness*. When she thinks about Dr Rowcliffe her strategy centres upon her body: '"I will make myself ill. So ill that they'll have to send for him. I shall see him that way"' (Sinclair 1985: 10). Ally's life is so tightly constrained by her father that her only means of physical expression is woefully inadequate: she channels her anger and pain into music. She plays Chopin's 'Grande Polonaise' (with more passion than skill) in order to attract Dr Rowcliffe's attention as he passes on his medical rounds. Her music becomes a vehicle by which she conveys her sensual needs, 'febrile and frustrate, seeking its outlet in exultant and violent sound [. . .] she flung out her music through the open window into the night as a signal and an appeal' (Sinclair 1985: 13). Ally's body becomes an instrument which she manipulates and controls as she does the piano, in order to have some 'sense of participation in determining the content of life' (Csíkszentmihályi in Ahmed 2010: 11). Ally is tormented by her thwarted youthful vigour and sexual desire; her body becomes an instrument for her torture as she becomes ill with hysteria, but also an instrument for her resistance: 'to let the Polonaise loose thus was Alice's defiance of the house and her revenge' (Sinclair 1985: 15). The joy of the music mediated through her body means that Alice demands that her desires be heard and felt; this mastery makes her as happy as her constrained circumstances permit. It is through music that Ally eventually achieves her ultimate *embodied* happiness. Ally accompanies Jim Greatorex, a Lawrentian spiritual-sexual figure, as he sings, and their musical union brings them together in ecstasy: 'It was essentially the same ecstasy; only, on Alice's face it was more luminous, more conscious, and at the same time more abandoned, as if all subterfuge had ceased in her and she gave herself up, willing and exulting, to the unspiritual sense that flooded her' (Sinclair 1985: 227). Their musical union leads to a sexual union, which in turn leads to her pregnancy. Sinclair's narrator explains the factors contributing to Ally's actions: 'She had yielded to his fascination partly through weakness, partly in defiance, partly in the sheer, healthy self-assertion of her suffering will and her frustrated senses' (Sinclair 1985: 250). Ally's happiness is truly ecstatic in the sense of *extasis* – to put out of place, to be outside of oneself and outside of social acceptability. By pursuing happiness outside of social norms she achieves a freedom impossible within them. Sinclair does not condemn Ally; rather she condemns the conventionally happy sister, Mary, who shuns Ally even after she marries Greatorex. Sinclair rewards Ally with a happy, fulfilling marriage and a joyful motherhood: 'In the fine sanity of happiness she showed herself as good as gold' (Sinclair 1985: 181).

Sinclair's depiction of Ally's sexual frustration and eventual *embodied happiness* also permits Sinclair a means of criticising the medical establishment of her time and its pathologising of women's sexual needs. Sinclair was an early supporter of psychoanalysis and conceded that sexual libido – what she calls 'Life-Force' or 'Will-to Life' – motivates both men and women's actions (Sinclair 1917: 4). Sinclair, informed by her reading in Freud and especially Jung, thought that frustrated sexual desire could lead to physical and mental illness, and women in particular should not be condemned as hysterical due to societal constraints on sexual expression. In order to see and be seen by Dr Rowcliffe, Ally starves herself of food, mirroring the lack of love in her life (parental or romantic). Dr Rowcliffe diagnoses Ally with hysteria, which he suggests stems from a repression of her appetites: 'You see, she isn't ill because she's been starving herself. She's been starving herself because she's ill. It's a symptom. The trouble is not that she starves herself – but that she has been starved' (Sinclair 1985: 77). For Rowcliffe unhappiness is a symptom, and being happy the cure: 'I don't say she's going to die. But – in the state that she's in – she might get anything and die if something isn't done to make her happy' (Sinclair 1985: 180). Happiness-as-cure, Rowcliffe seems to suggest, is a euphemism for sexual release, but that promise of happiness is only permitted within the confines of marriage: 'I mean of course – to get her married' (Sinclair 1985: 180). Sinclair makes it clear that the expression of libido is a natural impulse, as Gwenda and Rowcliffe agree: 'there's nothing wrong with Ally, she's as good as gold' (Sinclair 1985: 181). This discussion of women's desires offers a fictionalised version of the real-world issues faced by suffragettes within Sinclair's historical moment. Sinclair wrote her essay *Feminism* (1912) for the Women Writer's Suffrage League, wherein she addressed the sexual double bind constraining women as either over- or under-sexed; what Mina Loy calls the 'division of women into two classes — the mistress, & the mother' (Loy 1996: 154). Sinclair responds to famous immunologist Sir Almroth Wright's letter to *The Times* (1912) in which he stated that sexual frustration was at the heart of women's agitation for votes: 'no doctor can ever lose sight of the fact that the mind of woman is always threatened with the reverberations of her physiological emergencies' (Sinclair 1912a: 8). May Sinclair points out that men were as likely to have 'physiological emergencies' as women, and exasperatedly asserts: 'he argues as if there were no such thing in the world as self-control' (Sinclair 1912a: 9). Self-control and sublimation become central to a further stage of development for women which moves beyond 'physiological emergencies' and towards *perfect* happiness. Gwenda Carteret represents this development.

Gwenda, the middle sister, is the character who, through sacrifice and suffering, attains brief moments of *perfect* happiness. In contrast to Mary's conventional feminine charms and Ally's frustrated libido, Gwenda's self-awareness and emotional independence allow her to be more free than her sisters. Her inner freedom is reflected in her physical strength and her long walks over the North Yorkshire moors. Thinking of meeting Dr Rowcliffe, as her sisters do, Gwenda thinks: '"I will go out on to the moor again. I don't care if I am late for Prayers. He will see me when he drives back and he will wonder who is that wild, strong girl who walks by herself on the moor at night and isn't afraid." She thought (for she knew what she was thinking), "I shall do nothing of the sort. I don't care whether he sees me or not"' (Sinclair 1985: 10). Gwenda's independent spirit yearns for freedom, both physically (walking alone on the moors), and spiritually (missing prayers). Importantly, Gwenda is aware of her desires; she knows she wants to be seen by Rowcliffe and to be appreciated for her healthy physicality, her courage and her mystery; qualities at odds with Mary's 'Angel in the House' form of femininity, and Ally's ill-health.

Rowcliffe and Gwenda fall in love; Rowcliffe in his 'romantic youth' has potential as Gwenda's husband, but their incompatibility is ultimately revealed through their different orientations towards happiness.

Their different perspectives on love and marriage as a necessary good are illustrated by the symbol of the moon. Gwenda sees the poetry and beauty of the moon and this becomes a spiritually elevating experience for her. Rowcliffe, however, is irritated because Gwenda does not see the earthly pleasures that Rowcliffe offers her at the same moment. Rowcliffe snaps, '"You don't know how to be in love with anything – even the moon. But I suppose it's all right as long as you're happy"' (Sinclair 1985: 160). According to Rowcliffe, Gwenda doesn't feel happy in the right way. When orientated towards a 'proper' object of happiness, i.e. a suitable man, she *feels wrongly*, in that she is detached and controlled. When she is ecstatic and filled with passion, it is for an improper object, i.e. the natural world around her, symbolised by the moon. Gwenda defends herself against his emotional attack; to Gwenda real happiness is a self-created state which is linked to freedom, not things: '"Happiness isn't in the things you've got. It's either in you or it isn't"' (Sinclair 1985: 160). Rowcliffe, on the other hand, associates happiness with socially prescribed goods: '"Because you haven't got anything to *make* you happy"' – meaning himself, love, marriage, financial security – the things he prescribed for Ally (Sinclair 1985: 160, emphasis added). Gwenda, as a modern New Woman, adds, '"Anyhow, I've got my liberty [. . .] it covers most things"' (Sinclair 1985: 160). Freedom and liberty are at the centre of happiness for Gwenda. To *make* someone happy often means to expect them to feel happy about similar objects, and can also suggest a disapproval of the objects that the other finds pleasing. *Making* someone happy reveals the coercion at the heart of *inherited happiness*. Rowcliffe's character shifts at this moment from a potential suitor worthy of Gwenda, to a man at the mercy of his 'physiological emergencies'. Sinclair thereby dramatises the point she made to Wright that 'in matters of sex feeling and of sex morality [. . .] man is different from and inferior to woman' (Sinclair 1912b: 559).

Unlike Rowcliffe, who suffers because of his thwarted love for her, Gwenda is able to sublimate her love for him into her affinity with nature, which offers her access to *perfect happiness*. By denying herself *embodied happiness*, she achieves an awareness of a greater Reality behind nature: 'cut off from contacts of the flesh', Gwenda's 'woman's passion, forced inward [. . .] sustained her with an inward peace, an inward exaltation' (Sinclair 1985: 340, 339). Gwenda's sense of self dissolves and she has no words for the experience; it becomes pure feeling and sensation: 'It seemed to her that she *was* what she contemplated, as if all her senses were fused together in the sense of seeing and what her eyes saw they heard and touched and felt' (Sinclair 1985: 340). Importantly, Sinclair wishes readers to differentiate between the surrender of individual will to another's will, as in most marriages, and Gwenda's oneness with a larger reality, in which she becomes pure will. A greater comprehension of reality allows Gwenda to resist the demands placed upon her within the domestic sphere. For 'she shook off the slave-woman who held her down [. . .] In those hours her inner life moved with the large rhythm of the seasons and was soaked in the dyes of the visible world; and the visible world, passing into her inner life, took on its radiance and intensity. Everything that happened and that was great and significant in its happening, happened there' (Sinclair 1985: 339). Sinclair's *hierarchy of happiness* is informed by Sinclair's concept of 'higher sublimation value' (Sinclair 1917: 34). Sinclair characterised sublimation as 'the striving of the Libido towards manifestation in higher and higher forms' (Sinclair 1916: 119). Adapting the work of Freud and Jung, Sinclair posits that the life force can be consciously willed into channels other than the sexual: 'All religion, all art, all literature, all science are sublimations in various stages of perfection. Civilisation is one vast system of sublimations' (Sinclair 1916: 119). For Gwenda her will-to-live is channelled into her physical activity, her union with nature, and her sacrifice in giving up Rowcliffe for the wellbeing of her sister, Ally. Sublimation is what enables people to evolve towards *perfect* happiness.

Mary Olivier's Progression to Perfect Happiness

Sinclair's idea of *perfect happiness* finds its fullest expression in *Mary Olivier: A Life*. Sinclair consolidates aspects of all three Carteret sisters into one protagonist: Mary Olivier. *Mary Olivier* is a *Künstlerroman* told through the single consciousness of Mary. The novel follows her from infancy to middle age, tracing her perpetual battle to develop and retain a sense of self. Her mother, 'Little Mamma', is pious, cold and emotionally inaccessible to Mary. Activities appropriate to Mamma's Victorian conceptions of femininity, such as sewing and religious observance, precipitate a battle of wills between Mary and her mother. Little Mamma's love is entirely dependent upon her ideas of being good: '[Mamma's] face left off disapproving and reproaching and behaved like it did on Christmas Days and birthdays. She smiled now as she sat still and sewed, as she watched you sitting still and sewing' (Sinclair 2002: 298). Mary asks her: '"Why do you look at me so kindly when I'm sewing?"' and her mother replies '"Because I like to see you behaving like a little girl, instead of tearing about and trying to do what boys do"' (Sinclair 2002: 81). Little Mamma reinforces gender norms by passing down her values with her happy objects. These become a social good bequeathing a gender performance that she herself has inherited. If 'where we find happiness teaches us what we value rather than simply what is of value' (Ahmed 2010: 13), then Little Mamma values a 'good girl': one who performs her goodness by being submissive, domestic and religious. In other words, Little Mamma wants Mary to resemble herself.

From the age of seven through adolescence, Mary experiences a form of *embodied happiness*, a mystical vision of the Idealist Reality behind nature that enables Mary to slip the net of her mother's affective inheritance. She calls this joyous sense of freedom her 'secret happiness'. Mary sees 'a queer white light over everything, like water thin and clear'; the grey fields around her home are transformed and saturated with colour and vibrancy (Sinclair 2002: 57). She experiences an affective arrest quickly followed by a rush of pleasure, which culminates in a perceptual and emotional transformation: 'She saw the queer white light for the first time and drew in her breath with a sharp check. She knew that the fields were beautiful' (Sinclair 2002: 57). Beauty affects Mary; happiness floods her body: 'Suddenly, without any reason, she was so happy that she could hardly bear it [. . .] Her happiness was sharp and still like the white light' (Sinclair 2002: 58). Mary's happiness is embodied and emotional, filled with vitality. She becomes porous, visions of beauty flow in and her feelings of happiness flow out. Mary's collision with Beauty, her sudden vision of it, produces an affective access to what May Sinclair called the Absolute, to God. Mary refuses her mother's Christian dogma and discovers her own God, who 'had to do with beauty, absolutely un-moral beauty, more than anything else' (Sinclair 2002: 434). Mary's struggle to escape her mother's control and establish an autonomous personality mirrors the struggle of modernist artists to assert their aesthetic vision against the weight of their Victorian predecessors. Mary fights for her own modern forms of happiness, which she associates with the joy of creativity but which others consider abhorrent: 'Happiness, the happiness that came from writing poems; happiness that other people couldn't have, that you couldn't give to them; happiness that was no good to Mamma, no good to anybody but you, secret and selfish; that was your happiness' (Sinclair 2002: 271). Just as many modernist aesthetic products lay beyond the comprehension of an older audience raised on Victorian values, Little Mamma is enraged by Mary's will to autonomy. Mary experiences the violence of a historical-cultural transition in personal terms: 'Ever since I began to grow up I felt there was something about Mamma that would kill me if I let it. I've had to fight for every single thing I've ever wanted. It's awful fighting her, when she's so sweet and gentle. But it's either that or go under' (Sinclair 2002: 287). The Olivier mother-daughter relationship epitomises the possible violence at the heart of *inherited happiness*. Mary's experience of her embodied 'secret' happiness improves her life to an extent, but as long as Mary is emotionally attached to her mother she is never truly free. Mary's experience of the *perfect happiness* of her maturity is an attempt to escape that affective legacy.

In order to be free and happy, one must be unaffected, i.e. un*moved*, by external forces; especially the love of and from another. In her manifesto Mina Loy also warns of the dangers of loving, stating: 'Women must destroy in themselves, the desire to be loved' (Loy 1996: 155). Mary pursues the destruction of this need by her self-shattering experiences in the blackness of her mind. In moments of extreme conflict between her own desires and the necessities that compel her – for example, between her desire for her lover Richard and her love and duty to her mother – Mary turns inward and extinguishes her passions. She experiences a 'queer' blackness. As she lies in darkness, willing her body out of existence, 'wave after wave' of darkness fills her, 'blotting out everything but your self and your will'; Mary wills herself into a detached state (Sinclair 2002: 434). She attempts to distance herself from her embodied, sensual passions and enter into a perfect cerebral joy, which means an abandonment of body and emotions. She associates this death-like trance with her ability to make things happen, her power to change circumstances; for example, losing her own need for Richard, or healing her mother's illness. Being without attachment is having 'inconceivable freedom', and the power brings her a sense of 'exquisite security, clarity and joy' (Sinclair 2002: 422, 300). Sinclair seems to suggest that real freedom pertains to mental and emotional freedom, regardless of physical constraints. As Mary explains to her brother Mark, '"My body'll stay here and take care of [Mamma] all her life [. . .] but my *self* will have got away"' (Sinclair 2002: 290). If one escapes from the need for love, then there is freedom: '"There mayn't be much left when I'm done, but at least it'll be me"' (Sinclair 2002: 290).

To fully understand Mary's choice and her idea of *perfect happiness*, it is useful to turn to Baruch Spinoza's *Ethics*. Mary reads Spinoza propped against the weighing scales in her kitchen, mixing domestic duties and philosophy, demonstrating that whilst intelligence might not be gendered, the circumstances that cultivate it certainly are. Mary Olivier's experience of *perfect happiness* at the end of the book is closely linked with Spinoza's idea of perfection, freedom and will; Mary concludes that, 'if you were part of God your will was God's will at the moment when you really willed. There was always a point when you knew it: the flash point of freedom' (Sinclair 2002: 433–4). According to Spinoza, the highest good for humans depends upon knowing God intellectually and with a rational love. Mary reads this in her kitchen: 'He who clearly and distinctly understands himself and distinctly understands himself and his emotions loves God, and so much the more in proportion as he more understands himself and his emotions' (Sinclair 2002: 306). It is a necessary part of human nature to experience passions, he posits, our affects are inevitable; but we must control them in order to know God and experience our greatest happiness. Passions are the affective transitions that alert us to a change in being, a shift in our *conatus*. The Latin root of passion, *passio*, supports this understanding of passion as being without action, passive, whereas the late Latin *passionem* (nominative *passio*) also suggests 'suffering, enduring'. In order to escape the 'human bondage' of the passions, which for Spinoza means to be moved by forces outside of the self, one must adequately understand the cause of one's actions (Spinoza 2001: 161). Despite Mary glimpsing a flash of divinity in the crystalline mind of Richard, her lover, happiness with him is earthly, sensual and produces 'ungovernable want' which is to be tied to passion (Sinclair 2002: 262). For Spinoza, freedom is freedom of the mind: 'The free man is the one conscious of the necessities that compel him' (Scruton 1986: 91). As Mary puts it, 'Free-will was the reality underneath the illusion of necessity. The flash point of freedom was your consciousness of God' (Sinclair 2002: 434). To know God adequately, without illusion or passion, is to therefore experience *perfect happiness*: 'Joy is man's passage from a less to a greater perfection', and this is the greatest good for human beings (Spinoza 2001: 147). Mary's *perfect happiness* therefore involves an increase in *conatus*, an increase in the power to act, which means a detachment from human passion. This increases the intellectual and emotional ability to realise (meaning to know and to make real) the divine within in the material world.

Ironically, in attempting to escape from emotion, Mary uses her affects as evidence of the reality of her mystical oneness with God. Mary explains to Richard that she loves him but her 'queer' willing has stopped her wanting him: '"But Richard, it makes you absolutely happy [. . .] It's how you know [. . .] That there's something there. That it's absolutely real"' (Sinclair 2002: 422). To offer proof that relies on feelings is also to rely upon the unreliable body. Mary claims to have certainty about the meaning of true happiness at the close of the novel: 'All her life she had gone wrong about happiness. She had attached it to certain things and certain people – but none of them had brought her the happiness she foresaw' (Sinclair 2002: 435). Mary prefers an asexual, spiritual union with Richard; he had become 'part of the kingdom of

God without ceasing to be himself' because she had loved him enough to let him go (Sinclair 2002: 436). Mary is unable to doubt the reality of her experience because she's happy despite not having Richard: 'giving Richard up and still being happy. That was something you couldn't possibly have done yourself [. . .] all at once, making that incredible, supernatural happiness and peace out of nothing at all, in one night, and going on in it, without Richard' (Sinclair 2002: 423). Giving up Richard becomes part of the circular logic which justifies giving up Richard.

The 'happy ending' of *Mary Olivier* offers one of the greatest challenges to Sinclair's readers. Mary falls in love and takes as her lover the poet Richard Nicholson, yet she declines to marry him because of her duty to her mother. Richard is her intellectual equal and poetic counterpart, the person with the crystalline mind that she has longed for throughout her adult life. Mary choosing her duty to her mother over Richard appears self-effacing and much more akin to repression than sublimation. As Katha Pollitt points out, 'it is hard to think of a renunciation less necessary than Mary's refusal to marry Nicholson' and it is 'almost too much for a modern reader to bear' (Pollitt in Sinclair 2002: xi–xii). Yet Mary characterises her union with the Reality behind everyday reality in romantic terms: 'philosophers have refused to see God as he is: the wild poetic genius of eternity', whereas Mary's creative genius chooses an unworldly poetic union rather than a human one (Sinclair 1922: 304). Sinclair replaces earthly, *embodied happiness* with cerebral, *perfect happiness*, and in doing so creates an alternative form of affective consolation for the unavoidable constraints of life. Sinclair's differently happy ending aimed to frustrate readers' expectations by refusing the conventional happy ending of a marriage. Sinclair thereby forces readers to confront their own desires for traditional forms of narrative conclusion, and instead offers new narrative norms that conclude a woman's life with a bliss that is not constituted by marriage. She had begun this new narrative with Gwenda in *The Three Sisters* but it found its fullest, most perfect expression in *Mary Olivier*. Mirroring Mary's rejection of Richard, the close of *Mary Olivier* performs the final affective untangling within the novel: the tie between Mary and the reader.

The longest relationship throughout the novel is the one between the reader and the text. Sinclair performs this detachment by being less linguistically intimate with the reader. We are offered fewer and fewer details from Mary's mind, and larger gaps of time are introduced. At the start of the final section, for example, Mary has travelled for a year and leased her own house, and Mary's 'ecstasy of space' is dismissed in one sentence – we are being closed out, as Richard was closed out (Sinclair 2002: 428). The shift in reader-character intimacy means that the reader, like Mary, must deal with the separation from the 'mother' of the authorial consciousness into which the reader has been submerged. Sinclair creates a challenging modern reading experience in that the reader, mirroring Mary's self-development, is forced to reflect on this 'differently happy' ending, becoming aware of their own affective reactions in order to become free from authorial authority. At the close of *Mary Olivier*, Mary believes herself to be absolutely secure in her knowledge of God, of the existence of a perfect, Idealist realm of Reality behind the unreality of the everyday world. And so, as the ambiguous close of the novel suggests, the reader must also find their own happiness beyond the boundary of traditional constructions of narrative happiness.

The Degeneration of Happiness in *Life and Death of Harriett Frean*

In contrast to *The Three Sisters* and *Mary Olivier: A Life*, in *Life and Death of Harriett Frean* Sinclair explores how a failure to develop an individual sense of self can foster a degenerate form of happiness. Harriett's attempts to adhere to the 'happiness script' of a dutiful daughter means that she is crushed by the responsibility for making others happy (Ahmed 2010: 59). Unlike Mary Olivier, who strives to develop a sense of self – which means she is marked by society as disobedient – Harriett Frean has only one moment of disobedience, which results in her giving up her will completely thereafter. A decisive event in Harriett's development is when, at the age of ten, Harriett strays beyond prescribed domestic boundaries as she gathers red campion flowers. Harriett imagines her mature sexual self: 'she swung her hips and made her skirts fly out. That was her grown-up crinoline, swing-swinging as she went' (Sinclair 1980: 17). Sinclair's imagery moves from the white froth of cow-parsley (childhood innocence), and the 'red tops' of the red campion (vivid female sexuality), to a 'waste ground covered with old boots and rusted and crumpled things' with a 'dirty little brown house' (Sinclair 1980: 18). The house is inhabited by a man that Harriett feels scared of: 'He was the frightening thing' (Sinclair 1980: 18). The figure represents the fear and fascination of adult sexual experience. Harriett's parents wish her to forget a world that might contain dangers, but do not realise that in so doing she must also forget her own desires and her independence. After her small rebellion, her mother regularly takes her to see the red campion, protecting and policing Harriet's burgeoning sexuality. Harriett's mother takes control of her daughter's sexual experience, offering the flowers as a safe screen from the masculine sexuality and poverty Harriett had trespassed upon. To wish to protect Harriett from things that she is not old enough to experience is understandable, but the Freans are not preparing Harriett for the world. Rather, they are teaching her to repress her natural curiosity and desires, and replacing them with the empty promise of happiness resulting from behaving beautifully.

Harriet's natural curiosity and spiritedness is restrained by the threat of her mother's unhappiness. Harriett is told by her father not to return to see the red campion alone, '"Because it makes your mother unhappy. That's enough why"' (Sinclair 1980: 22). Harriet's father places the burden of affective labour upon Harriet's shoulders, and it is used as a means of tying Harriett to the values of the family. Harriett is aware of this emotional control but feels powerless against it: 'She would always have to do what they wanted; the unhappiness of not doing it was more than she could bear. [. . .] *Their* unhappiness was the punishment. It hurt more than anything' (Sinclair 1980: 23). Harriett's father hopes she will self-regulate: 'we trust you to do what we wish. To behave beautifully' (Sinclair 1980: 23). Harriett accepts the inheritance of her parents' script for happiness. Her will is no longer her own. Harriett's failure to move beyond her parents' wishes means she does not develop the skills to build her own moral edifice. The tragedy of Harriett is not that she is unhappy, but that she is unhappy without understanding the reasons. In the Spinozian sense, Harriett has an inadequate idea of her actions; hence she is at the mercy of external pressures and passions. Lacking emotional and intellectual courage, Harriett refuses to look squarely at reality and so her unconscious motivations manifest affectively: 'She had no clear illumination, only a mournful acquiescence in her own futility, an almost physical sense of shrinkage' (Sinclair 1980: 148). Harriett's psychic and somatic edifice, which she built upon her understanding of her 'beautiful and honourable self', crumbles around her (Sinclair 1980: 149). This is her tragedy.

To surrender intellectual and emotional freedom to others is to regress. In *A Defence of Idealism*, Sinclair states that it is part of each person's duty to add something to the collective consciousness of the race: 'by the one fact that [. . .] I lifted my head above the generations and added another living being, another desire, another will, another experience to the sum of human experiences [. . .] I prove the superiority of my sublimation' (Sinclair 1917: 35). Harriett's failure, then, is a failure to add anything to the sum of human experience or knowledge. To 'simply refuse to grow up and persist in being a child' or to go back to 'the dead generations' is, according to Sinclair, to be degenerate: 'to be degenerate is to fail to add the priceless gift of individuality to the achievement of the race' (Sinclair 1917: 35). Harriett's personal dilemma reflects a cultural challenge, namely the difficulty (and sometimes failure) to move from the 'dead generations' of Victorian values into the modern era. When Harriett's mother dies, Harriett feels that she has to 'retrace the footsteps of her lost self' (Sinclair 1980: 110). Harriett replaces her dead mother with a surrogate, her maid Maggie. Harriett regresses to a childlike state of *embodied happiness*; she grows 'ecstatic under Maggie's flickering fingers as they plaited her thin wisps of hair' (Sinclair 1980: 164). Harriett, unable to withstand the social and familial pressures to behave beautifully, becomes degenerate by Sinclair's standards.

May Sinclair, in her psychological novels, constructs a *hierarchy of happiness* which reveals the coercion at the heart of happiness, but which also offers a means to affective freedom. In the spirit of Loy's explosive 'Feminist Manifesto', Sinclair unmasks the illusion that certain social norms, such as marriage and the family unit, are the only route to happiness. Sinclair demonstrates that other people attempting to *make* you happy, or trying to *make others* happy yourself, can lead to repression and control. Instead, Sinclair depicts women fighting to forge intellectual and spiritual freedom through emotional self-awareness. Sinclair suggests that one must understand one's own motivations and cultivate 'intelligent curiosity and courage in meeting and resisting the pressure of life' (Loy 1996: 156). By striving to add something to the sum total of human experience one increases the power to act, increases *conatus*, which produces joy. For the modern reader the idea of escaping oppressive power structures by leaving behind the body and retreating into *perfect happiness* might be unsatisfying, or even seem delusional. But Sinclair's affective militancy does not leave the body behind entirely – feelings are both psychic and somatic, and in attempting to depathologise female happiness (sexual and cerebral bliss), she also resists the reduction of women to their 'physiological emergencies'. *Perfect happiness* might not be desirable for everyone; but in her fiction Sinclair offered *perfect happiness* as a way to facilitate a radical shift in consciousness, which Sinclair felt was necessary for both social and aesthetic emancipation.

Note

1. The phrase 'Angel in the House' originated with Coventry Patmore's poem about his wife (originally published 1854, revised 1862). There are numerous works discussing this Victorian ideal, but Deborah Gorham's definition is particularly useful: 'The ideal woman was willing to be dependent on men

and submissive to them, and she would have a preference for a life restricted to the confines of the home. She would be innocent, pure, gentle and self-sacrificing. Possessing no ambitious strivings, she would be free of any trace of anger or hostility. More emotional than man, she was also more capable of self-renunciation' (Gorham 1982: 4–5).

Works Cited

Ahmed, Sara (2010), *The Promise of Happiness*, Durham, NC and London: Duke University Press.
Gorham, Deborah (1982), *The Victorian Girl and the Feminine Ideal*, Bloomington: Indiana University Press.
Loy, Mina [1914] (1996), 'The Feminist Manifesto', in Roger L. Conover (ed.), *The Lost Lunar Baedeker*, New York: Farrar, Straus and Giroux, pp. 153–6.
Nadler, Steven (2006), *Spinoza's Ethics: An Introduction*, Cambridge: Cambridge University Press.
Raitt, Suzanne (2000), *May Sinclair: A Modern Victorian*, Oxford: Clarendon Press.
Scott, Bonnie Kime, ed. (1990), *The Gender of Modernism: A Critical Anthology*, Bloomington: Indiana University Press.
Scruton, Roger [1986] (2002), *Spinoza: A Very Short Introduction*, Oxford: Oxford University Press.
Sinclair, May (1912a), *Feminism*, London: The Women Writer's Suffrage League.
Sinclair, May (1912b), 'A Defence of Men', *English Review* 11, 556–66.
Sinclair, May [1914] (1985), *The Three Sisters*, New York: The Dial Press.
Sinclair, May (1916a), 'Clinical Lecture on Symbolism and Sublimation – I', *The Medical Press and Circular* 153, 118–22.
Sinclair, May (1916b), 'Clinical Lecture on Symbolism and Sublimation – II', *The Medical Press and Circular* 153, 142–5.
Sinclair, May (1917), *A Defence of Idealism: Some Questions and Conclusions*, New York: The Macmillan Company.
Sinclair, May [1919] (2002), *Mary Olivier: A Life*, New York: New York Review Books.
Sinclair, May (1922), *The New Idealism*, New York: The Macmillan Company.
Sinclair, May [1922] (1980), *Life and Death of Harriett Frean*, London: Virago.
Spinoza, Baruch [1677] (2001), *Ethics*, trans. W. H. White, revised trans. A. H. Sterling, London: Wordsworth Classics of World Literature.
Wright, Almroth E. (1913), *The Unexpurgated Case Against Woman's Suffrage*, New York: Paul B. Hoeber.

Chapter 5

Architecture, Environment and 'Scenic Effect' in May Sinclair's *The Divine Fire*

Terri Mullholland

The Divine Fire (1904) was May Sinclair's third novel and the one that was to make her name. Ironically, as Suzanne Raitt notes, 'The novel which made her both famous and relatively wealthy [is] a critique of the bookselling industry in which she was now earning her living' (Raitt 2000: 77). Sinclair's novel is, in fact, an astute engagement with the commercialisation of modern life and consumer culture. This chapter will focus on how, within the confines of the realist novel and a fairly traditional plot, Sinclair uses carefully staged representations of architectural space to highlight the play between illusion and reality, exterior and interior, and the commercial versus the domestic. I explore how Sinclair utilises 'scenic effect' (Sinclair 1904: 276), in particular the vibrant imagery of modernity, such as the lighting and window displays of the new department stores, in order to create particular textual environments, and how these function to demonstrate the subtleties of Sinclair's commentary on the commercialisation of modern life.

The Divine Fire is the story of Savage Keith Rickman, 'a cockney poet' (24) who drops his aitches and is not 'exactly what you'd call a gentleman' (119). At the start of the novel, Rickman works at his father's bookshop and is sent to catalogue the private family library of Sir Frederick Harden. Sir Harden's daughter, Lucia, has requested the catalogue while her father is abroad, not knowing that her father has mortgaged the library to cover his debts. Rickman, however, does know this information and he knows also that Dicky Pilkington, to whom the library is mortgaged, is going to offer his father the opportunity to buy the Harden library cheaply. Rickman falls in love with Lucia and is tortured by the duplicity of his situation. When Lucia's father dies and she is forced to sell the library for far less than it is worth, Rickman walks out on his father and the bookselling business over the sale. His father ends up mortgaging the library and his death leaves the debt in Rickman's hands. Rickman's feelings of moral responsibility lead him to sacrifice everything in order to buy the library back for Lucia. He lives in squalor and almost starves to death in the effort to reclaim the library and, with it, Lucia's love.

One early review of Sinclair's novel noted that the whole book is a study of 'the struggle with environment' ('The Divine Fire by May Sinclair' 1905: 120). In particular it is the struggle between commercial and domestic environments. In *The Divine Fire* the commercial is pitched against the domestic not only in the conflict between Rickman's bookshop versus the Harden private library, but also in the distinction between Court House, the Harden family home, and the commercialised domestic space of Mrs Downey's boarding house, where Rickman lives for much of the novel. Sinclair contrasts the Harden library, with its unique, irreplaceable collection hidden from public view, against Rickman's shop, filled with piles of mass-market volumes displayed for anyone to see and purchase. This theme of consumption and display is extended to the domestic realm. Goods circulate in the book trade in the same way as people circulate in the boarding- and lodging-house world, and like the shop window displays that are designed to tempt customers to part with their money, Mrs Downey advertises her boarding house by displaying her boarders prominently in her well-lighted windows to entice passing trade.

The splendour of modernity evoked by the new shop window displays recalls the first world exposition held in London in 1851 and the monumental Crystal Palace, in which consumer goods were displayed as art objects. At these events, Susan Buck-Morss writes, 'the crowds were conditioned to the principles of adventurousness: "Look, but don't touch," and taught to derive pleasure from the spectacle alone' (Buck-Morss 1989: 85). For Walter Benjamin, the great exhibitions were where his concept of the 'phantasmagoria' first found expression. Writing out of the rapid growth of mass culture and consumerism that defined the early twentieth century, Benjamin defined the commodity as a phantasmagoria, a term derived from magic lantern shows and exhibitions of optical illusions. Displayed in the shopping arcades with their dreamlike promise, these phantasmagorias became objects of collective consumer desire. Like the goods on show at the great exhibitions, they traded not on their market value, but on their value as spectacle to captivate the masses: 'Everything desirable, from sex to social status, could be transformed into commodities as fetishes-on-display that held the crowd enthralled even when personal possession was far beyond their reach' (Buck-Morss 1989: 82). Benjamin conceives of modernity under capitalism as a dream world from which society must awake into political consciousness. The commodity is thus posited as an illusionary object of fetishised desire for a dreaming collective.

Lighting was considered 'an essential prop' for Benjamin in the creation of these displays of phantasmagoria and, as Simon Gunn comments, 'in the staging of the dream world of urban modernity' (Gunn 2002: 271). Sinclair utilises lighting to similar effect when she introduces the reader to Keith Rickman by describing the flamboyance of his father's shop, 'a gigantic modern structure, with a decorated façade in pinkish terra-cotta, and topped by four pinkish cupolas' (18). Outside the shop, 'Isaac Rickman New & Second-hand Bookseller' is 'blazoned in letters of gold' (26), and the whole spectacle is one of dazzling exterior display. From whichever direction the shop is approached:

> you could see nothing else, so monstrous was it, so flagrant and so new. Though the day was not yet done, the electric light streamed over the pavement from the huge windows of the ground floor; a coronal of dazzling globes hung over the doorway at the corner. (18)

In a self-deprecating description, Rickman references the vulgarity of the shop, declaring himself to be: 'A poet one day out of seven; the other six days a potman in an infernal, stinking, flaring Gin-Palace-Of-Art' (37). Gin palaces in the nineteenth century were places of surface illusion, with an exterior façade usually considered far grander than the interior, featuring both external and internal gas lighting and utilising large mirrors to increase the overall illumination (Tames 2003: 10). In calling himself a mere 'potman', Rickman distances himself from the ruthless commercial aspects of the bookshop: 'I'm ashamed of the shop [. . .] of this gaudy, pink concern. It's so brutally big. It can't live, you know, without sucking the life out of the little booksellers' (35).

In contrast to the showy and superficial exterior, Rickman is positioned in the interior of the shop seated at a table that is raised up 'on a sort of platform' (19) above the retail business that surrounds him. He is daydreaming and detached from the scene. Sinclair's emphasis is on the distinction between the inner, spiritual life of the mind and the exterior world of commerce. Rickman's presence attracts 'a certain group of young men' (19) who frequent the shop, treating it like a salon, a social space in which to exchange ideas, rather than to buy books: 'they were not the least bit of good to the shop, those customers' (19). As a salesperson, Rickman is 'not the least bit of good to the shop' either. He could have sold many books to the young men on their visits, but 'Surrounded by wares whose very appearance was a venal solicitation, he never hinted by so much as the turn of a phrase that there was anything about him to be bought' (20). The items surrounding Rickman are not for sale and neither is Rickman himself. The question of ownership is one that is raised throughout Sinclair's novel, for there are certainly those who would like to possess Rickman, or at least to claim ownership of the discovery of his poetic talent. Even Rickman's father feels that he has bought Rickman's services behind the counter by having paid for his education: 'which *I* gave *you* to put into *my* business' (389).

The shop has not always been such a brightly illuminated commercial space; in its earlier incarnation in Paternoster Row it had been a 'dark little second-hand shop', where in 'agreeable dusty twilight, outwards forms were dimmed with familiarity and dirt' (22). In this first shop, the public space of the shop and the private domestic space of the home overlapped to create Rickman's early world:

> He had been born over the shop, nursed behind the shop, and the shop had been his schoolroom ever since he could spell. It was the books found in the shop and studied in the shop that first opened his eyes to the glory of the world, as he sat on the step-ladder, reading his Shakespeare or puzzling out his first Greek by the light of a single gas-flare. (77)

It was in this dark shop that Rickman 'first saw what light there was to be seen' (72), experiencing the internal illumination of books and ideas rather than the artificial brightness of the gin palace. The Harden library is a similar place of muted and faded colour, the walls 'of one blackness with the oak floor and ceiling' (83), and the darkness illuminated only by natural sunlight. Throughout the novel Sinclair returns to the symbolism of a light shining into the darkness, or a movement from dark to light; this spiritual and intellectual illumination is also emphasised by the contrast between natural and artificial means of lighting. The poetic world is aligned with purity and truth, while the commercial world is soiled and deceitful.

In his father's new shop, the purity of the higher realms of thought and contemplation are apt to be disturbed:

> Here all that beautiful world of thought lay open to the terrific invasion of things. His dreams refused to stand out with sufficient distinctness from a background of coloured bindings, plate glass and mahogany. They were liable at any moment to be broken by the violent contours of customers. (22)

In describing Rickman's thoughts as violently invaded by the very materials that construct his father's shop, the goods they sell and the customers who keep them in business, Sinclair stresses how brutal the intrusion of these commercial concerns are to Rickman's poetic sensibility; a contemplative sensibility that must be protected from the encroaching threat of commercialisation.

Rickman is depicted as physically elevated from the bookshop as if on a small stage, but rather than make him part of the display, Sinclair's setting serves to emphasise the disconnection between Rickman's body, physically located in the shop, and his mind, wandering freely in poetic reverie. Rickman rejects being an object for display; he 'did not like being looked at' and, when observed, 'his eyes were all over the place, seeking an escape' (20). Sinclair describes his personal appearance as 'the shy, savage beauty of an animal untamed, uncaught' (19). His discomfort in the vulgar shop is intensified by his positioning, and like the books in the window display, he feels 'exposed on his little dais or platform, in hideous publicity' (23), of which he refuses to be a part. These scenes of exposure continue in Rickman's home 'in a fifth-rate boarding-house in Bloomsbury' (176). Like the dazzling brightness of the bookshop that overwhelms the street in which it stands, Mrs Downey's boarding house is 'the light of Tavistock Place' and a spectacle to behold:

> In the brown monotony of the street it stood out splendid, conspicuous. Its door and half its front were painted a beautiful, a remarkable pea-green, while its door knob and door-knocker were of polished brass. Mrs Downey's boarding-house knew nothing of concealment or disguise. Every evening at the hour of seven, through its ground-floor window it offered to the world a scene of stupefying brilliance. The blinds were up, the curtains half-drawn, revealing the allurements of the interior. From both sides of the street, the entire length of the dinner-table was visible. (275)

The window is illuminated by 'as many as three gas-jets [that all] burned furiously at once', lighting the faces of the boarders in its 'intense illumination' (275), and becomes a framing device for the theatrical staging of Mrs Downey's nightly dinners where the 'table was disposed with a view to scenic effect' (276). The phrase 'scenic effect' aptly sums up Mrs Downey's careful curating of her home, and is also useful for thinking about the ways in which Sinclair utilises 'scenic effect' in her narrative. In particular, Sinclair highlights what could be called 'theatres of domesticity' – that is, scenes of domestic life, created purely for 'effect'. These theatres of domesticity are performed by the various women with whom Rickman becomes involved and, as we shall see later in this chapter, even Rickman himself is not immune to creating 'scenic effects' in his domestic environment.

The 'scenic effects' created by the window displays in Rickman's shop and Mrs Downey's boarding house are brought together by Sinclair's explicit links between window dressing and costume. Like the books in Rickman's window display, clothed in their finery, where 'the newest of new books stood out, solicitous and alluring, in suits of blazing scarlet and vivid green, of vellum and gilt' (18), Mrs Downey displays the youngest and the best-dressed inhabitants of her boarding house in a similar way, placing them in the centre of the table beneath the dazzling lights where their 'brilliant appearance of an evening was as good as an advertisement for Mrs Downey's' (276); while seating herself 'at the most obscure' end of the table and gathering around her 'the older and less attractive members of her circle' (276).

These nightly window displays are a live performance in which Mrs Downey can present her wares, combining 'the splendid publicity of an hotel with the refinements of a well-appointed home' (276). In contrast to the 'hideous publicity' experienced by Rickman in the shop, Mrs Downey views the exposure of her boarders as 'splendid publicity'. She has a commercial awareness of the human spectacle she is creating. In placing her young, attractive boarders strategically in a brightly lit window designed to create the illusion of an intimate dinner party in a bourgeois private home, Mrs Downey converts her boarders into commodities. They become the advertisement that will tempt passers-by off the street, and Mrs Downey hopes 'wandering persons in hansoms, lonely persons having furnished apartments, persons living expensively in hotels or miserably in other boarding-houses, might look in, and long to be received into Mrs Downey's, to enjoy the luxury, the comfort, the society' (278).

In her discussion of the development of consumer culture, Rachel Bowlby writes about the new use of glass technology and lighting in department-store window displays:

> Glass and lighting [...] created a spectacular effect, a sense of theatrical excess coexisting with the simple availability of individual items for purchase. Commodities were put on show in an attractive guise, becoming unreal in that they were images set apart from everyday things, and real in that they were there to be bought and taken home to enhance the ordinary environment. (Bowlby 1985: 2)

Mrs Downey's use of 'scenic effect' exhibits a definite 'sense of theatrical excess', and in staging her nightly dinners her boarders take on a similarly unreal quality as mere stage props: 'remarkable as they were collectively, individually, Mrs Downey seldom thought of them' (278). Mrs Downey is not only exhibiting her house and inhabitants as goods; she is displaying her own services as landlady. There is a strong sexual element in this display; the brightly lit window is suggestive of a brothel, which calls into question what else Mrs Downey might be selling.

The sexual undertone inherent in the display and transaction of commodities is a theme that Sinclair utilises in her description of the Harden library. Even though the Harden library must be sold, the uniqueness of its collection sets it apart from the easily bought and replaced mass-market volumes in Rickman's bookshop, and determines its value:

> The great Harden Library would come virgin into the market, undefiled by the touch of commerce, the breath of publicity. It had been the pure and solitary delight of scholar lovers who would have been insulted by the suggestion that they should traffic in its treasures. Everything depended on his keeping its secret inviolate. (95)

The chaste 'virgin' nature of the Harden library is something that can only be touched by 'scholar lovers'; unlike the promiscuous mass-market volumes that are available to everyone, these volumes are irreplaceable. Sinclair also emphasises the division between 'the touch of commerce' and the handling of the 'scholar lover' in Rickman's distinctions between the types of work he does in the two different spaces. While he is simply a 'potman' in the bookshop, suggesting rough and mindless treatment of objects, when working in the Harden library he becomes a scholar: 'handling the book as a lover handles the thing he loves' (103). In *The Human Condition*, Hannah Arendt makes a distinction between the terms 'labour' and 'work'. Labour activities are those which are 'undertaken not for their own sake but in order to provide the necessities of life'; in contrast, work is an individualising occupation that 'transcends both the sheer functionalism of things produced for consumption and the sheer utility of objects produced for use' (Arendt 1958: 83, 173). Rickman's poetry is an 'individualizing occupation'. Bowlby explains that poetry could transcend the commodity because it rarely paid the author enough to live on, making 'questions of the market [. . .] relatively insignificant. Poetry, as a result, could be identified as a place kept pure, the locus of "art for art's sake," uncontaminated by the profit motive or by the vulgar requirements of the popular market' (Bowlby 1985: 9). Rickman refuses to charge Lucia the market rate for his cataloguing and prostitute himself and his task. By asking for only a nominal fee of fifteen pounds 'to accomplish three weeks' expert work to the value of fifty pounds' (108), his work becomes elevated from the marketplace and maintains the virgin purity of art.

Rickman wants to apply the same poetic values to the production of the catalogue; spiritually cleansing it of the commercial purpose for which he knows it will be ultimately used against Lucia. The reason he leaves the bookshop is because he is unable to reconcile his father's conception of the way the business should be run with his own higher ideals. Isaac Rickman does not understand why he should be made to pay more for the Harden library simply because of his son's promise to do his best for Lucia. For him, emotions have no part in business: 'The book trade was not a matter for high spiritual romance; it was simply the way they got their living, as honest a way as any other' (77).

As the Harden library circulates throughout the novel, Sinclair demonstrates that history is not immune from commercialisation, and the unique objects in the library can be bought and sold as easily as the mass-market novels. However, when Rickman's father is unable to pay his debts the library is mortgaged once again to Dicky Pilkington, pausing its circulation and sale:

> And yet for the time being [. . .] it was safe, the great Harden library, once the joy of scholars, loved with such high intellectual passion [. . .] Now that the work of sacrilege was complete, housed at last in the Gin Palace of Art, it stood, useless in its desecrated beauty, cumbering the shelves whence no sale would remove it until either Rickman's or Pilkington let go. (324)

The Harden library is entombed within the Gin Palace of Art, which becomes a mausoleum for 'its desecrated beauty'; the scholar lovers can no longer touch the books, and the knowledge within them becomes useless. It is ironic that this gaudy pink monument to commercialism should preserve the library not only from being read, but also from being dispersed and sold as individual items, preserving the other aspect of its uniqueness, that it is a collection. When Rickman finally returns the library to Lucia, he acknowledges that the collection is no longer complete; 'a few very valuable books were sold before the mortgage and could not be recovered' (613). To Rickman the true value of the library is that it is the 'Harden' library; it has become a memory-artefact, and as such is the preservation of the family memory: 'The library belonged to her race and to their historic past' (170).

Rickman's refusal to labour for adequate payment on the library catalogue is also due to his desire to separate his pure love for Lucia from the taint of the commercial. As Raitt has argued, Rickman 'undercharges for his services because he longs to be near her [. . .] Lucia represents the possibility of non-commercial economies: economies of learning and of love' (Raitt 2000: 88–9). In Rickman's mind, Lucia is aligned with the qualities of the Harden library: chaste, pure and untarnished by the world of commerce. Like the books in the library, Lucia is also unique and unattainable.

Lucia is also Rickman's muse and, as her name suggests, his 'light' and the source of his 'divine fire': a term that refers both to his love and his intellectual genius and inspiration. The sense of a 'divine' connection is also evoked; the muse is, after all, a goddess, and Lucia is given similar otherworldly qualities: she is 'the Lucia who had divined and would divine him still' (345). Rickman writes a series of poems, 'the best things I've written' (482), for which she is the source of inspiration. The poems are available in a single handwritten version with no copy. This is not an item that Rickman can ever sell for his own gain, no matter how destitute he becomes; instead he gives it to Lucia, for her to choose what becomes of the manuscript. Rickman knows that it is 'only valuable because it's unique' (483), and sees in it the potential to pay off his debt to Lucia for the loss of the Harden library.

The reproducible commodity and the unique art form are deliberately contrasted throughout Sinclair's novel, from the books Rickman works with to the journal articles and poetry he writes and the women he chooses. Before he meets Lucia, Rickman is involved with Miss Poppy Grace, another character who, like Mrs Downey, trades on illusion and theatrical excess. The reader is introduced to Poppy through her rooms, which are located next door to Rickman's, their balconies adjoining. Poppy is a performer at the Jubilee Variety Theatre, and both her balcony, heavy with its dramatic Shakespearean imagery, and her accommodation are extensions of the stage. Poppy lives up to her name, being 'like a flower' (52), and blossoming in the dreary landscape of respectable Bloomsbury. In the description of her rooms, Sinclair emphasises how one room:

> had been once an ordinary Bloomsbury drawing-room, the drawing-room of Propriety. Now it was Poppy's drawing-room. You came straight out of a desert of dreary and obscure respectability, and it burst, it blossomed into Poppy before your eyes. Portraits of Poppy on the walls, in every conceivable and inconceivable attitude. (54)

There is something fantastical about Poppy's imagery. In addition to the portraits on the walls, there were also '[t]wo immense mirrors facing each other' and reflecting 'Poppy, when she was there, for ever and ever, in diminishing perspective' (54). Poppy is reflected to the reader through these multiple visual representations, and her body is very much part of the interior design of her room and part of its scenic effect. The interior of Poppy's room looks like the outside of a theatre, covered with advertising posters, and merging the boundaries between her domestic private space and the public space of the street and the theatre. Rickman is also unable to think of Poppy without thinking of her image as represented in her publicity posters, a static version of the real thing, stage lit:

> He had a sudden vision of Poppy as he was wont to meet her in delightful intimacy, instantaneously followed by her image that flaunted on the posters out there in the Strand, Poppy as she appeared behind the foot-lights, in red silk skirts and black silk stockings, skimming, whirling, swaying, and deftly shaking her foot at him. (25)

In his well-known essay 'The Work of Art in the Age of Its Technical Reproducibility', Benjamin observes that in the age of photography and film, a work of art can be technologically reproduced and circulated endlessly, substituting 'a mass existence for a unique existence', but all these images lack the authenticity, the 'aura' of the original (Benjamin 2008: 22). This applies equally to human beings, for whom 'the mirror image has become detachable from the person mirrored, and is transportable [. . .] [t]o a site in front of the masses' (Benjamin 2008: 33). The image then becomes owned and controlled by the masses, leading to the self-estrangement of the individual.

The multitude of images in Poppy's room suggests an endlessly reproducible Poppy Grace, and Rickman's fetishised image of Poppy seems interchangeable with the real thing. Poppy is simply another commodity that can be viewed for a price. But while Rickman and the whole audience at the Jubilee Theatre may have fallen for the allure of the phantasmagoric Poppy, Sinclair wants the reader to know that there is more to Poppy than just her image, for Poppy is aware of her commercial worth. On the stage, Poppy acts the part of various characters, but rather than being simply a copy, 'she always played the same part in the same manner; but her manner was her own' (50). In drawing attention to the uniqueness of Poppy's method of imitation, Sinclair is also pointing to the complexities of the represented image in modern life; although Poppy may be 'authentic' and the artist of her own creations, she reproduces her performances time and again, knowing that this is what her audience demands. Poppy may have no control over the independent circulation of her image in its reproduction both on posters and prints, and in the minds of her audience, but on the stage she knows that it is within her power to manipulate that image for her own profitable gain.

When the audience call out the name 'Poppy Grace', Rickman is uncomfortable. It reminds him that Poppy is a popular entertainer: 'To Rickman's mind the name was an outrage; it reeked of popularity; it suggested – absurdly and abominably – a certain cheap drink of sudden and ephemeral effervescence' (52). There is the suggestion that Rickman wants Poppy to exist for him alone, an object for his scholarly contemplation, but instead he sees that her role is simply to intoxicate the masses. The notion of the popular versus the scholarly is one that also defines the journals for which Rickman writes. Setting out the aims of *The Museion*, the editor, Lucia's brother Horace Jewdwine, argues that: 'It would, therefore, be unique. Yes; it would also be unpopular. Heaven forbid that anything he was concerned in should be popular' (311). Sinclair is clearly mocking Jewdwine's views of the popular here; even though throughout the novel she is expressing her distaste for the commercialisation of art, she is also aware of the uselessness of producing work that is never read. She plays out the conflict that faces the writer who feels forced to choose between making art or money. For Jewdwine, writing that appeals to the masses is to be avoided for its vulgar connection with the commercial, for *The Museion* is not 'a commercial speculation' (313), and in its place would be articles that 'would be examples of the purity it preached' (311). However, even these high-minded ideals cannot hold out against changing consumer demands; *The Museion* becomes *Metropolis* in 'the race for money and position' (412), a title that deliberately evokes the bustling urban city and the movement of modern life. Jewdwine explains this change of direction: 'We certainly want to draw a rather larger public than we have done; and to do that we must make *some* concessions to modernity. There's no doubt that the paper's interests have suffered from its tradition. We have been too exclusive, too detached' (414–15). Rickman chooses to leave *Metropolis* because his beliefs and that of the journal are in conflict and he is unwilling to provide 'the sort of opinion I'm paid to give' (565). In this, Sinclair is clearly critiquing aspects of the popular press for not having the courage of their convictions, but she is also suggesting that there is an alternative; and, as she herself discovered with the publication of *The Divine Fire*, commercialisation and writing for an audience does not always lead to inauthenticity on the part of the writer.

Kathleen Wheeler has observed that for many modernist women writers, 'houses or rooms, are all sources of symbolic enrichment of the narrative, and often almost become central characters, or at least embodiments of the heart and soul of a central character' (Wheeler 1994: 13–14). *The Divine Fire* is intrinsically concerned with modernity and the new modes of representation of modern life, and even in this early-twentieth-century novel, we can see Sinclair is attentive to the spaces that her characters inhabit and fully exploits the power of her own brand of 'scenic effect' in constructing the story. Sinclair's descriptions of physical environments are subtly aligned with her characters, often revealing qualities theatrically through visual props and clues. Throughout the novel Sinclair articulates for the reader how Rickman and Lucia perceive each other, and the intricacies of the relationship between them, through architectural and environmental allusion, particularly in the design of her narrative interiors as theatres of domesticity.

The greatest obstacle between Rickman and Lucia is not the sale of her father's library, but the class difference between them. Sinclair emphasises this divide by the way Rickman moves through the space of Court House. The gulf between him and Lucia is described in spatial terms. When he is invited to have coffee with Lucia and her friend Kitty Palliser in the in the drawing room, he finds himself in a room that

> was almost dark except for a small fire-lit, lamp-lit square at the far end. Lucia was sitting in a low chair by the fire-place, under the tall shaded lamp, where the light fell full on her shoulders [...] He had to cross a vast, dim space before he reached that lighted region. With what seemed to him a reeling and uncertain gait, he approached over the perilously slippery parquet. (167)

Rickman must metaphorically move through the darkness towards the light represented by Lucia. That he might be walking on thin ice is suggested by Sinclair in the slippery parquet floor, and when Rickman does slip, he is able to make a joke about it: 'if you fall, it breaks the ice' (169). 'Breaking the ice' becomes an act of speech as well as movement for Rickman. In *The Practice of Everyday Life*, Michel de Certeau connects the act of walking to the act of speech, arguing that walking is a 'spatial acting-out of the place' and speech is an 'acoustic acting-out of language', offering a 'definition of walking as a space of enunciation' (De Certeau 1988: 97–8). Walking and speech are both a means for the articulation of space. Rickman's speech, in particular his pronunciation, is what deters him from moving with ease through the space of Court House.

Lucia first hears about Rickman through her cousin Horace Jewdwine when he visits her at Court House with the first two acts of Rickman's *Helen in Leuce*. When Lucia suggests that her cousin might invite Rickman to Court House he exclaims, 'I don't think it would do [...] You see, for one thing, he sometimes drops his aitches' (10). Rickman's spoken words define and place him: as George Orwell writes, the English working class are 'branded on the tongue', their accent revealing their class status (Orwell 1947: 10). Rickman's disarticulation, the gulf between him and Lucia, is the gulf where the spoken 'H' should be; the gulf around which he must stutter and stumble with 'a reeling and uncertain gait' (167). Lucia is more understanding than her brother, and in describing Rickman's failure to enunciate the 'H' she alludes again to the instability of his movement across the parquet floor: 'she wouldn't go as far as to say he *dropped* them; he slipped them, slided them; it was no more than a subtle slur, a delicate elision' (173).

Yet in writing, Rickman is word-perfect, and when he adopts a foreign tongue he avoids the pitfalls of English. Reading Euripides to Lucia in the library:

> He began to quote softly and fluently, to her uttermost surprise. His English was at times a thing to shudder at, but his Greek was irreproachable, perfect in its modulation and its flow. Freed from all flaws of accent, the musical quality of his voice declared itself indubitably, marvellously pure. (104)

Diana Wallace has argued that the space of the library is an important one in Sinclair's novel: 'Rickman's dropped aitches and Lucia's gender should equally exclude them from the Harden library, which, tellingly, is famous in part because it has never yet been inherited by a woman. Instead, Sinclair transforms the library into the only space where they can meet on anything like equal terms' (Wallace 2006: 55). It is the continued link with the library that ensures they will continue to meet during the course of the novel, as the library becomes a privileged space where class and commercial interests no longer apply.

Although they come together in the space of the library, Lucia is set apart from the other women in Rickman's life. This is emphasised by Sinclair's description of the interior design of Lucia's drawing room: the room was 'furnished with an extreme simplicity, such bareness as musicians love. He was struck by that absence of all trivial decoration, all disturbing and irrelevant detail. In such a room, the divinity of the human form was not dwarfed or obscured by excess of furniture' (170). This is the opposite of Miss Poppy Grace's rooms and its 'litter of coffee cups' and shoes on the tea table (54). Lucia's room in its simplicity is like the rarefied space of the museum awaiting its curios for display. In his essay 'Valéry Proust Museum', Theodor Adorno discusses Proust's vision of the museum as the perfect blank space for the display of art, as opposed to the cluttered space of the home. Proust writes that: 'the masterpiece observed during dinner no longer produces in us the exhilarating happiness that can be had only in a museum, where the rooms, in their sober abstinence from all decorative detail, symbolise the inner spaces into which the artist withdraws to create the work' (Adorno 1981: 179). Lucia's room, with its 'absence of all trivial decoration', acts in a similar way to display its inhabitant as art object. But the connection is also a spiritual one; the blank canvas represents Lucia's purity, and the room's similarity to the artist's mind or studio places her in the position not only of muse, but also of art object. The lack of 'trivial decoration' is far removed from the dazzling showiness of the gin palace, and devoid of all distractions, Lucia becomes the focal point of the interior. Rather than grounding her in the room, the effect of Sinclair's description is to enable Lucia to transcend the physicality of the room and to emphasise the 'inner spaces' and her spiritual qualities.

In contrast to the bare simplicity of Lucia's rooms, when Rickman briefly becomes engaged to Flossie Walker, another resident of Mrs Downey's boarding house, Sinclair depicts Flossie's crazed buying spree to create her own theatre of domesticity by furnishing her house with the newest of new things:

> Her ceaseless winding in and out of shops, her mad and furious buying of furniture, her wild grasping at any loose articles that came in her way, from rugs to rolling-pins, appeared to him as so many futile efforts to construct a dam. (468)

Rickman calls Flossie 'the beaver'. Although originally referring to her 'plumpness', her practicality and her 'secretive ways' (373), the nickname quickly becomes symbolic of her desire to build her fantasy house. Before a beaver can build its home, it must first build its dam, and Flossie constructs hers out of consumer goods. Didier Maleuvre has argued that in the nineteenth century it was through ownership that the bourgeois individual inhabited the home: 'It is as an *owner* of a great many objects that the bourgeois individual inhabits the home. To dwell is to possess' (Maleuvre 1999: 115). The pile of objects is Flossie's protection and defence, and the more she purchases, the further ensnared Rickman is: 'He had committed himself more deeply with every purchase [. . .] There was something in the Beaver's building after all' (477).

Sinclair reveals Flossie to Rickman through her homemaking. If Lucia is aligned with the books in the Harden library, Flossie is one of the mass-market books in Rickman's shop – the word 'flossy' meaning excessively showy. Flossie is a consumer with a desperate desire to buy the dreams of her future. Her dreams are very precise, and firmly grounded in the material:

> To be married (to a person hitherto unspecified in fantasy, whose features remained a blur or a blank), to be the mistress of a dear little house (the house stood out very clear in Flossie's fancy), and the mother of a dear little girl (a figure ever present to her, complete in socks and shoes and all the delicious details of its dress). (349)

The details of the husband are insignificant compared to that carefully imagined house, and the daughter is simply a figure to dress up in the latest fashions. Although the husband may be 'a blur', Flossie has a clear mental image of the furnishings for the house: the drawing room would be 'imitation rosewood and tapestry' and the dining room 'stamped velvet and black oak (imitation, too)' (424). The furniture is all imitation; it is a copy of the fine furnishings and real wood that would exist in a bourgeois home like Court House. The department store is also laid out in an imitation of home, to enable the dreaming consumer to see their vision in carefully constructed domestic settings: 'the little rosewood tea-table (spread, for the heightening of the illusion, with a tea-service all complete)' (425). Flossie involves herself in this theatre, pretending to pour out tea and 'smiling over the teapot in the prettiest delight. [. . .] (It did not occur to him that at the moment Flossie was only smiling at the teapot' (425). Here the faceless husband is superfluous to Flossie's imagined scene of conventional domesticity; her smile is for the teapot that helps create her teatime illusion, not for the recipient of the tea. Indeed, it seems that Flossie is not a part of her dream house either; it exists independently, as an accumulation of household goods. The furnishings are not there to express her taste or her personality, but to create them.

Sinclair tells us that Rickman is 'peculiarly sensitive to his surroundings' (426), and this is highlighted when Flossie and Rickman disagree over the choice of house: Flossie wants a 'brand-new, red-brick villa, with nice clean white paint about it', while Rickman wants an 'old-fashioned brown-brick house' (425–6). Rickman wants a house with a history; Flossie wants somewhere bright and new to showcase the mass-produced furnishings: 'What's wrong with the house? It won't suit the furniture, that's what's wrong with it' (426).

Rickman, however, is focused on his need for a space in which to write, a house that accommodates his inner life, rather than one that displays his possessions. When Rickman points out the perfect room in the old-fashioned house in which he could 'get away to write' (426), Flossie interprets this as 'When you want to get away from me, you mean' and looks at the room 'with angry eyes, as if jealous of the place, and all that he meant to do in it' (426). The room looks as if was once a nursery, and it is in that room that Flossie sees her own future child: 'Never had Flossie had so poignant a vision of Muriel Maud' (427). She gives in to Rickman on the house, but tells him he cannot have the room 'I want to keep it empty [. . .] To store things in' (428), as if the room itself has become the receptacle for her dream of Muriel Maud. The daughter of whom Flossie dreams is another piece of her dam of furnishings, shoring up and stabilising her relationship and her identity. Muriel Maud simply becomes another prop in her theatre of domesticity. The fairytale quality of Flossie's wish for happiness is built on the creation of an illusion. Like the Gin Palace of Art, from the outside the house, crammed with all her new possessions, is a dazzling display of the ideal of married life, but inside it is empty of the very thing that cannot be purchased: Rickman's love.

Although he dismisses Flossie's purchasing of the furnishings of her dream life as dam-building, Rickman is not immune to the importance of 'scenic effect', and Sinclair demonstrates that he is also aware of the importance of creating environmental illusions and his own theatre of domesticity. When Lucia arrives at Mrs Downey's boarding house to stay with her former tutor and Rickman's fellow boarder Miss Roots, Rickman offers Miss Roots the use of his library in which to relax with

Lucia. Here the power of objects in creating 'scenic effect' is demonstrated through Rickman's careful curating of the room. After first 'removing or concealing the unlovelier signs of his presence and profession' (438–9), Rickman purchases new items for Lucia's use, striving to make them look old: 'He did things to them to make them look as if they had been some little time in use. He caused a wrinkle to appear in the smooth blue cheeks of the sofa cushions. He rubbed some of the youth off the edges of the tea-table. He made the brass kettle dance lightly on the floor, until, without injury to its essential beauty, it had acquired a look of experience' (439). In battering the kettle to give it 'a look of experience', he is attempting to create a room with a sense of history. Although it cannot compete with the Harden library and its 'historic past' (170), it can still create an air of traditional bourgeois comfort.

However, it is not only Lucia's comfort and well-being that are being considered. Rickman is also thinking about how these surroundings will enhance the beauty of his visitor and how Lucia will appear against his carefully selected cushions, 'chosen with a distinct prevision of the beauty of the white face and dark hair against that particular shade of greenish blue' (446). In her exploration of the housewife as modern artist in turn-of-the-century Paris, Lisa Tiersten argues that the '[d]ecorating handbooks and magazine columns so emphasised the need for aesthetic harmony and unity between the woman and her home that the body of the bourgeois housewife became an integral part of the interior' (Tiersten 1996: 30). Rickman practises this role as modern artist, designing an interior that stresses the 'aesthetic harmony and unity' between Lucia's colouring and the soft furnishings of the room: 'Bourgeois wives were not to select the fabrics in vogue, but to pick those which best blended with their hair-color and skin tone' (Tiersten 1996: 31). When he meets Lucia in the library, Sinclair presents Rickman as a detached observer, admiring his scene-setting: 'He had done his work so thoroughly well that the place looked as if it had been ready for her since the beginning of time' (446). His purchasing and subsequent distressing of these new consumer goods points to Rickman's role as both consumer and producer of commodities and images, as his attempts to create an aesthetic ideal result in him commodifying his muse into art object. In his need to protect Lucia from the crass world of commercialisation, Rickman turns her into a commodity that, like the goods displayed at the Crystal Palace, can be looked at and desired, but not touched. Throughout *The Divine Fire* Sinclair's engagement with the themes of modernity, particularly her awareness of the ways in which modern life was moving towards increasing commercialisation and her nuanced articulation of the role of display and scenic effect, seems prescient of the themes of the modernist literature that was to follow. Georgina Downey argues that '[t]hrough making rooms, we display to ourselves and others where we fit in the social and material world' (Downey 2013: 4). The rooms in *The Divine Fire* not only display where the characters 'fit', but also draw attention to the very notions of display and commerce that are changing the construction of the world in which they live.

Sinclair closes the novel with Lucia and Rickman about to be married, but Diana Wallace has argued that this is not the traditional fairytale closure, writing that 'The novel offers a number of indications, including the title itself, that it is to be read on a symbolic rather than purely realistic level' (Wallace 2006: 53). Sinclair has modernity at the heart of her symbolic world. She goes beyond the classical symbolism of the novel to depict the paradox of the modern subject's striving for individualism and self-actualisation in the increasingly fragmented nature of modern life that has replaced dreams of the future with phantasmagoria.

In writing about the phantasmagorias that captivated the masses, Benjamin argues that 'what emerges in these wish images is the resolute effort to distance oneself from all that is antiquated – which includes [. . .] the recent past' (Benjamin 2002: 4). In *The Divine Fire*, Sinclair demonstrates this relentless desire for the new and the modern against the values of the old. Raitt has argued that in this novel Sinclair's characters are searching 'to preserve a sense of the sacred in everyday life', and she suggests that Sinclair was 'looking for a modernity in which she could believe' (Raitt 2000: 86). Sinclair was writing at a time of rapid change, and in her use of the imagery of modernity – the commodities, the dazzling lights, the decor – to create 'scenic effect', she reveals society's growing obsession with surface illusion and 'the new'. But alongside this Sinclair also reveals an alternative world that still values art and the spiritual values it represents, a world she hopes can still survive the bright lights of commercialisation now dominating modern life.

Works Cited

Adorno, Theodor W. (1981), 'Valéry Proust Museum', in Adorno, *Prisms*, trans. Samuel and Shierry Weber, Cambridge, MA: The MIT Press, pp. 173–86.

Arendt, Hannah (1958), *The Human Condition*, Chicago: University of Chicago Press.

Benjamin, Walter (2002), *The Arcades Project*, trans. Howard Eiland and Kevin McLaughlin, Cambridge, MA: Harvard University Press.

Benjamin, Walter (2008), 'The Work of Art in the Age of Its Technical Reproducibility' [Second Version], in Michael W. Jennings, Brigid Doherty and Thomas Y. Levin (eds), *The Work of Art in the Age of Its Technological*

Reproducibility and Other Writings on Media, Cambridge, MA: The Belknap Press of Harvard University Press, pp. 19–55.

Bowlby, Rachel (1985), *Just Looking: Consumer Culture in Dreiser, Gissing and Zola*, New York and London: Methuen.

Buck-Morss, Susan (1989), *The Dialectics of Seeing: Walter Benjamin and the Arcades Project*, Cambridge, MA: The MIT Press.

'The Divine Fire by May Sinclair' (1905), *The Sewanee Review* 13, 119–20.

Downey, Georgina (2013), 'Introduction', in Downey (ed.), *Domestic Interiors: Representing Homes from the Victorians to the Moderns*, London and New York: Bloomsbury, pp. 1–12.

Gunn, Simon (2002), 'City of Mirrors: The Arcades Project and Urban History', *Journal of Victorian Culture* 7:2, 263–75.

Maleuvre, Didier (1999), *Museum Memories: History, Technology, Art*, Stanford: Stanford University Press.

Orwell, George (1947), *The English People*, London: Collins.

Raitt, Suzanne (2000), *May Sinclair: A Modern Victorian*, Oxford: Clarendon Press.

Sinclair, May (1904), *The Divine Fire*, London: Archibald Constable and Co.

Tames, Richard (2003), *The Victorian Public House*, Oxford: Osprey.

Tiersten, Lisa (1996), 'The Chic Interior and the Feminine Modern: Home Decorating as High Art in Turn-of-the-Century Paris', in Christopher Reed (ed.), *Not at Home: The Suppression of Domesticity in Modern Art and Architecture*, London: Thames and Hudson, pp. 18–32.

Wallace, Diana (2006), '"A Sort of Genius": Love, Art, and Classicism in May Sinclair's *The Divine Fire*', in Andrew J. Kunka and Michele K. Troy (eds), *May Sinclair: Moving Towards the Modern*, Aldershot and Burglington, VT: Ashgate.

Wheeler, Kathleen (1994), *'Modernist' Women Writers and Narrative Art*, Basingstoke and London: Macmillan.

Part II
Abject Bodies

Chapter 6

Disembodying Desire: Ontological Fantasy, Libidinal Anxiety and the Erotics of Renunciation in May Sinclair

Faye Pickrem

> She envied her youth its capacity for daydreaming, for imagining interminable communions. Brilliant hallucinations of a mental hunger. Better than nothing [. . .] Your mind would die in a delirium of hunger. (Sinclair 1980a: 314)

Ontological Fantasy

In a well-travelled passage of *The Phenomenology of Spirit*, Hegel writes, 'The true is the whole, But the whole is nothing else than the essence consummating itself through its development. Of the Absolute, it must be said that it is essentially a *result*, that only in the *end* is it what it truly is' (1979: 11–12). Franco Moretti echoes this passage in his theory of the classical *Bildungsroman*. Arguing that the novel of formation neatly dovetails 'the ending and the aim of narration' (55), he emphasises that, 'for Hegel the marriage of Truth and the Whole is celebrated *at the end of a story*' (1987: 60). While Moretti critiques this narrative of wholeness, May Sinclair invests in such 'interminable communions', adhering to the trajectory of '"idealised and transfigured embodiment"' (John Elof Boodin, quoted in Sinclair n.d.: 20). Performing her own alchemical transposition of philosophy into literary theory, ontological significance – indeed, subjectivity itself – is posited as the achievement of the 'whole, gorgeous, concrete, and abundant life' of Hegel's Absolute (Sinclair 1917: 349). Sinclair's narratives seek this transfiguring consummation in an attempt to guarantee what Jacques Lacan calls the *point de capiton*, a 'quilting point' to secure unified subjectivity: '[T]he point of convergence that enables everything that happens in this discourse to be situated retroactively and prospectively'

(1997: 268). In a textual bid for Hegelian wholeness, Sinclair employs philosophical idealism and psychology as tools for 'psycho-synthesis'.[1] Reader and protagonist are discursively 'situated' so as to be 'lured by the vision of that "Sublimation" which is held out before him as the end' (Sinclair 1916: 119).

Sinclair's narratalogical assumptions suggest the triumphant attainment of ontological transcendence: the tale not of a fragmented subject, but of desire fulfilled and lack overcome. But what if Sinclair's theoretical lure is merely a structural assertion that remains incommensurable with the body of the text? Her denouements frequently resonate with ambivalence, contradicting their narrative trajectory. What if the centre cannot hold, and Sinclair's perception of the *Bildungsroman* as the path of idealism and unified subjectivity is a chimera, a 'brilliant hallucination', as Mary Olivier reflects: in other words, an ontological fantasy? Lacan labels this elusive register the real: a psychic structure 'without fissure' (1988: 97), an 'unrent, undifferentiated fabric' that is 'full everywhere' (Fink 1995: 24), bearing traces of the phantasmatic embrace of the m/other, the lost originary object, and providing the illusion of ontological wholeness.[2] However, any entry into the symbolic order '*cuts into* the smooth façade of the real, creating divisions, gaps [. . .] laying the real to rest' (24). This plenitudinous real, rendered in Sinclair as 'Reality' or 'the Absolute', haunts the nascent subject as the psychic wound of lack, engendering a desire to resolve the split in the fabric of the psyche. Sinclair's fantasy of ontological wholeness represents the spectral trace of desire projected onto genre.

As a good Hegelian, Sinclair has a need for immanent truths. Her craving for 'Ultimate Reality' is 'the object of the metaphysical quest' (Sinclair 1917: 241). Yet as Slavov Žižek writes in *The Plague of Fantasies*, the subject's 'ontological status is that of a void, of a pure gap sustained by the endless sliding from one signifier to another', in which we

> get hooked on a particular object which thereby starts to function as the object-cause of [our] desire. How can infinite desire focus on a finite object? [. . .] [t]he object which functions as the 'cause of desire' must be in itself a metonymy of lack – [. . .] an object which is not simply lacking but, in its very positivity, gives body to a lack. (1997: 104–5)

In this economy of lack, the possibility of subjectivisation – the formation of a unified subject – through the traditional denouement is always already compromised. Both Sinclair's theory and *Bildungsromane* '[give] body to a lack', stitching symptoms of fragmentation into a tenuous whole – as in Audrey Craven's appropriation of others' personalities to repudiate her empty subjectivity, or in Sinclair's eroticising of renunciation not as 'an instinct or passion, but an acquired taste' (Sinclair 1904: 114).

Žižek observes that 'if our experience of reality is to maintain its consistency, the positive field of reality has to be "sutured" with a supplement which the subject (mis)perceives' (105). While Sinclair's *Bildungsromane* strive to produce 'consistency' through ontological fantasy, their sutures erupt through symptomatic textual discrepancies. Her beckoning narrative of wholeness cannot be transmuted into the Reality of 'full' subjectivity. Instead, Sinclairian desire 'get[s] hooked on a particular object', obsessively sliding from one truncated object, one metonym to another in a futile endeavour to stave off the lack and pain that are conditions of being and to anchor the subject ontologically. The rift between fantasies of fusion with a transcendent Absolute and the concession that such unity can never be anything but 'brilliant hallucinations of a mental hunger' constitutes one of the vexed tensions in Sinclair's theory and fiction. Faced with the status of 'pure gap', her proto-subject flees into denial, which may be expressed as Žižekian (mis)perception, but also as what Sinclair describes in 'The Way of Sublimation' as the hysterical 'fictions' of Adler's neurotic (c. 1915: 38). Disavowing the divided, mourning subject, she constructs a discourse of supplements centering on 'the unity of all things in the Absolute' (c. 1915: 44a). This is '[b]etter than nothing', says Mary Olivier, though she acknowledges, 'If this went on the breaking point must come. Suddenly you would go smash. Smash. Your mind would die in a delirium of hunger' (Sinclair 1980a: 314). As Suzanne Raitt presciently observes, 'The text's continual slippage into the second person registers the continual disintegration of consciousness' (2000: 221).

Gertrude Stein's *Autobiography of Alice B. Toklas* (1933) and James Joyce's *Finnegans Wake* (1939) are often touted as post-modern precisely because they mock ontological fantasy *qua* fantasy. However, in writers as diverse as Radclyffe Hall, Jean Rhys, Kate Chopin and Ernest Hemingway, while the trauma of the fragmented subject is outed, nostalgia persists for a narrative that can successfully suture subjectivity. Frantic to avoid the 'smash', Sinclair's narratives disavow, displace, repress and repudiate, hurling objects that are always substitutes for that which was never available – mere signifiers of lack – into the ontological void, seeking a *point de capiton* that can never be efficacious. Her work constitutes an excellent exemplar of ontological fantasy as prophylactic.

Libidinal Anxiety, Sublimation, Hysteria

> That world, the lost paradise of the libido, is the psyche's hell. (Sinclair 1916: 121)

Anxiety over libidinality itself structures Sinclair's ontological fantasy, founded in the perception of desire as an obscenity that betrays both excess and lack. Fear of primitive corporeal appetites haunts her writing, for the material body is a reservoir for longing and loss. This is the quintessential ground of Sinclair's work: the need to sanitise and expunge the materiality of desire in order to escape its anguish, rising above it to the mystical utopia of the Absolute. Unless desire is disembodied, libidinal appetite is almost always impossible to endure. To paraphrase Julia Kristeva, Sinclair's 'pain is the other side of [her] philosophy' (1989: 4). For Sinclair, the libido, 'this word so repulsive to the idealist' (122), is 'in conflict with itself and with its own sublimation' (1916: 120). In its Freudian form, libidinality is a site of revulsion and angst: an 'uncanny and unnatural thing' of 'gross flesh and blood', like Pauline in 'The Nature of the Evidence' (Sinclair 2006a: 120, 122). Sinclair recognises that the libido has no loyalty to anything but itself, for 'desire, conscious or unconscious, if it be strong enough, is the most powerful and designing thing in the universe' (2006b: 67). The unharnessed libido is frightening because it is indiscriminate and infinite: 'the one eternal and universal element is the sexual libido. It chooses its own symbols, saturates them with its own emotion and so fixes them' (Sinclair 1916: 118).

Although Jung was not convinced that the libido could be sublimated, Sinclair favours his portrayal of the libido as 'creative energy' (Sinclair 1916: 122 n. 5); notably, Jung broke with Freud over the latter's insistence that the libido is sexual. Sinclair's writing is fraught with anxiety that the libido will choose the primal pleasures of 'the dark underworld we came from' (121) rather than transcendental aims. Hence, the 'sinful, secret libido [must be] dragged out of its hiding-place in the Unconscious into full consciousness and thus made clean' (119). Sinclair posits sublimation as a psycho-philosophical mechanism to overpower and transform primitive bodily aims, saturating the libido not with the sexual muck of primal instincts but with symbols of Hegelian wholeness. She embraces the disembodied Absolute to cure the queasy malady of desire.

Nonetheless, the repressed Other emerges in Sinclair's hysterical fear of regression to 'the psyche's hell'. As she argues in *Feminism*:

> What I venture to dispute is the conclusion that for a woman there is only one kind of alternative between frustration and fulfilment of the Life-Force, and

that is – hysteria, neurosis, and the detestable manifestations of degeneracy. I dispute it without one moment blinking the frightful possibilities of the celibate and solitary life. (Sinclair 1912: 30)

Sinclair's vehement protestations resonate with her own '*bonheur manqué*' (1914: 82), conveying repressed panic at the vicissitudes of libidinality. This anxiety also leaks through in Sinclair's 'devastated' response to Charlotte Brontë's expression of 'emotional and erotic needs' in her letters to Héger (Miller 2001: 120), for she idealises the Brontës as 'virgin priestesses of art' (Rebecca West, in Boll 263 n. 33). Her repudiation of the primitive libido becomes a strained justification for the de-materialisation of desire, with isolation and virginity as 'the law, the indispensable condition' (Sinclair 1910: 117). This valorisation of sublimation as the 'way of genius' (117) constitutes a self-assuaging, legitimising supplement: a compensatory suture that is the discursive trace of libidinality 'succumb[ing] to repression and fixation' (Klein 1975: 77).

Like Adler's hysteric, whose aggressive fictions are 'the heroic efforts of the humiliated ego to assert himself, to redress the balance of his insufficiency' (Sinclair c. 1915: 38), Sinclair's defensive discourse invokes Freud's and Breuer's observation that hysteria 'develop[s] through the repression – motivated by defence – of an intolerable idea'. It requires 'the conversion of excitation' at 'something unpleasant' (2004: 287, 231). Sinclair's disavowal of desire and lack as 'detestable manifestations of degeneracy' certainly qualifies as 'something unpleasant', while her fantasy of wholeness defends against the 'intolerable idea' of the irreparably split subject. She imposes the rigid rhetorical carapace of sublimation to guard against the obscenity of a 'degenerate' desire that can overcome neither its own origins nor the wound of incomplete subjectivisation.

Sinclair herself defines hysterical neuroses as 'a drama of separation' and 'dissociations': the 'splitting off of the libido from the developed life of the psyche' (1916: 122). While acknowledging that Jung and Freud see mysticism as 'a history of neurosis' (1917: 262), she nonetheless uses the language of hysteria to describe the path of the mystic, including 'all perversions of instinct and desire, all suppression, obsessions and possessions' (258–9). Connecting mysticism and sublimation through the commonality of a transfiguring ecstasy, Sinclair's distinction between neurotic fiction and mystical sublimation is murky. The dissociative self-estrangement experienced by idealists such as Gwenda, Mary and the Brontës has much in common with the hysterical repression of Alice Carteret and Harriett Frean. Sinclair's distinction is that in neuroses, the libido regresses, while in mysticism it 'advances a little way', though 'it does betray a shocking tendency to revert' to madness (260, 249). Sublimation ostensibly 'ransoms' and 're-unites' the primal libido with the psyche (Sinclair 1916: 122). It aestheticises sullied desire into metaphysical passion, enabling 'the redemption of the flesh; the redemption of the psyche from the tyranny of the flesh' (120). However, given her horror of libidinal 'degeneracy', it is expedient for Sinclair to elide the boundary between the pathology of the 'ordinary' hysteric and the 'genius' of mystical ecstasy. She maintains that 'most repression [is] sublimation', and that Freud and Jung 'underrate [its] value' (c. 1915: 39b–40). Configuring hysterical (mis)perception as the higher aim of philosophical idealism, she co-opts repression and calls it sublimation.

Nonetheless, Sinclairian sublimation does not resolve the crisis of the split subject; it tries to create a less distressing symptom. In a related inflection, Raitt argues that Sinclair seeks to escape 'a nightmare world in which the pain of rejection and loss persists' (2016: 9). As Kristeva contends, sublimation 'weaves a *hypersign* around and with the depressive void' so that '[b]eauty emerges as the admirable face of loss' (9). Sinclair's ontological project signifies a 'hypothetical state of auto-enclosure' (Lacan 1988: 98). A hysterical fantasy of the real, it is inhabited by a pseudo-subject and governed by defensive (mis)perceptions: a symptomatology of compromise positions and reaction formations including anamorphosis, masochistic *jouissance*, hysterical bliss and what I term the erotics of renunciation. With its sometimes purple prose and lurid language, Sinclair's theory of sublimation is not the apotheosis of transfiguration but a visceral response to an anxiety regarding desire.

Disciplining Desire

> I want – I want – (Sinclair 1980a: 18)

Sinclair's discomfort with the 'tyranny of the flesh' is played out in *Two Sides of a Question* (1901). I am interested in the pathology of overdetermination here. The two stories offer contrasting studies in the channelling of the libido. In 'The Cosmopolitan', Frida Tancred, immolated in her father's petty patriarchal fiefdom, emerges from dull drudge to daring, self-sufficient idealist. She sails the world as a female Odysseus, practising a form of classical stoicism. Frida finds strength and passion in transcending the desires of the body. She learns to disdain corporeal love as inferior to the direction of her libido to a loftier plane: 'moments when the spirit is uplifted and rid for a splendid splinter of time of material consciousness' (Terry 2015). She is, nonetheless, put through

Sinclair's paces of self-sacrifice: asceticism, renunciation of romantic love, spiritual testing and death alone in India. 'The Cosmopolitan' offers an early conjugation of the quintessentially Sinclairian protagonist. Physically robust and self-sustaining, morally pure and committed to intellectual, creative and spiritual goals, they are frequently aligned with the huntress Artemis. Sinclair's protagonists are premised on what Raitt eloquently enunciates as the 'poetics of celibacy' (109), embracing sublimation as the path to emancipation, mystical communion and 'higher and higher' aims (Sinclair 1916: 119). They are idealised instantiations of ontological completeness.

Rather than accepting this narrative of sublimation as a given, my interest is piqued by the pathological disciplining of desire in the second story. 'Superseded' obsessively enacts the repression of the primal libido when it is invested in romantic sentimentality. Unlike Frida, Miss Quincey, a spinster of about forty-five, is not much of a figure at all. She resembles Harriett Frean, another of Sinclair's neurasthenic, withered pseudo-intellectuals. These bird-like creatures flutter through life in a curious mix of obstinacy and vulnerability, the enervated descendants of Dickens' Miss Flite. Miss Quincey's fault is that she mistakes Dr Cautley's professional visits for romantic interest, 'stir[ring] up the sediment of a lifetime's unused love' (Boll 1973: 176). 'Superseded' expresses contempt for those in whom the libido is neither harnessed nor sublimated, but directed to inferior aims. It is a complex, caustic, cautionary tale, with Miss Quincey as the locus of a diatribe on the obscenity of desire. One episode in particular crystallises this libidinal anxiety, revolving around two fetishised metonyms: Miss Quincey's purchase of a blouse and a cake in anticipation of Dr Cautley coming for tea.

Stirred by 'so terrible a solicitation of the senses [. . .] dim and germinal desires had burst and blossomed in this sinful passion for a blouse' (Sinclair 1901: 252–3). The blouse symbolically expands to embrace love, romance, sensual pleasure and plenitude: an economy of abundance. Schooled in an ideology in which 'the sumptuary laws are exceptionally severe', Miss Quincey castigates herself: 'It is a crime, a treachery, to spend money on mere personal adornment'. She buys the blouse, but 'it seemed that a spirit of obstinate malevolence lurked in that deceitful garment' (253–4). The blouse slips from one signifier to another – from a metonym of plenitude to a symbol of inadequacy: it 'repudiated the very idea of Miss Quincey'. She has to 'pinch, pull, humour and propitiate it before it would consent to cling to her diminished figure' (254–5). Given the infinite deferral of desire, the signifier of the blouse – the object on which she attempts to 'hook' her desire – is unstable. This supplement of plenitude slides away into its *unheimlich* opposite. As Miss Quincey repudiates desire, so the blouse repudiates her, pointing up a divided subject riven with lack: her inability to occupy desire is echoed in her inability to fit into the blouse, and 'she hid it away in a drawer out of sight, for the very thought of it frightened her' (255).

Nonetheless, on tea day, Miss Quincey appears: 'all shining and shimmering like a silver and mauve chameleon [. . .] a sight to take anyone's breath away'. She is immediately condemned by her aunt for 'mak[ing] an exhibition' of herself, 'like a whirligig out of a pantomime' (257–8). The excoriation continues until Miss Quincey acquiesces to libidinal anxiety: 'Criminal and crime, Miss Quincey and her blouse, seemed linked in an awful bond of mutual abhorrence' (259). Her primitive libido is 'dragged out of its hiding place' and scoured clean. She dons her old clothes, the uniform of repression; quashing pleasure, she moves from agency to abjection at 'her own ridiculous dimensions' (261). The blouse's power as a talisman of fulfilment and *jouissance* is crushed, and the project of disciplining desire is under way.

So too with the cake, 'crowned with a sugar turret and surrounded with almond fortifications', which 'spoke for itself, though in an unknown language' (257). This is the embattled language of desire, irrupting as the semiotic chora of instinctual drives, but silenced under Mrs Moon's gaze. She continues her laceration: the cake looks like wedding cake; the invitation lacks 'maidenly reserve' and reveals 'flightiness' (263). By the time the doctor arrives, Miss Quincey, metaphorically beaten and stripped, cannot even speak to him; 'she had understood and accepted' (263) the impossibility of desire.

The narrative voice softens momentarily:

> The lump sum of pleasure that other people get spread for them more or less thickly over the surface of the years, she had meant to take once for all, packed and pressed into one rapturous hour [. . .] the memory of it to be stored up and economised so as to last her life-time [. . .] She cut her cake with trembling fingers and offered it, blushing as the gash in its side revealed the thoroughly unwholesome nature of its interior. She felt ashamed of its sugary artifice, its treacherously festive air, and its embarrassing affinity to bride's-cake. (264–5)

Miss Quincey's coveted 'lump sum of pleasure' is inevitably appropriated. Both she and the day are confirmed as 'a waste and a failure' (265), with the blouse and cake marking the 'unwholesomeness' of her maidenly libido. Miss Quincey yearns for 'one rapturous hour' of plenitude to patch over the 'gash' of incompleteness. Denied even an illusory costume of subjectivity, she is left in tatters.[3] Similarly, the cake is transformed from an object of pleasure into a graphic sexual symbol of Miss Quincey's unsavoury interior: both the sexual gap of her spinsterhood and the psychic wound of lack that even treacherous 'artifice' cannot overcome. Blouse and cake are saturated with revulsion and anxiety, while Miss Quincey's body becomes the site for censoring the primal 'I want'. She neither controls nor transforms libidinal excitation, and there is no reward for characters who do not have the right mettle for sublimation. This early story punishes Miss Quincey not only for harbouring instinctual desire, but for the dissipation of libidinal energy in 'degenerate' aims. Inscribed with an almost physical disgust, it rehearses the anxiety underpinning Sinclair's need for an ontology that purifies and abstracts the gross materiality of the undisciplined libido.

In *The Combined Maze* (1913), libidinal panic runs amok. The novel enacts a wildly over-invested repudiation of the carnal libido and a corresponding over-determined reification of moral purity. Violet, Ranny's hyper-sexualised wife, is positioned against Winny, self-sacrificing paragon and idealised angel in the house. Violet is one of Sinclair's strongest degenerates. Mired in moral filth and depravity, she is ruled by the profanity of sexual drives. Protagonist Ranny Ransome, like Rickman in *The Divine Fire* (1904),[4] is also initially guilty of sexual lust, but is exonerated through his morally clean relationship with Winny.

Anxiety and ambivalence to primal libidinality emerge in Ranny's *fort/da* response to Violet's letter telling him that she is leaving for a sexual affair:

> the uncleanness was such that his mind turned from it instinctively as from a thing unspeakable [. . .] There rose before him a sort of welter of gray slime and darkness in which were things visible [. . .] faceless and deformed [. . .] These white things came tumbling and tossing toward him from the gray confines of the slime; urged by a persistent and abominable life, they were borne perpetually on the darkness and were perpetually thrust back into it by his terror. (Sinclair 1922: 237)

Ostensibly, Ranny's mind turns away from the 'white things' in the 'gray slime' of the primal libido in its 'persistent and abominable life'. However, as Luke Thurston aptly notes of the welter or vortex – the depository of libidinal energy – desire can be 'both enjoyed by a protagonist in a virtual fantasmatic moment and immediately denied in the real, disavowed as a disgusting, abject thing that infringes on the ego's limits and disfigures its self-projection as decent and integral' (2014: 33). Motivated by primitive drives, Ranny surreptitiously indulges in 'degenerate' libidinality, projecting squalid images of Violet and her lover on the 'Kantian screen' of his psyche (March-Russell 2006: 19). Simultaneously enjoying and denying this 'lost paradise', his 'unclean' libido threatens to overwhelm him.

Ranny's 'sinful, secret libido' re-surfaces when Violet returns, the metonym of his disavowed desire:

> It was his instinct, not his eyes that knew her [. . .] supple, sinuous, and shivering, she cowered like a beaten bitch.
> Yet she faced him. Shrinking from him, cowering like a bitch [. . .] where the rain beat her, she faced him for a moment [. . .] Her eyes, as she came, gazed strangely at him; eyes that cowered, bitchlike, imploring, agonised, desirous. (Sinclair 1922: 376)

Here again is the anxiety-ridden, haunting encounter with anarchic desire, the contaminant that must be purged for Sinclair's ontological fantasy to succeed. However, sublimation as a means of transversing fantasy is a shaky proposition. Although Ranny contends that 'he had no desire to look at [Violet], he looked. He stared rather'. She 'stirred in him some sense, subtler or grosser than mere sight' (377). He experiences the conflicted appetitive desire that attracted him to Violet in the first place. 'Imploring, agonised, desirous', Violet is the over-determined representation of the Freudian libido, the vertiginous source of libidinal anxiety that Sinclair is driven to metamorphosise through sublimation.

Having ransomed his primal libido for 'higher aims', Ranny ought to have no difficulty ousting Violet. However, his will is paralysed; 'instinct' and 'terror' dictate his response, contradicting the trajectory of sublimation. The mental reins that Sinclair insists harness and transform the libido are loosened, and the living spectre of desire engulfs Ranny, returning to him the unclean aspects of himself. His language changes register radically, reverting to primitive sexual aims as he voices the obscenity of the 'beaten bitch' that is repudiated desire. Fed on repression, libidinality expands from maggot to 'sinuous' serpent – a threatening, feminised force repulsive in its sensual materiality. Violet's ever-shoddy 'mask of womanliness' (Rivière 1929: 38) slips to reveal the ugly, unchaste drives of the id. Violet is abhorrent because she *wants*: the ravenous, devouring Other that is primal desire.

The Erotics of Renunciation, Masochistic *Jouissance*, Hysterical Bliss

> You know I love you – that's why I've been such a brute to you. (Sinclair 1982: 324)

The arc of *The Three Sisters* (1914) comprises a doomed romance plot in which Alice, Mary and Gwenda (the Brontë-esque protagonist) are forced to vie for a sole eligible male, Dr Steven Rowcliffe. Like Frida

Tancred, Gwenda's task is to spin the energy of the libido into the golden fleece of sublimation. The traditional marriage plot is constructed for her, but she is made to renounce Steven in order to show the ostensible rewards of sublimation. The text attempts to institute mystical ecstasy as compensation, but Gwenda is caught in the net of longing and repudiation that typifies anamorphosis, that potent elixir of torment and teasing that endlessly defers union with the love object. Instead of sexual consummation, an erotics of renunciation is instituted and reified, through which carnal desire is eliminated from the body and re-cathected onto an abstract metonym of desire: nature, immanence, the Absolute. Once the libido has been bathed clean through displacement, it can re-enter the body as the transcendental piercing of masochistic *jouissance*.

Thus, when Steven and Gwenda visit Karva after an argument, pleasure and pain are co-mingled. We are cued to the mysticism of the moment by the fact that Gwenda's symbolic tree is flowering – that mix of blood-sharp thorns and ethereal blossoms that Sinclair calls thorn trees:

> The moon was hidden in the haze where the gray day and the white night were mixed [. . .] the thorn trees were in flower. The hot air held them like still water. It quivered invisibly, loosening their scent and scattering it. And of a sudden she saw them as if thrown back to a distance where they stood enchanted in a great stillness and clearness and a piercing beauty.
> There went through her a sudden deep excitement, a subtle and mysterious joy. This passion was as distant and as pure as ecstasy. It swept her, while the white glamour lasted, into the stillness where the flowering thorn trees stood. (Sinclair 1982: 320–1)

The discourse of sexuality is pervasive; consummation is acknowledged in the flowering of the trees and in the post-coital 'stillness' after the 'deep excitement' of Gwenda's passion. Gwenda longs for Steven, but under the rubric of sublimation, their communion must be without touch: a meeting of minds and spirits, not hearts and bodies. The thorn trees become the cathected object through which their souls can come together in disembodied consummation, for they 'have to get rid of [their] bodies first' (Sinclair 2006: 123). Libidinal pleasure is not foreclosed, but sexual arousal is to be diverted via Gwenda's idealist stance into transcendental penetration. Sexual desire is transferred from her body to nature in mystical, not physical intercourse: a transsubstantiation into so-called higher aims.

This displacement simultaneously removes Gwenda's embodied desire and allows her to identify with it 'as if' it is purified passion: ecstasy made safe through distance. Psychoanalyst Christopher Bollas calls such pathological avoidance of the sexual 'hysterical bliss': 'the exchange of carnal sexuality – specifically, the genital drive – for spiritual sexuality. Where once the body and its drives prevailed upon the self to accept the animal within, the hysteric vigorously refuses this logic' (2000: 25). Re-framing Raitt's poetics of celibacy, I read this recurring trope less as a conscious, disinterested choice essential to creative genius than as the unconscious dictates of libidinal panic and a foundational discomfort with corporeal desire. The result is a need to rationalise the shift of desire away from the body. However, in the erotics of renunciation, rather than the de-sexualisation of libidinal aims that sublimation and celibacy promise, instinctual pleasures and primitive aims remain in place.

This displacement of carnal love requires that Gwenda take her pleasure in pain; in Steven's logic, he has 'been a brute' to Gwenda *because* he loves her. In the erotics of renunciation, pleasure is attached to suffering and self-denial, just as the pricking thorns of the hawthorn are inseparable from the lush sensual pleasure of its blossoms. *Jouissance* – albeit masochistic – comes disguised in the 'white glamour'. The desiring body, pierced by a metonymic object in a symbolic ritual, ostensibly remains morally intact and clean of sullied carnality. Yet as James Thrall notes, when 'Sinclair mixed the sexual with the mystical, the frankness of her writing could be shocking' (2005: 3). Rather than transformation to 'a divine and spiritual [object]' (Sinclair 1917a: 257), desire retains all the lubriciousness of sexual intercourse and orgasm. Denied on a conscious level, sexuality is subversively enjoyed through its inscription as transcendental ecstasy, despite the fact that sublimation supposedly de-sexualises libidinal aims. Or, as Bollas phrases it, 'Between the violence of the nun and the violence of the prostitute, the hysteric lives' (144) – an apt characterisation of the perverse voluptuousness that characterises both Sinclairian renunciation and sublimation. When Gwenda returns to Karva, she tries to 'recapture the magic [. . .] But it had gone and she could not be persuaded that it would come again' (Sinclair 1982: 370). The cost of Sinclairian sublimation is clear. In Gwenda's 'dreadful duologue', the psychic split that typifies both mystical belief and hysterical dissociation is played out: 'Is it going to be taken from me like everything else?' Perhaps the bliss 'never *had* anything but what you gave it [. . .] Am I to go on giving [. . .] Am I never to have anything for myself?' (370). Whatever masochistic *jouissance* Gwenda experienced deserts her, and the erotics of renunciation have lost their appeal: 'You should have taken. You had your chance [. . .] Do you call this living?' (370). The hypersign of sublimation fails as inoculation against desire. Greatorex commiserates at the transience of ecstasy, but reminds Gwenda that only through pain might she experience bliss again: 'Ef yo soofer enoof mebbe it'll coom t'yo again. Ef yo're snoog and 'appy sure's death it'll goa' (369). Having foreclosed normative paths of pleasure,

Gwenda succumbs to self-interment, an abject servant to the punitive code of the novel. Ontological completion is exploded as the idealised 'hypothesis of pre-established harmony' (Lacan 1988: 98). More anti-*Bildungsroman* than exemplification of Hegel's transfiguring 'result', the denouement places Gwenda closer to his master/slave dialectic than to 'Truth and the Whole'.

The Three Sisters ends with a return to 'the silence, the darkness and the secrecy of all ultimate habitations' (Sinclair 1982: 1), but this is repetition with critical difference. Alice and Mary are gone, into their own lives, and Gwenda and her father form an arid third couple in whom corporeal desire is repressed while libidinality is perversely enjoyed through the posture of purity. Gwenda's hollow existence resonates in the foreboding sense of waiting for transcendence that never comes. The sublime beauty of the thorn trees is supplanted by her knowledge that they possess 'a power that before long would make her suffer' (387). This is a bleak vision for a novel that seeks to celebrate the ecstatic matriculation of the subject through sublimation and philosophical idealism. It is at odds with the Sinclairian fantasy of transcendence, instead invoking the impossibility of fulfilment that haunts her novels. At best, the narrative 'result' is not epiphanic, ecstatic 'Unitive Life' (Sinclair 1917: 273), but an ambivalent experience in which Gwenda's agency and subjectivity are questionable. Significantly, the fertile life born of Essy's primal libidinality closes the novel, functioning both as a voice for Gwenda and as a rebuke to her barren solitude:

> As if she had seen what had happened to [Gwenda] she hurried the child in out of her sight [. . .] And, loud through the quiet house, [Gwenda] heard the sound of crying and Essy's voice scolding her little son, avenging on him the cruelty of life. (Sinclair 1982: 387–8)

The inescapable pain of life is displaced onto Essy's son, who cries out the unutterable, unsublimated anguish of Gwenda's ontological emptiness. The final image of nature reinforces Gwenda's ambivalent future: 'under the risen moon, the white thorn-trees flowered in their glory' (388). Perhaps this can be read as a symbol of ineffable transcendence, but the trees also invoke the earlier images of masochism and meaningless renunciation. The only flowering is a fruit(less life) of painful thorns, where capricious blooms occasionally flower in a world bereft of sound and colour. Gwenda's and Steven's disparate discourses on the moon prove to be insurmountable for the lovers, constituting gaps in both their ontological fantasies. The sensual materiality of nature is bathed in brilliance, but it is offset by a cool remoteness, blanched and unnatural, ominous and surreal.

Ritual, Simulacrum, Performance, Disappearance

Why did I smash it all up? [. . .] I've killed myself. (Sinclair 1980a: 349)

Sinclair describes will, symbol and ritual as the 'golden bridge' to wholeness; language is the 'Orphic song' (Sinclair 1916: 121–2) that escorts the libido from the pleasures of primal regression to the airy cerebration of sublimation, imbuing assertions of ecstasy with transcendental life. In *Mary Olivier*, three such rituals are performed. Firstly, having renounced Richard, Mary attempts the mystical through symbolic speech acts: the seductive song of language. The text proffers ecstasy – or escape – through rhetoric. Her hypnotic 'If I could get out of it all' becomes the hinge by which denial of ontological emptiness is enacted, swinging away from entrapment in quotidian life to the opening of a transcendental door:

> Her crying stopped with a start as if someone had come in and put a hand on her shoulder [. . .] She had a sense of happiness and peace suddenly [. . .] Not so much her own as [. . .] of an immense, invisible, intangible being [. . .] She knew somehow, through It, that there was no need to get away; she was out of it all now, this minute. There was always a point where she could get out of it and into this enduring happiness and peace. (Sinclair 1980a: 375)

Mary is provided not with a rational solution, but with a mysticised rhetorical flourish as the answer to despair. The simile is significant: it is 'as if' someone is with her; the 'happiness and peace' are not hers, but those of an 'intangible being'. A simulacrum of transcendence is rhetorically sutured into the fabric of language. This is subjectivisation by simile. Instead of sublimation, we find the transfer of libidinal energy to a metonymic substitute, with Mary re-writing her life's narrative *as if* it has had meaning.

In the second ritual, Mary, like Gwenda, seeks to exchange carnal sexuality for Bollas's 'spiritual sexuality', and thereby to retain the moral purity of sublimation. She symbolically disembodies desire, but it is displaced and re-invested in doubt. Rather than Gwenda's passive despair over uncertainty, however, Mary actively panders to it, voluptuously enjoying libidinality:

> Last night I began thinking about it again, I stripped my soul; I opened all the windows and let my ice-cold thoughts in on the poor thing; it stood shivering between certainty and uncertainty.
>
> I tried to doubt away this ultimate passion, and it turned my doubt into its own exquisite sting, the very thrill of the adventure.

Supposing there's nothing in it, nothing at all?
That's the risk you take. (Sinclair 1980a: 379)

Mary's language is sexually charged and masochistically driven. She 'strip[s]' her soul, personifying it as her naked body 'shivering between uncertainty and certainty'. Ostensibly escaping the body, Mary plunges into the vortex of libidinality, transforming herself 'into an event', 'a form of erotic theatre' (Bollas: 125). A striking elision occurs between soul and body; at the very least, this is a highly embodied and eroticised soul. Using uncharacteristically vital language, Mary revels in lack. She indulges in intra-subjective anamorphosis for masochistic pleasure. In the 'exquisite sting' of doubt lies not only the 'very thrill of the adventure', but also the frisson of erotic delight, derived by deploying philosophical uncertainty as a tantalising scourge for self-flagellation. Mary harnesses the libidinal energy of her own ambivalence, savouring it as a field of transgressive ecstasy in which everything is suspended except for *jouissance*. Her active participation in this erotic 'adventure' of uncertainty constitutes perhaps her only moment of subjectivity, albeit in 'delirium of hunger' in which 'the mind dies'. A split subject speaking about herself as Other, she hovers fleetingly as both abject subject and fetishised object.

Mary is certainly desirous, but is her pleasure demonstrative of re-direction of the libido, or an expression of raw libidinal energy couched in spiritualised terms, *sans* 'higher aims?' Or is this perhaps hysterical bliss? Mary is applauded for sublimation, but the text simultaneously reverses the ideology of disembodied desire, subverting the 'pure' erotics of renunciation into perverse pleasure and masturbatory fantasy. Her language invokes both Christian martyrdom and the orgasmic plenitude of the carnal body; mystical and material pleasures become interchangeable. However, except in this brief flicker of subversive subjectivity, it is unclear whether ecstasy exists as more than a phantasmatic gaze back towards a simulacrum (a fantasy of a fantasy of plenitude) or a pathological self-encoffining to 'get out of it all'.

In the final ritual, Mary embraces symbolic death as a conduit to the metaphysical unity of the Absolute, using incantory language as the bridge: 'blotting out your body and the world, blotting out everything but your self and your will, that was a dying to live; a real dying, a real life' (Sinclair 1980a: 377). In her arduous quest for subjectivity, Mary rejects her body and its desires, not as 'a body untenanted by meaning' (Kristeva 1989: 101), but as polluted terrain to be 'blotted out' so that she can be filled and made whole by the master signifier of the sublime Other. She either fades into or blooms through darkness. Sinclair positions these moments as ontological arrival and metaphysical ecstasy. I read them as asphyxiating blackouts of hysterical self-entombment. Sinclair contends that the mystical idealist's 'inward look' (257) provides 'a peculiar certainty' (267) of Reality, despite its location in the 'country of abnormal consciousness' (1917: 259). I acknowledge Sinclair's longing for ontological synthesis, but I mistrust her disembodied abstraction of desire, which I read as the unconscious pathology of her 'fiction' of subjectivisation.

Mary's symbolic rituals become incantations for the dissolution of being; her wilful 'dying to live' postulates subjectivity as dissociation, a splitting off rather than a reconciliation of body and mind. Her escape from libidinal anxiety epitomises aphanisis – the eclipse, 'fading,' and 'petrifying' of the subject, whereby 'the subject manifests himself in this movement of disappearance that I have described as lethal', both in Ernest Jones's context as the disappearance of sexual desire due to separation trauma and neuroses, and as the 'constitution of the subject' solely 'in the field of the Other' (Lacan 1981: 208). Similarly, I read Mary's pronouncement that she has 'suicided' under Kristeva's black sun of trauma: 'In order to protect mother, I kill myself' (28). Renouncing embodiment, Mary embraces the lethal 'delights of reunion that a regressive daydream promises itself through the nuptials of suicide' (14).

Fictionalising aphanisis as sublimation and (mis)perceiving it as transcendence, Sinclair's sublimative hypersign inscribes ontological erasure as metaphysical beauty. Her narratives redound with protagonists who suffocate their emerging subjectivity, and whose contradictory language is emblematic of the anguish of lack, libidinal panic and hysterical denial of death-in-life. At best, they might be recuperated as Sinclair's 'third alternative' for the mystic sublimator: a 'divided and disintegrated personality' (Sinclair 1917: 259). Like her mystic, Sinclair and her protagonists venture into the hysteric's 'dissociative space into which is inserted an imaginary figure of desire' (Bollas: 55).

Both fiction and theory inadvertently betray the inefficacy of Sinclairian sublimation as a solution for the modernist subject. Sinclair's cure for desire brings about neither authentic subjectivisation nor ontological wholeness. Her protagonists can only ventriloquise plenitude, while her texts iterate the embodiment of lack. As in gender performance, if sublimation is 'instituted through acts which are internally discontinuous, then the *appearance of substance* is precisely that, a constructed identity of performative accomplishment' (Butler 1988: 520). Sinclair's protagonists encounter a narrative demand to perform compensatory rituals that give the appearance of attainment of the Absolute, while knowledge of the performance *qua* performance remains repressed so as not to interrupt the suspension of disbelief. However, their status as subjects cannot be secured by performances of plenitude, nor can the *Bildungsroman* or its denouement function as a *point de capiton*. If there are moments of efficacy, hesitations in the endless slide of signifiers, these are unpredictable and uncertain, for 'the hysteric resists closure, producing ever new conversions and ever-changing narratives' (Bronfen 1999: 54). Ontological wholeness remains the 'spectacle of private sublimations' (Gilman 1918: 288), where Sinclair's protagonists 'substitute theatrical display' for actual wholeness and 'lack authentic being' (Strychacz 2008: 30).

As Claire Drewery observes, this space of sublimation and ecstasy is liminal – a 'threshold state' that both 'reveals[s] profound conflicts of identity' (12) and is 'a challenge to the limits of subjectivity' (2011: 2). A Žižekian void that can be filled temporarily, it is also a neo-Platonic echo chamber of the unreachable real. Thus, Thurston pursues in Sinclair 'a point of vitality *in excess* of a discursive structure' (6), 'a radical ontological otherness [. . .] extimate to the field of signifying representation' (2012: 109). Adela Pinch positions Sinclair as 'an idealist philosopher who articulated a compelling version of "love thinking": a particular kind of cognition that produces not knowledge, but ethical, mystical bonds' (2010: 46). And Raitt explores moments of uncanny empathic bridging, as in 'The Intercessor', where '[t]he child who has been ruthlessly rejected and suppressed is finally brought out of the unconscious into the world of conscious remembrance' (2016: 33), a poignant analogy of Sinclair's repressed desire to mend her own shriven subjectivity through the incarnation of her dream of wholeness.

Perhaps Sinclair's 'way of sublimation' constitutes a provisional subject. If so, the agency of her sublimators is largely abject or false. Allison Pease observes that Sinclair's solution to the problem of subjectivisation is 'the emptying out of one's self' (57), the 'self-evacuation from desire and power' (2012: 62) – a receptacle awaiting completion at the whim of the Absolute. Even Sinclair's preferred protagonists become ossified, unable to emerge as authentic subjects who are active agents of their own lives. As Jean Radford (1980) writes, the ending of *Mary Olivier* might be described 'not as a triumph of sublimation but as a defeat of desire', while Thrall notes the 'difficulty in reading Mary's final mystic achievement' (2005: 8). Rewriting Mary's introjected desire, *Harriett Frean* mocks sublimation as a narcissistic delusion of 'behav[ing] beautifully' (Sinclair 1980b: 21) that breeds cancer and hysterical paralysis. And Theophilus Boll writes of Sinclair 'renouncing renunciation, deriding sublimation' in *The Allinghams* (296). Sinclair's ontological fantasy of wholeness, paradoxically, can be read as Jean Baudrillard reads Lacan, espousing 'a philosophy of disappearance. The obliteration of the human, of ideology, the absent structure, the death of the subject' (1990: 160–1).

Despite disavowal of the pain and mourning that attend it, the defining enunciation of the Sinclairian subject remains 'I want'. Yet a dialectical tension exists between the desire for and the negation of subjectivity. In her relentless rehearsal of the crisis of subjectivisation, Sinclair's lust for the metaphysical unity of 'Truth and the Whole' competes with her desire for the bliss of disembodiment and the dissolution of desire altogether. Sinclair might then be read as Bronfen's hysteric, 'performing, as she does, the interface between narrative representation and its limitations, precisely because her stories revolve around the impact of traumatic woundings to the psychic apparatus' (54). Sinclair ultimately strains beyond the Hegelian ending of the *Bildungsroman* towards a spectral, seamless fourth dimension that escapes epistemology, alternately trusting and doubting rhetorical incantation to launch her into the liminal. If there is a restorative dimension, it is extremely precarious, requiring not only the violent and persistent invocation of symbolic ritual to materialise it, but also the passivity of endless waiting for it to be bestowed. Nor does it seem to provide solace or compensation for the burdens of desire and divided subjectivity. What remains is an externalised, idealised chimera that floats as an ephemeral possibility across the anxious psychic landscapes of Sinclair's texts.

Notes

1. As if 'buy[ing]' her theories at 'some remote ontological bazaar' (Sinclair 1917: vi), Sinclair also mines discourses of aesthetics, the supernatural, religious ecstasy, heredity, even physics, in her quest for phenomenological alterity. Her published and unpublished theoretical texts restate her ideas, sometimes using the same vocabulary. See Battersby (2002) for a careful assessment of Sinclair's philosophical arguments.
2. While outside the scope of this paper, the engendering of the maternal 'Thing' haunts Sinclair's work and also inflects my argument.
3. See also Jean Rhys's fine story, 'Illusion' (1927), regarding sartorial expressions of desire.
4. Rickman wrestles his carnal libido, learning to 'stamp down' its 'dull red fire' (Sinclair 1904: 167) and displace it via the erotics of renunciation and profoundly masochistic suffering. He ultimately wins Lucia – a rare Sinclairian consummation of sexual and sublimative aims.

Works Cited

Battersby, Christine (2002), '"In the Shadow of His Language": May Sinclair's Portrait of the Artist as Daughter', *New Comparison: A Journal of Comparative and General Literary Studies* 33:4, 102–20.
Baudrillard, Jean (1990), *Cool Memories*, trans. Chris Turner, London: Verso.
Boll, Theophilus (1973), *Miss May Sinclair: Novelist: A Biographical and Critical Introduction*, Cranbury, NJ: Associated University Presses.
Bollas, Christopher (2000), *Hysteria*, New York: Routledge.
Bronfen, Elizabeth (1999), *The Knotted Subject: Hysteria and its Discontents*, Princeton: Princeton University Press.
Butler, Judith (1988), 'Performative Acts and Gender Constitution: An Essay in Phenomenology and Feminist Theory', *Theatre Journal* 40:4, 519–31.
Drewery, Claire (2011), *Modernist Short Fiction by Women: The Liminal in Katherine Mansfield, Dorothy Richardson, May Sinclair and Virginia Woolf*, Burlington, VT and Farnham: Ashgate.
Fink, Bruce (1995), *The Lacanian Subject: Between Language and Jouissance*, Princeton: Princeton University Press.
Freud, Sigmund, and Josef Breuer [1895] (2004), *Studies in Hysteria*, trans. Nicola Luckhurst, London: Penguin.
Gilman, Lawrence (1918), 'The Book of the Month: May Sinclair's New War Novel', *The North American Review* 207.747, 284–8.
Hegel, Georg Wilhelm Friedrich [1807] (1979), *The Phenomenology of Spirit*, trans. A. V. Miller, Oxford: Oxford University Press.
Jung, Carl [1912] (1916), *Psychology of the Unconscious*, trans. Beatrice Hinkle, London: Kegan Paul, Trench, Trubner.
Klein, Melanie (1975), *Love, Guilt, and Reparation, and Other Works, 1921–1945*, New York: Dell.
Kristeva, Julia (1989), *Black Sun: Depression and Melancholia*, trans. Leon S. Roudiez, New York: Columbia University Press.
Lacan, Jacques [1973] (1981), *The Seminar of Jacques Lacan, Book XI*, ed. Jacques-Alain Miller, trans. Alan Sheridan, New York: Norton.
Lacan, Jacques [1978] (1988), *The Seminar of Jacques Lacan, Book II*, ed. Jacques-Alain Miller, trans. Sylvana Tomaselli, Cambridge: Cambridge University Press.
Lacan, Jacques [1981] (1997), *The Seminar of Jacques Lacan, Book III*, ed. Jacques-Alain Miller, trans. Russell Grigg, London: Norton.
March-Russell, Paul (2006), 'Introduction', in May Sinclair, *Uncanny Stories*, London: Wordsworth Editions, pp. 7–21.
Miller, Lucasta (2001), *The Brontë Myth*, London: Jonathan Cape.
Moretti, Franco (1987), *The Way of the World: The Bildungsroman in European Culture*, London: Verso.
Pease, Allison (2012), *Modernism, Feminism, and the Culture of Boredom*, Cambridge: Cambridge University Press, http://ebooks.cambridge.org (last accessed 22 June 2016).
Pinch, Adela (2010), *Thinking About Other People in Nineteenth-Century British Writing*, Cambridge: Cambridge University Press.

Radford, Jean (1980), 'Introduction', in May Sinclair, *Mary Olivier: A Life*, London: Virago.
Raitt, Suzanne (2000), *May Sinclair: A Modern Victorian*, Oxford: Oxford University Press.
Raitt, Suzanne (2016), '"Dying to live": remembering and forgetting May Sinclair', in Rebecca Bowler and Claire Drewery (eds), *May Sinclair: Re-Thinking Minds and Bodies*, Edinburgh: Edinburgh University Press, pp. 21–38.
Rivière, Joan [1929] (1986), 'Womanliness as a masquerade', in Victor Burgin, James Donald and Kora Kaplan (eds), *Formations of Fantasy*, New York: Routledge, pp. 35–44.
Rhys, Jean (1927), *The Left Bank and Other Stories*, London: Jonathan Cape.
Sinclair, May (1901), *Two Sides of a Question*, New York: J. F. Taylor.
Sinclair, May (1904), *The Divine Fire*, New York: Henry Holt.
Sinclair, May (1910), *The Creators*. New York: The Century Co.
Sinclair, May (1912), *Feminism*, London: Women Writers' Suffrage League.
Sinclair, May [1912] (1914), *The Three Brontës*, New York: Houghton Mifflin.
Sinclair, May [1913] (1922), *The Combined Maze*, New York: Macmillan.
Sinclair, May [1914] (1982), *The Three Sisters*, intro. Jean Radford, London: Virago.
Sinclair, May (c. 1915), 'The Way of Sublimation', May Sinclair Collection, Rare Book and Manuscript Library, University of Pennsylvania, Box 23, Folders 436–8.
Sinclair, May (1916), 'Clinical Lecture on Symbolism and Sublimation – I', *The Medical Press and Circular* 153, 118–22.
Sinclair, May (1917), *A Defence of Idealism: Some Questions and Conclusions*, London: Macmillan.
Sinclair, May [1917] (2006a), Letter to the *Journal of the Society for Psychical Research*, 26 April 1917, in George M. Johnson, *Dynamic Psychology in Modernist British Fiction*, London: Palgrave Macmillan, p. 67.
Sinclair, May [1919] (1980a), *Mary Olivier: A Life*, London: Virago.
Sinclair, May [1922] (1980b), *Life and Death of Harriett Frean*, London: Virago.
Sinclair, May [1923] (2006b), *Uncanny Stories*, London: Wordsworth Editions.
Sinclair, May (n.d.), 'The Higher Pragmatism', May Sinclair Collection, Rare Book and Manuscript Library, University of Pennsylvania, Box 22, Folder 414.
Strychacz, Thomas (2008), *Dangerous Masculinities: Conrad, Hemingway, and Lawrence*, Gainesville: University Press of Florida.
Terry, Alice (2015), personal email correspondence to Faye Pickrem, 2 June 2015.
Thrall, James Homer (2005), 'May Sinclair: Mystic Modern', Available at: www.aarmysticism.org/documents/Thrall.pdf (last accessed 22 June 2016).
Thurston, Luke (2012), *Literary Ghosts from the Victorians to Modernism: The Haunting Interval*, New York: Routledge.
Thurston, Luke (2014), 'Clouds and Power: May Sinclair's War', *Journal of Modern Literature* 37:3, 18–35.
Žižek, Slavoj (1997), *The Plague of Fantasies*, London: Verso.

Chapter 7

May Sinclair and Physical Culture: Fit Greeks and Flabby Victorians
Rebecca Bowler

Mary Olivier, the work which most critics claim marks the transition between the fin-de-siècle novels of the young May Sinclair and her later modernist efforts, is a novel about activity overcoming lethargy. Mary Olivier is in thrall to her mother, who wishes her to stay at home, to sew and to become a ladylike and passive young lady. Mary, however, is an intellectual. She is in love with the process of learning as adventure, and she is also in love with the athletic and dynamic power of her own body, a body which 'could excite itself with its own activity and strength' (Sinclair 1919: 226). Mary's dilemma is that the passive domesticity that her mother wants for her, and the life of intellectual adventure that she wants for herself, are both antithetical to an active life. As her brother Mark warns her, '"if you stodge like that you'll get all flabby"' (Sinclair 1919: 84). In Mary's quest to become a modern woman and to shake off her mother, her very own 'Angel of the House', she must find and embrace both athleticism and intellectualism; she must figuratively and literally escape the boundaries of the home and stretch her legs in the public world. This emphasis on freedom and activity is a part of what makes *Mary Olivier* so modern.

However, Sinclair had explored these themes in a much earlier work. *The Combined Maze*, published in 1913, is an allegory about two possible futures for the human race. One possible future is to continue along Victorian lines, with working men and women either 'weedy, parched, furtively inebriate' like the hero Ranny's father, or with the 'flabbiness' of his father's chemist assistant, Mercier (Sinclair 1913: 1; 24). The alternative is for young people to throw off their Victorian shackles, to stride forth into the world, to run and jump, and to establish their lives upon the principles of moral and physical fitness.

The hero of *The Combined Maze*, 'John Randall Fulleymore Ransome, and Ranny for short' (Sinclair 1913: 1), is not just an athlete, but a clerk, whose work is abhorrent to him; he works so that he can live, and so that, in the evenings, he can go to the Polytechnic Gym and absorb himself in the 'fusion of all faculties in one rhythm and one vibration, one continuous transport of physical energy' (Sinclair 1913: 23). He sees the world as divided into the fit (physically and morally) and the flabby or weedy (also physically and morally), and lives in fear of detecting in himself a deterioration in his physical fitness: 'The thing that young Ransome most loathed and abhorred was Flabbiness, next to Flabbiness, Weediness. The years of his adolescence were one long struggle and battle against these two' (Sinclair 1913: 2). In *The Combined Maze*, and elsewhere in Sinclair's oeuvre, she presents physical activity, strength training and joy in movement as the solution to moral, psychological and physical flabbiness. As she says of Ranny, if you asked him why he was so active, 'he would say you did it because it kept you fit, also (if you pressed him) because it kept you decent. And to know how right he was you had only to look at him, escaped from his cage' (Sinclair 1913: 4). He is continually disgusted by the 'flabbiness' of Mercier, or 'old Eno', and he implies that this flabbiness and his frequenting of music halls, his sensuousness and immorality, go together. If 'old Eno' would join the Poly. Gym., he tells him, he 'would be a lot decenter' (Sinclair 1913: 23). He tries to appeal to Mercier's appreciation of women to tempt him to join the gym, but he does not quite understand what he is saying because he does not yet understand the appeal of the opposite sex:

> He [Mercier] liked young ladies. Among them (he intimated) his flabbiness might not excite remark. Girls (he pondered it) were flabby things.
> Chivalry constrained him to a mental reservation: Winny Dymond and the young ladies of the Poly. Gym. excepted. (Sinclair 1913: 24)

Ranny's downfall in *The Combined Maze* is that he does not marry Winny, who is fit, intelligent, active and sensible. Instead he becomes infatuated with Violet, a feminine, curvaceous and flirtatious (and therefore shallow, lazy and morally corrupt) woman. His lack of understanding about the mysteries of sex, feminine performance and sensuality means that when Violet begins her flirtation with him he is unable to see through the masquerade: there was 'something about her'; 'something helpless that implored and entreated and appealed to his young manhood for protection' (Sinclair 1913: 72). In contrast to Winny's independence, and her 'fugitive' spirit (Sinclair 1913: 18), Violet communicates a vulnerability and a dependence which is flattering to the young man.

Ranny's fatal choice destroys his life because it represents a backward turn. Ranny chooses a feminine, old-fashioned woman over an independent and active woman. He chooses the nineteenth century over the twentieth; and he chooses physical weakness and inactivity over strength and movement. In this choice, this chapter will argue, he also privileges the aesthetic over the ascetic; Victorian decadence and waste over a kind of modern efficiency with echoes of the Classic past: the balance and harmony of an idealised Greek lifestyle, with athleticism and intellectual endeavour bolstering each other.

Modernity and Physical Culture in *The Combined Maze*

At the end of the nineteenth century and the beginning of the twentieth century there was a widespread anxiety about the effects of modernity: not only the fast pace of life as lived, or the modernist crisis of vision (in which to see was no longer, in the Cartesian sense, to know), but anxiety about the 'artificial, morally corrupting living conditions of the modern city' (Zweiniger-Bargielowska 2011: 25). One of the side effects of living and working in this modern, early-twentieth-century city was the sedentary lifestyle: men caught the omnibus to work at the Bank, or the office, and then sat down at work all day; women felt unsafe on the streets and so took carriages or hansoms everywhere (when they didn't just stay at home and have the tradesmen, and visitors, come to them). In *The Combined Maze* both sexes work for long hours in cramped offices. The response to this anxiety about the dangers of the sedentary lifestyle was a sudden and intense interest in physical culture, exercise and fitness. As Ina Zweiniger-Bargielowska points out, the turn of the century witnessed a mass appearance of centres for physical fitness: 'The National Physical Recreation Society listed 115 gymnasia in the 1890s. Of these some were privately owned, 33 were military, and others were run by charitable organisations including 23 clubs operated by the YMCA' (41). By the early twentieth century there were many more. Similarly, at the turn of the century, affordable magazines devoted to physical culture appeared on the market. *Health and Strength* was launched in 1898, and *Vim* in 1902. Both were aimed at 'a lower-middle- and working-class readership', and both railed against the corrupting influence of modern city life, with its polluted air and lack of opportunities for exercise. In *Health and Strength*, for example, regular articles appeared that promoted an idea of 'the "simple life"'. The '"dust-laden and smoke-begrimed air" of the city, confinement within the "four walls of an office or shop", and the customary "abominable clothes (particularly collars!)"' were set against healthful activities in nature: outdoor swimming, sun bathing and fresh air (41).

The magazines *Health and Strength* and *Vim* reflected the burgeoning 'life reform' movements, in which modernity was characterised by an attention to 'hygiene': free-flowing garments (in the dress reform movement), vegetarian diets and new relations between the sexes. Valentine Wannop, in Ford Madox Ford's *Parade's End*, is a devotee of physical exercise. Her father, a 'classical don at Cambridge', has brought her up to be an 'athlete' ('because father, being a brilliant man, had ideas' [Ford 2012: 82]). During the First World War, Valentine works as a gym teacher in a girls' school. She is equipped for the job because her father was such an advocate of physical education as a mentally and morally strengthening practice that he based her entire education around running and learning Latin. In Valentine's mind, this late-nineteenth-century enthusiasm for producing intelligent and moral citizens by making them do 'physical jerks' is a troubling one: 'the brilliant Victorians talked all the time through their hats. They evolved a theory from anywhere and then went brilliantly mad over it' (534). She worries too that the war has 'exaggerated' the importance of physical education as mental and spiritual panacea to ridiculous degrees: 'for the last four years she had been regarded as supplementing if not as actually replacing both the doctor and the priest' in her teaching of children how to exercise (535). At the turn of the century, Pehr Henrik Ling's system of Swedish Drill exercises became popular in Britain in schools and amongst the upper classes. Women also began to exercise at home, as Sylvia Tietjens does when she is trying to atone for her extramarital affairs in *Parade's End*:

> Her personal chastity she now cherished much as she cherished her personal cleanliness and persevered in her Swedish exercises after her baths before an open window. [. . .] Indeed, the two sides of life were, in her mind, intimately connected: she kept herself attractive by her skillfully selected exercises and cleanlinesses; and the same fatigues, healthful as they were, kept her in the mood for chastity of life. (149–50)

The Combined Maze is about this rise of physical culture (the year is 1902 when it opens) and the anxieties that caused it. It is also about physical exercise and body-building as a type of sublimation. Every issue of *Health and Strength* featured a column about sex. The narrative of these columns is that sex is healthy, but that lust is unhealthy. The libido is a part of the natural life force that sustains and energises the body, and stifling it and denying it its outlet (or its existence) is just as harmful to physical and psychic health as abstaining from exercise. The magazine promoted sex education for children: 'The subject of sex is taboo in our public schools. It is buried in darkness, and we know what noxious creatures breed in the dark' (8 Aug 1931: 175). It also advocated honour and decency in sexual relations, and it did so in terms that recall psychoanalysis's 'sublimation'. In an article entitled 'Is Man Really Polygamous?' the author writes that a monogamous relationship between a man and a woman is 'natural and ideal', but that promiscuity – for a man to sleep with a woman purely to 'slake' his 'appetite' – is 'to dishonour, degrade and desecrate her': 'all civilisation is built upon a mass of restraints which man has gradually imposed upon himself in his search after a better, less brutish and more human kind of life' (21 Nov 1931: 606). *Health and Strength* is not just about 'physical culture' in the sense of weight-lifting and muscle-building, then; it championed higher ideals, encouraging its readers to become the best specimens of humankind that they could possibly be, physically, spiritually, and morally.

In her essay 'Symbolism and Sublimation', printed in the *Medical Press* in 1916, Sinclair describes sublimation as 'the striving of the libido towards manifestation in higher and higher forms' (119). Any surplus libido, instead of being repressed (and thus left to 'breed in the dark'), should be channelled into active and creative endeavour. Creative endeavour includes art, science and literature; active endeavour includes most other forms of productivity. Historically, Sinclair says, the sublimation of generations past has given us the 'superstructure' of our current civilisation:

> Civilisation is one vast system of sublimations. The houses we live in, the pavement we walk on, the steamships, trains and motor cars we travel by, chairs and tables, machinery and the products of machinery are so many examples of sublimation carried out in the concrete. (119)

In 'primitive man', Sinclair says, much of the libido must have been channelled into 'the energies of battle and hunting and later of agriculture' (120). She presents a model of sublimation in which the libido, in creative and intellectual people, manifests itself as cultural production, and in less intelligent people manifests as 'concrete' production or as physical activity. In both of these types, sublimation is linked to morality. The physical results of the cultural, concrete or active production that sublimation enables are connected always with 'the passion for beauty or for truth or for goodness; all the emotions which, for want of a better word, we call moral' (120). In her presentation of Ranny, Sinclair demonstrates how sublimation can work in an unintellectual lower-middle-class man. Ranny is dedicated to the production of his own body as efficient and strong, and in this production he cultivates also his finer feelings: his 'passion' for decency, truth and honesty.

Ranny is precisely the kind of man who would read *Health and*

Strength. He is lower-middle-class, a member of the 'London Polytechnic Gymnasium', not very intellectual, working in a dull job for small wages, but committed to being the best he can be: physically, by building his muscles; and morally, by building his muscles. Sinclair writes: 'In all cities there are many thousand Ransomes, more or less confined in mahogany cages, but John Randall Fulleymore stands for all of them' (Sinclair 1913: 3). She consciously presents Ranny as just one of many examples of the modern phenomenon of a physical culturist, who was a figure much discussed. He is a familar fin-de-siècle modern 'type': a symbol of youth striving to overcome its restrictions and establish new ways of living, working and loving. He is also emblematic of the young lower-middle-class man with low wages and no prospect of career advancement, spending long and boring days totting up accounts in a stuffy and repressive office: 'That stillness was abhorrent to young Ransome. So was the bowing of his head, the cramping of his limbs, and his sense of imprisonment in his pen' (63). The more his job depresses him the more he keeps himself 'fitter than ever', doing 'dumb-bell practice in his bedroom', sprinting 'like mad', and rowing 'hard' on the river in the evenings (64). His exercise is a form of non-intellectual, non-artistic sublimation, which enables him to 'stick it' at his work and in his active life: '"Stick it!"', Sinclair tells us, 'was the motto of his individual recklessness and of the dogged, enduring conservatism of his class' (22). As Zweiniger-Bargielowska states, physical culture and life reform were enthusiastically embraced by 'skilled manual workers' and by lower-middle-class clerks because they believed in 'self-discipline and temperance as a sign of respectability' (11). Similarly, the 'physical beauty' that was the by-product of exercise was seen to denote 'harmony between body and soul' and 'was grounded in virtues such as cleanliness, moderation, and self-control' (19).

Ranny's physical beauty, his self-control and his decency are contrasted with the weakness and degeneracy of his inebriate father the chemist, who works in a dark, gothic and chemically pungent dispensing room at the back of the chemist's shop where the family also live. He is, Ranny thinks, 'a miracle of unfitness', with his 'sallow, sickly face', 'peevish nostrils' and 'thin and irritable mouth': 'He was weedy to the last degree' (38). He is also, however, when he is in public, respectable and well-dressed. He goes to church and hands around the collection plate, and he has a good standing in the community. However, without any outlet for his libido and his life force, he drinks more and more and his health deteriorates. The chemist's business becomes bankrupt, and the man himself becomes very ill. The proprieties that led him to conceal his drinking and to parade his respectabilities and his reputation as 'wise and good' (46) are what kills him. He is the epitome of all that was wrong with the nineteenth century for Sinclair: a case study of how repression manifests in undesirable ways and eventually kills.

Mercier, Ranny's father's assistant, is young and unfettered by ideas of propriety. He is modern, and he does not repress his libido: instead he indulges it. He visits music halls, entertains women, dresses himself up as a dandy, and strolls about town looking for fun. He is a 'black-haired, thick-set youth with heavy features in a heavy, pasty face, a face oddly decorated by immense and slightly prominent blue eyes, a face where all day long the sensual dream brooded heavily' (22). Mercier's flabbiness is seen by Ranny to be as bad as, or worse than, his father's weediness. He is the modern countertype to Ranny's moral and physical fitness. Zweiniger-Bargielowska identifies two countertypes or 'negative stereotypes' to the 'hegemonic ideal of masculinity' at the turn of the century: the 'physique of the stunted, narrow-chested urban casual labourer' and the 'obese, flabby body of the sedentary white-collar worker or businessman'. In other words, Ranny's twin horrors: weediness and flabbiness. Fat, in particular, signified not only physical but cultural degeneration: 'The obese man whose fat denoted greed, self-indulgence, and effeminacy threatened dominant codes of manliness based on restraint and self-control. Obesity was frequently linked with inferior racial groups, crime, and moral trangression' (19). Mercier has an 'abominable smile' (34) and Ranny dislikes him. Mercier thinks that it is because Ranny thinks of him as dangerous: a woman-stealer. Actually, Ranny is disgusted by his physical presence: 'To Ranny, Jujubes in his increasing flabbiness, was too disgusting to be dangerous. And his conversation, his silly goat's talk, was disgusting, too' (187). The silly goat's talk is talk about sex – jokes about women and about 'improprieties' – talk that Ranny, with his firm belief in the twin ideals of fitness and decency, abhors.

A large part of Ranny's character is the fact that he is what his mother calls 'venturesome'. He is 'fond, fantastically and violently fond of danger, of adventure' (5). In 1902, he also starts to realise that women are attractive:

> But in the spring of nineteen-two something stirred in him, something watched and waited; with a subtle agitation, a vague and delicate excitement, it exulted and aspired. The sensation, or whatever it was, had as yet no separate existence of its own. So perfect, in this spring of nineteen-two, was the harmony of Ranny's being that the pulse of this unborn thing was one with all his other pulses; it was one, indistinguishably, with the splendor of life, the madness of running, and the joy he took in his own remarkable performances on the horizontal bar. (9)

He starts paying attention to the girls at the Polytechnic Gym, particularly Winny, who he admires because she is fit: 'What he first noted in her with wonder and admiration was the absence of weediness and flabbiness. Better known, she stirred in him, as a child might, an altogether indescribable sense of tenderness and absurdity' (12). Winny is alternately infantilised and portrayed as maternal and loving and strong: as a woman with 'sound practical common sense' (225). The two end up dancing together in the 'Combined Maze' of the title, a dance which is chalked out on the floor of the gymnasium as 'Seven mystic, seven sacred circles' and which is run by all the members of the gym, 'young men and young girls', 'together with the racing of the stars, for the unloosening of the holy primal energies in a figure and a measure and a ritual old as time' (26).

This ancient pagan dance is a spiral dance, and it mirrors 'the spiral patterns that nineteenth-century astronomers [. . .] began to discover in many star systems' (Materer 1979: 16). These same spiral patterns in the stars were considered by scientists in the early twentieth century to mirror other forms of energy and patterning in nature – the 'widespread law compelling matter to flow in these forms' (15) – and this is what Sinclair means when she calls the 'figure', or pattern, of the dance one that is as old as time. The discovery of the spiral pattern in astronomy, and endlessly repeated in nature, is also the inspiration behind Ezra Pound's increasing fascination with the figure of the vortex as the pattern of all life, energy, change and renewal. Pound's launch of Vorticism in *BLAST* was in 1914, but the ideas behind it had been circulating for him for some time: rhythm, vibration and energy as originating from the centre of a spiral vortex; and these energies and rhythms as crucial to a modern awareness of the bodily and creative self. As Pound and Wyndham Lewis write in the 1914 *BLAST*: 'WE ONLY WANT THE WORLD TO LIVE, and to feel it's [sic] crude energy flowing through us' (1914: 7); and later, 'The vortex is the point of maximum energy,/ It represents, in mechanics, the greatest efficiency' (153).

Pound first used the motif of the vortex in his 1908 poem 'Plotinus', and Sinclair would have been aware of his interest in the spiral pattern as originatory form at the time of writing *The Combined Maze* in 1913. The two knew each other from around 1908, shortly after Pound arrived in London, and were corresponding 'as early as March 1909' (Raitt 2000: 193). By 1917 she was referring to the vortex (the feminist vortex, the social vortex of commuunal school life and the vortex of the trenches) as a product of the crowd and the 'collective feeling' that threatens the 'clearness and hardness' of the individual soul, but in 1913, pre-war, she was fascinated by the power of the image of the surrender of the ego (Sinclair 1917: 124). The 'combined maze' dance also has similarities to Lewis's early *Creation* painting (exhibited in 1912), 'which shows a highly stylised male and female couple engaged in a fertility dance within its whirling planes' (Materer 1979: 18). It is possible that Sinclair was thinking of this when she wrote the description of the dance of the 'combined maze' at the polytechnic gym.

The men and women dance, in circles and then in spirals. They return to the centre of the maze, the centre of the vortex, only to be 'flung' out again from it and create with their running bodies 'the great Wheel of Eight Spokes, the Wheel of Life' (Sinclair 1913: 29):

> And the ancient rhythmic rush and race of the worlds, and the wheeling of all stars, the swinging and dancing of all atoms, the streaming and eddying of the ancestral stuff of life was in the whirling of that living Wheel; it was one immortal motion, continuous and triumphant in the bodies of those men and maidens as they ran. And they, shop-girls and shop-boys and young clerks, slipped off their memories of the desk and counter, and a joy, an instinct, and a sense that had no memory woke in them, savage, virgin, and shy; the pure and perfect joy of the young body in its own strength and speed; the instinct of the hunter of the hills and woodlands. (29)

The movement of the dance enables the participants to cast off their egos and any individual memories and to become a part of something larger: they mirror the movement of the stars and of atoms and thus become connected with 'the ancestral stuff of life'. For Ranny, the dance has an extra pleasure in that it keeps returning him to Winny's side and the pattern means that often he is following her through the spiral motions of the vortex, looking as he runs at the 'slender, innocent movement of her hips' (30). This coupling, Sinclair is quick to state, 'precluded passion' (31), because the libido is sublimated in the wild movement of the dance and there is no surplus. It is also not about individual passion because the bodies in the dance are not acting out their individual wills but rather responding to what Pound called in *BLAST* 'MOMENTUM, which is the past bearing upon us, RACE, RACE-MEMORY, instinct charging the PLACID, NON-ENERGISED FUTURE' (1914: 153). However, the dance does make Ranny realise that he has 'tender' feelings for Winny, and feelings of 'comradeship' with her (Sinclair 1913: 31). The motif of the 'combined maze' recurs in the novel, as Suzanne Raitt points out, and becomes a figure 'for the deterministic influence of sex and environment' (Raitt 2000: 186). The vortex of the dance is also the vortex of the early twentieth century, in which individuals are flung about by societal pressures and financial worries.

Ranny loves Winny, and decides he is going to save up to marry her. However, this means a long wait, and the long wait means that his libido has been first stimulated and then given no outlet. Into this tense situation steps another woman, Winny's friend Violet. Violet has soft flesh, and long dark eyelashes, and beautiful dresses. She is very sensual, with an 'incomparable softness', and a 'band of velvet round her full white neck' (73). She is not the kind of woman that Ranny thought that he liked, with his horror of flabbiness, but she enchants him. She convinces him, too, that he disapproves of Winny's athletic performances, on the parallel bar:

> Some of his innocence had gone. She had taken it away from him. He was beginning to understand how Winny's performance had struck her. It was magnificent, but it was not a thing that could be done by a nice woman, by a woman who respected herself and her own womanhood and her own beauty; not a thing that could be done by Violet Usher. (85)

Ranny marries Violet, and immediately Violet begins to feel unhappy. She has a baby, which she despises, and she sits at home all day, allowing the house to get dirty and dilapidated. She neglects the baby so much it falls ill. She doesn't want to be a housewife – she is averse to housework – and wants her old life back: going to music halls, working as a female clerk, having her freedom. When she does make an effort at housework it improves the shape of her body (and also stops her from being so discontented), but she does not really want to improve her body or her soul:

> It was not that the light work Violet did was unbecoming to her. On the contrary, Violet bloomed in Granville. She had had to own that the unaccustomed exercise was a good thing, giving a fineness and a firmness to outlines that had been a shade too lax. It was that you can have too much of a good thing when you have it every day; too much of light washing and light cooking, of the lightest of light sweeping, of dusting, and the making of even one double bed. (145)

Violet and Mercier then run away together to Paris. They are both of the same modern type: the flabby, the thrill-seeking and the decadent. Ranny saves up for a divorce, but it takes him five years, and in the meantime he proposes to Winny. They are both very happy for a while, but then on the eve of the divorce proceedings Violet turns up again. She's been misused: first by Mercier, who has left her because he couldn't marry her, and then by an artist 'gentleman' who has beaten her. Ranny takes pity on her, and takes her back.

The fall of Violet is precipitated by her boredom, and by her flabbiness. The flabbiness causes the boredom: she will not go out on bike rides with Ranny, and she is bored by the countryside. She therefore ends up sitting in her suburban house hating herself, her husband and her children. As Allison Pease points out, the 'detailed, often tedious portrayals of wasted female lives' (Pease 2012: 61) is a Sinclairian motif. May Sinclair's fiction is full of bored women. *The Three Sisters*, which is loosely based on an account of the early life of the Brontë sisters, features three women shut up in a parsonage, slowly going mad; *The Creators* aims to show what happens when women of genius are thwarted and cocooned in domesticity (they slowly go mad) and *Life and Death of Harriett Frean* is a boring novella *about* boredom. Violet is another of these trapped, bored and repressed women who has no outlet for her emotions, or her libido. She cannot sublimate her libido into intellectual work because she is not very clever, and she will not sublimate it into physical activity.

Fit Greeks

Ranny's embrace of physical culture as an outlet for his libido and as a way of harmonising the physical and the moral in his life is a modern activity which is in fact a return to a Classical past. The athleticism of the ancient Greeks seemed, from the perspective of the nineteenth century, to complement and enhance their intellectual achievements. In 1896 the first modern Olympic Games was held in Athens, reflecting (and further feeding) the fin-de-siècle interest in Classical athleticism. Charalambos Anninos, writing in the Official Report of the first Games, praised the native discus players in terms of their affinity with their ancestors: 'Mr Versis in particular showed a harmony and a dignity in his attitudes, which would not have disgraced an Ancient discus thrower. He himself is beautiful of form like an ancient statue' (O'Mahony 2012: 33). The photographer Albert Meyer, who documented these games, shot the athletes in the poses of ancient statues instead of showing them in more modern attitudes, reconstructing, as Mike O'Mahony writes, 'the image of the modern athlete within a classical vocabulary that evoked ancient tradition, thus conflating modernity with the glories of a classical past' (33). The public fascination with Greek athletics grew all the more after the revival of the Olympics. In 1910, E. Norman Gardiner wrote in the Preface to his *Greek Athletic Sports and Festivals*:

> It is my hope that the present volume may prove of interest to the general reader as well as to the student of the past. For though its subject may seem at first sight purely archaeological, many of the problems with which it deals are as real to us today as they were to the Greeks. The place of physical training and of games in education, the place of athletics in our daily life and in our national life, are questions of present importance to us all, and in considering

these questions we cannot fail to learn something from the athletic history of a nation which for a time at least succeeded in reconciling the rival claims of body and of mind, and immortalised this result in its art. (vii)

For Gardiner a study of the athletic and intellectual practices of the ancient Greeks must necessarily be instructive to any consideration of the mental and physical fitness of modern people. To draw a comparison between the practices of the Greeks and the inferior practices of 1910 England is to inspire improvement: not only for the individual, but for 'national life'. In the early twentieth century, this admiration for a Greek body–mind harmony was transferred too onto aspirational bodily aesthetics:

> Beauty ideals were based on a classical Greek aesthetic and two competing conceptions of male beauty were represented by the muscular frame of Hercules [...] and the lithe figure of Apollo [...] The dominant female beauty ideal extolled by doctors and hygienists was the Venus de Milo. The Venus' straight-waisted torso contrasted sharply with the conventional corseted female figure of the turn of the century. (Zweiniger-Bargielowska 2011: 4–5)

To be Greek is to be muscular and to be natural, and to be modern (as opposed to Victorian) one must similarly be strong, natural, healthy and unconstrained by corsetry. Ranny is likened several times to Greek gods and Greek athletes. On the very first page of *The Combined Maze* the narrator says that he should 'have been born in lands of adventure [...] he should have run, half-naked, splendidly pagan, bearing the torch of Marathon' (Sinclair 1913: 1). He is 'half pagan in his "zephyr"'; and is an 'indomitable and impassioned worshiper of the body and the earth' (3). When he appears as the 'apex' of a gymnastic display, with his feet in the air, he looks like 'the body of a young immortal descending with facile precipitancy to earth' (21). His friend Booty, the second-best athlete at the Poly. Gym., is also Greek, pagan and mysterious, with 'the face of a beardless faun'. (5) The women are Greek-like too, although for Sinclair the figure of Artemis, the slender and virginal huntress, was a greater inspiration than that of Venus. Winny is a runner and not a soft, voluptuous Venus-type. She moves always with a 'swiftness', an air of never wanting to be captured, and she can run as fast as, or faster than, Ranny himself (67). The swift, strong and slender woman recurs in Sinclair's fiction, and often she is explicitly described as an Artemis figure. One dancer in *The Combined Maze* has 'the questing face and wide-pointing breasts of Artemis' (27). Gwenda in *The Three Sisters* 'carried herself like a huntress; slender and quick, with high, sharp-pointed breasts' (Sinclair 1915: 39); 'like Artemis carrying the young moon on her forehead' (40). Mary Olivier is a fast runner and is 'exquisitely light and slender' (Sinclair 1919: 244); and the resilient farmer Anne Severn has a body 'slender but solid', and a 'strong white neck' which 'carried her head high with the poise of a runner' (Sinclair 1922: 34). Her body has a 'forward springing look' which in its 'very stillness' 'suggested movement': 'Her young breasts sprang forward, sharp pointed' (57). This emphasis on the 'sharp pointed' breasts is an emphasis on virginity and youth. Sinclair's Greek heroines are not sexual or maternal Venus-figures, they are independent and active women. Their very breasts convey a sense of continual springing forward.

The Classical emphasis on the slender and fit-for-purpose body has its counterpoint. Gardiner uses the same word as Sinclair uses in *The Combined Maze* to describe the other side of this coin: 'The Greek, with his keen eye for physical beauty, regarded flabbiness, want of condition, a sign of neglected education' (88). In the late 1920s and the early 1930s, this disgust for flabbiness as the counterpoint to strength, beauty and efficiency was increasingly used in the rhetoric of eugenicists and race hygienists, and the notion of the beautiful and fit ancient Greek became an issue of race. In a 1931 *Health and Strength* article called 'No Need to Envy the Physical Perfection of the Ancient Greeks', this is made explicit:

> Gymnastics originated with the ancient Greeks, who made the proper exercising of the body one of the most important duties in life. Not so that they might produce an army of athletes, but that a race of strong, healthy and beautiful men and women might people their land, a race capable of attending to all the affairs of life with that energy and vigour which is the birthright of the human race. [. . .]
> The Spartans required their women to be gymnasts as well as the men, and, indeed, forbade them to marry unless they were. If, in spite of these precautions, a child was born defective, mentally or physically, it was destroyed at birth. Would that we to-day took such an interest in the welfare of our people! (8 Aug 1931: 179)

Sinclair's presentation of Ranny and of Winny in *The Combined Maze* as the future of the race, healthy, active and morally sensible, is then an example of the very beginnings of the kinds of thought that lead to eugenics, racial cleansing and extreme social Darwinism. The horrific events of Nazi Germany in the 1930s and 1940s did not spring from a vacuum: they had as their root a pan-European desire to improve the health, intelligence and moral capacity of 'the race' through life reform. This kind of discourse is echoed in *The Tree of Heaven*, where the mother, Frances, is very relieved that her children don't seem to have the taint of the 'flesh and blood' of her brother Morrie, who has mental health problems (Sinclair

1917: 15). They are, she thinks happily, 'slender and clear and hard', with none of the 'fluffiness and fuzziness and fatness' of other children (25). In *Mary Olivier*, the fear of genetics and heredity is so great that Mary reads 'Herbert Spencer's *First Principles*, the *Principles of Biology*, the *Principles of Psychology*; Haeckel's *History of Evolution*; Maudsley's *Body and Mind, Physiology and Pathology of Mind, Responsibility in Mental Disease*; and Ribot's *Heredity*' (Sinclair 1919: 288) as well as 'Darwin's *Origin of Species*' (289) so that she knows one way or the other if she will 'go like' her mad Aunt Charlotte (291).

Mary Olivier is a *Bildungsroman*, and as such it is about Mary's aspirations and her development. Her aspirations are to be fit, to be strong and to be learned. Elise Thornton has demonstrated, in this volume, just how Mary's ambition to learn Greek is an ambition to be an intellectual, unfettered by gender constraints. Mary's fascination with Greek, however, goes hand in hand with a fascination with the Greeks themselves:

> There were such a lot of gods and goddesses that at first they were rather hard to remember. But you couldn't forget Apollo and Hermes and Aphrodite and Pallas Athene and Diana. They were not like Jehovah. They quarrelled sometimes, but they didn't hate each other; not as Jehovah hated all the other gods. They fitted in somehow. They cared for all the things you liked best: trees and animals and poetry and music and running races and playing games. (78–9)

Mary wants the poetry and the wisdom of the ancient Greeks, but she also wants their 'running races and playing games'. For her, this ancient civilisation represents a perfect synthesis of body and mind, with the one enhancing the other. If intellectual pursuit and the maintenance of a strong body sometimes seem antithetical (as Ranny suspects 'the votaries of intellectual light' of 'Weediness, if not of Flabbiness' [Sinclair 1913: 7]; as Valentine wonders if too much exercise makes for an 'overoxygenated brain' [Ford 2012: 535]; as Mary is told 'if you stodge like that you'll get all flabby' [Sinclair 1919: 84]), at other times physical health saves Mary from intellectual and spiritual despair:

> Somebody talked about a soul dragging a corpse. Her body wasn't a corpse; it was strong and active; it could play games and jump; it could pick Dan up and carry him round the table; it could run a mile straight on end. It could excite itself with its own activity and strength. It dragged a corpse-like soul, dull and heavy; a soul that would never be excited again, never lift itself up again in any ecstasy. (226)

The physical conditioning of the body allows for the soul to recover, and it allows too for the effort of intellectual pursuit that Mary embarks upon when she orders three volumes of Hegel's *The Logick* and sits down to read them. Her mind, she thinks, is 'like a robust, energetic body, happy when it was doing difficult and dangerous things, balancing itself on heights, lifting great weights of thought, following the long march into thick, smoky battles' (277).

Both intellectual activity and physical activity are conceived in terms of adventure. The central tension of *Mary Olivier* is that Mary is a seeker of thrills and new experiences, but that her circumstances rarely allow for any such activity. She wants to show off to her brother's friend Mr Ponsonby when she is a child, and she shows him her flexed muscles:

> 'I say – *what* a biceps!'
> 'Yes, but,' Mark said, 'you should feel his.'
> His was even bigger and harder than Mark's. 'Mine,' she said sorrowfully, 'will never be as good as his.'
> Then Mamma came and told her it was bed-time. (84)

Mary's mother censors her muscle-flexing much as she censors her reading of Greek in the public space of the drawing room. Mary's showing off to Mr Ponsonby is also a childish flirtation, aimed at 'the nicest looking person she had ever seen' (84). Because it is cut short and she is made to leave the room she must find a new way of performing her athleticism to this desirable male. The next opportunity she has to show off has rather more potential for disaster:

> 'Mr Ponsonby. Mr Ponsonby! Stay where you are and look!'
> From the window at the end of the top corridor the side of the house went sheer down the lane. Mary was at the window. Mr Ponsonby was in the lane.
> She climbed on to the ledge and knelt there. Grasping the bottom of the window frame firmly with both hands and letting her knees slide from the ledge, she lowered herself, and hung for one ecstatic moment, and drew herself up again by her arms.
> 'What did you do it for, Mary?'
> Mr Ponsonby had rushed up the stairs and they were sitting there. He was so tall that he hung over her when she leaned.
> 'It's nothing. You ought to be able to pull up your own weight.'
> 'You mustn't do it from top-storey windows. It's dangerous.'
> 'Not if you've practised on the banisters first.' (86)

Mary's innocence as to the sexual impetus for her performance and her earnest declaration that pull-ups from high window ledges are something that everybody should be able to do are meant to be amusing, but there is a deeper message here: if the libido of a child is stifled it will manifest itself in potentially unsafe ways. Mary needs to sublimate her surplus libido somehow, and if her reading is disallowed, and her physical exercise is disallowed, she will go to greater lengths to find an outlet for it.

Luckily for Mary, the countryside around her home gives her opportunities for the sublimation of the libido through physical exertion. She is free outside to run, holding hands with Mr Ponsonby, jumping over brooks 'in a business-like way. Mr Ponsonby took brook-jumping as the serious and delightful thing it was' (87). Gwenda in *The Three Sisters* also enjoys brook-jumping. Mr Rowcliffe sees her one day 'short-skirted and wild, jumping the wide water courses as they came, evidently under the impression that she was unobserved. And he smiled and said to himself, "She's doing it for fun, pure fun"' (Sinclair 1914: 40). Gwenda does not necessarily believe herself unobserved. She does walk out on the moor by herself, but it has crossed her mind that doing so, and giving the impression that she is jumping across brooks for 'pure fun', would make her attractive in Rowcliffe's eyes: 'he will wonder who is that wild, strong girl who walks by herself on the moor at night and isn't afraid' (10). The open countryside becomes the site for sexual encounter as well as for the free exercise of body and mind, unobserved and unpoliced.

May Sinclair's characters are continually negotiating the boundaries between their free and wild pagan selves and their higher ideals; of intellectual or of moral and spiritual beauty. For Ranny in *The Combined Maze* the struggle is one with society's financial and moral strictures: he needs to earn money so that he can marry, and he needs to keep up his household as a site of respectability, but this is at odds with his desire for freedom, for movement and for adventure. For Mary in adolescence, the negotiation of these boundaries is a negotiation between different societal pressures. There are, she thinks, several 'persons that were called Mary Olivier'. One is her mother's daughter, 'proud of her power over the sewing-machine'; there is 'the little girl of thirteen' who is about to become a woman but does not quite understand what that means; and there is Mark Olivier's sister, 'who rejoiced in the movements of her body, the strain of the taut muscles throbbing on their own leash, the bound forwards, the push of the wind on her knees and breast, the hard feel of the ground under her padding feet' (Sinclair 1919: 94). There is also the Mary who experiences 'secret happiness'; who sees mystical visions of the Absolute and who is driven by the need to find out what this is. All these versions of Mary are inflected by other people's perception of who she is and who she can be, but all of them are, nonetheless, genuine selves. The self which desires her mother's happiness and who tries to be as 'good' as possible in order to secure it is antithetical to the selves that desire physical and intellectual freedom, and the task of Mary, in her *Bildungsroman*, is to reconcile these conflicting impulses. She nurses her mother through her final illness, and finally gains her freedom (Ranny too has a moment of reconciliation with his father before his death; a 'final act of humility and contrition' [Sinclair 1913: 333]). In so doing she enacts a form of compassionate closure: an embracing and then banishing of the Victorian past and a step towards the new, modern world.

Works Cited

Ford, Ford Madox (2012), *Parade's End* [1924], London: Penguin.
Gardiner, E. Norman (1910), *Greek Athletic Sports and Festivals*, London: Macmillan & Co.
Materer, Timothy (1979), *Vortex: Pound, Eliot, and Lewis*, Ithaca, NY and London: Cornell University Press.
O'Mahony, Mike (2012), *Olympic Visions: Images of the Games throughout History*, London: Reaktion Books Ltd.
Pease, Allison (2012), *Modernism, Feminism, and the Culture of Boredom*, Cambridge: Cambridge University Press.
Pound, Ezra, and Wyndham Lewis (1914), *BLAST*, Modernist Journals Project, http://modjourn.org/render.php?id=1158591480633184&view=mjp_object (last accessed 22 June 2016).
Raitt, Suzanne (2000), *May Sinclair: A Modern Victorian*, Oxford: Oxford University Press.
Robinson, David J. W. (1931), 'No Need to Envy the Physical Perfection of the Ancient Greeks', *Health and Strength: The National Organ of Physical Fitness* (8 August 1931).
Sinclair, May (1913), *The Combined Maze*, New York and London: Harper & Brothers.
Sinclair, May [1914] (1915), *The Three Sisters*, London and New York: Macmillan & Co.
Sinclair, May (1916), 'Clinical Lecture on Symbolism and Sublimation – I', *The Medical Press and Circular* 153, 118–22.
Sinclair, May (1917), *The Tree of Heaven*, London and New York: Macmillan & Co.
Sinclair, May (1919), *Mary Olivier*, London and New York: Macmillan & Co.
Sinclair, May (1922), *Anne Severn and the Fieldings*, London: Hutchinson & Co.
Standwell, T. W. (1931), 'Is Man Really Polygamous? An Ever-Recurring Question', *Health and Strength: The National Organ of Physical Fitness* (21 November 1931).
'You and I. by the Editor' (1931), *Health and Strength: The National Organ of Physical Fitness* (8 August 1931).
Zweiniger-Bargielowska, Ina (2011), *Managing the Body: Beauty, Health, and Fitness in Britain, 1880–1939*, Oxford: Oxford University Press.

Chapter 8

Dolls and Dead Babies: Victorian Motherhood in May Sinclair's *Life and Death of Harriett Frean*

Charlotte Beyer

May Sinclair's Mothers

This chapter examines May Sinclair's representations of mother figures and maternity in her 1922 novel *Life and Death of Harriett Frean*.[1] My discussion focuses specifically on Sinclair's critique of idealised Victorian motherhood in the novel, and on its portrayals of mothering practices, femininity and class.[2] I explore Sinclair's novel as a modernist work of historical fiction, analysing its use of modernist thematic and textual strategies in reassessing Victorian values and representations.[3] Such themes reflect a more general preoccupation in modernist women's writing with motherhood, agency and sexuality. This concern can be seen in Virginia Woolf's novels *To the Lighthouse* (1927) and *Mrs Dalloway* (1925), and Katherine Mansfield's short story 'Bliss' (1918), where mother-figures struggle against invisibility and idealised maternity in a patriarchal society which frequently diminishes them, and yearn to express their creativity and sexuality. In her discussion of Coventry Patmore's poem 'The Angel in the House' in relation to Victorian constructions of femininity, Annie Cossins concludes that Patmore 'lauded the selfless devotion and submissiveness of the Victorian feminine ideal woman and modelled the angel on his wife, Emily, the "perfect" woman' (Cossins 2015: 63). Patmore's poem was highly influential and continued to resonate into the twentieth century (Cossins 2015: 64). My chapter examines Sinclair's critique of the continued influence and impact of these pervasive Victorian ideals and values into the modernist period. Like Virginia Woolf, who struggled with the emotionally and creatively limiting legacies of the Angel in the House, Sinclair also battled Victorian ideals, both in her writing and her personal life. For both authors, these questions were centred on motherhood. My analysis focuses on two contrasting yet interconnected dimensions of Sinclair's portrayal of the maternal in *Harriett Frean*: namely the Victorian idealisation of motherhood, and Sinclair's depiction of baby farming, the dark repressed side of Victorian maternity.[4]

Harriett Frean portrays the life of Harriett, a middle-class woman growing up during the latter half of the nineteenth century. Harriett is brought up in adherence to the traditional Victorian values of 'beautiful behaviour' (Sinclair 1922: 23) for women, and looks up to her parents as ideals. She foregoes marriage and motherhood, and never moves out of her parents' house; yet memories and images from her childhood continue to return to haunt her throughout her life, demonstrating Sinclair's interest in the psychological dimensions of existence. Suzanne Raitt says of the novel: 'Sinclair uses psychoanalytic paradigms to expose the Victorian family and domestic ideology for the destructive force they were for women such as Harriett' (Raitt 2000: 254). Alongside these subjective, psychological perspectives, *Harriett Frean* explores the potential of the *Bildungsroman* and historical fiction, challenging the format of both these genres to depict motherhood and the maternal with the complexity it warrants (Mosimann 2015: 198). Representations of motherhood in Sinclair's *Harriett Frean* are both complex and emotionally compelling.[5] The examination of Sinclair's portrayal of psychological themes has long been key to feminist readings of her work. Terry Phillips offers a detailed reading of Sinclair's novel and her treatment of the topic of motherhood. She writes that Sinclair's interest was 'directed towards the psychological development of women in families and the conflict between their ascribed family roles and the development of their individual consciousnesses. Mothering is of course crucial to these interests' (Phillips 1996: 128). Phillips also comments that Sinclair's portrayal of mothers reflects a degree of ambivalence: some portrayals are unsympathetic, whereas others engage 'sympathetically with the plight of women as mothers' (Phillips 1996: 128). Discussing *Harriett Frean*, Peter Childs highlights the significance of Harriett's relationship to her father: 'Harriett grows up idolizing her father and remains a dutiful daughter, staying a spinster to her own death, long after his demise' (Childs 2000: 34). Childs concludes that Sinclair's *Harriett Frean*, along with several other works of hers, are preoccupied with what he terms 'the overthrow of the Electra complex' (Childs 2000: 34). However, whereas Childs concentrates on Sinclair's portrayal of the relationship between Harriett and her father within the traditional patriarchal Victorian family, my chapter takes a different focus by examining the mother-daughter relationship, arguing that the novel is centrally preoccupied with motherhood and the maternal, and that Harriett's complex relationship with her mother is crucial to the novel.[6]

There has been less critical engagement with Sinclair's preoccupation with the wider social and cultural constructions of maternity, or with the literary language and textual techniques employed to represent these relations. This relative neglect of the subject of Victorian motherhood has been commented on by critics. Klaver and Rosenman maintain:

> In spite of its importance, however, maternity itself is one of the least-studied aspects of the Victorian era [. . .] Although maternity is routinely placed at the center of constructions of femininity and domesticity, it has received surprisingly little attention as a distinct conception or experience. (Klaver and Rosenman 2008: 1–2)

Through the image of 'dolls and dead babies', this chapter investigates the conflict between the idealisation of the mother-figure and an emphasis on feminine appearance and conduct on the one hand and, on the other, the erasure of motherhood through the hidden and hushed-up practice of baby-farming. The portrayal and context of the two main maternal figures in *Harriett Frean*, namely Harriett's mother and the maid Maggie, is key to the investigation of this conflict. By setting her novel retrospectively in the nineteenth century, well before the monumental changes caused by modernism and the First World War, Sinclair contests the popular conception of the Victorian era as the peak of the British Empire (Haydock 2008: 14). In contrast, Sinclair exposes the hidden shame of the period's repressions and inequality, through her depiction of the grim realities of baby-farming. Sinclair has previously used this retrospective strategy; as Susanne Stark asserts: 'it is one of the author's recurring topics to look back on the Victorians from a modern, twentieth-century point of view' (Stark 1992: 265). In her scrutiny of the Victorian past in *Harriett Frean*, Sinclair critically examined and rejected the 'dolls and dead babies' legacies of the Victorian period, and the insidious ways in which constructions of idealised femininity and maternity established during this period continued to not only inform, but also damage, women's identities in 1920s Britain. Through this preoccupation, Sinclair's novel articulates a critique of British society and culture, reinforced via imaginative and creative means, through her modernist challenge to traditional narrative forms. My chapter examines these compelling dimensions of the novel, through the various cracks which appear in the narrative fabric constructed by Sinclair's textual experimentation, which allow the reader to engage with the contradictions and complications to the sanctioned social and cultural construction of Victorian maternity.

Dolls: The Idealisation of Motherhood

The image of dolls forms the focal point for the present investigation of Sinclair's modernist portrayal of Victorian motherhood in *Harriett Frean*, and is a recurring symbol in Sinclair's work.[7] Sinclair employs the doll motif in *Harriett Frean* to portray the relationship between mother and baby and to problematise motherhood and its representation. In the novel, the doll represents an insidious idealisation of motherhood (chiefly illustrated through Harriett's mother), allowing Sinclair to establish a sense of distance between the Victorian era and the modernist period. The doll symbolises invisibility and the erasure of the mother and the maternal body, but also provides a means through which to examine representations of the mother-daughter relationship that challenge patriarchal authority. Furthermore, the symbol of the doll alludes to Henrik Ibsen's doll's house, in which the Victorian maternal and domestic ideal is presented as a performance of femininity in accordance with patriarchal expectations against which the female protagonist finally rebels. However, Sinclair's depiction is also intended to uncover the extent to which women in the 1920s were still affected by the Victorian values and ideals that shape social and cultural conceptions of motherhood and femininity in *Harriett Frean*. As we shall see, despite the powerful influence wielded by the cult of femininity, the novel also provides moments in which female and maternal oppression is resisted.

An early episode in *Harriett Frean*, describing the young Harriett's complicated relationship with her two dolls Ida and Emily, foregrounds the mother role and the centrality of the doll motif in the novel. Harriett loves her doll Ida passionately, but is given a new doll for her birthday called Emily; however, she does not connect with the latter emotionally. Despite this, when Harriett has her friend Connie Hancock over to play, Mamma admonishes Harriett that she must share her best beloved doll Ida with Connie, despite Harriett's protestations: '"My darling, you mustn't be selfish. You must do what your little guest wants"' (Sinclair 1995:6). As Harriett is forced to relinquish her exclusive relationship with Ida, she copes by imagining that the doll has died: 'She thought "If I can't have her to myself I won't have her at all." [. . .] She pretended Ida was dead; lying in her pasteboard coffin and buried in the wardrobe cemetery' (Sinclair 1995: 7–8). In this scene Harriett enacts a prohibition on excessive maternal emotional attachment, and cautions herself against forming an exclusive mother-baby relationship that constitutes a threat to the patriarchal order. This portrayal reflects Marianne Hirsch's assertion that the portrayal of hidden or silenced mother-daughter narratives forms a prominent subject in modernist women's writing, seeking to: 'reframe the familial structures basic to traditional narrative, *and* the narrative structures basic to traditional conceptions of family, from the perspective of the feminine and, more controversially, the maternal' (Hirsch 1989: 3). The trivialisation of attachment in the scene means that, for Harriett, the doll comes to symbolise the loss of exclusive emotional attachment between mother and baby. Thus, the two separate images, the doll and the dead baby, merge in this deeply affective scene, made more powerful still by Sinclair's writing, which in its pared-down minimalism is reminiscent of Imagist poetry, echoing Pound's insistence that the image should constitute 'an intellectual and emotional complex in an instant of time' (Pound 1913: 200–1).[8] Whilst emotionally powerful in its simplicity, the passage has the effect of underlining maternal erasure through its very lack of affective evocation.

Visuality is central to *Harriett Frean*'s portrayal of the erasure or invisibility of the mother's body. In its examination of this problem, *Harriett Frean* focuses intensively on the physical appearance and serene beauty of Harriett's mother, and her gentle demeanour, both of which are illustrations of the idealisation of Victorian maternity. Klaver and Rosenman explore the prominent profile given to the idealised mother-figure in the Victorian period, and the context of that figure. In their examination of representations of nineteenth-century motherhood, they argue: 'As the sanctification of motherhood gained its full ideological force in the nineteenth century, the successful or failed performance of maternity became the ubiquitous subject of social debate and textual representation' (Klaver and Rosenman 2008: 1). Lillian Craton comments further on the problematic and potentially destructive implications of the 'sanctification of maternity' that Klaver and Rosenman describe, emphasising how 'the selflessness associated with motherhood was often exaggerated and stylised within Victorian culture to an unhealthy degree' (Craton 2008: 293). The erasure of Victorian maternal corporeality is also highlighted in photographic work from the time which foregrounds this cultural anxiety around visibility and the maternal body. A 2013 book of photography by the artist Linda Fregni Nagler, entitled *The Hidden Mother*, illustrates the practice of erasing the maternal body. Fregni Nagler's book displays over one thousand photographs, taken from the nineteenth century up until 1920, which all conceal the mother within the photograph of her child.[9] This social and cultural erasure of the mother's body that we see depicted and problematised in Fregni Nagler's images is echoed in *Harriett Frean*. We also see a similar critique of the invisible maternal body in fellow modernist woman writer Katherine Mansfield's 1920 short story 'Bliss'.

Here, the female protagonist Bertha rebels inwardly against the restrictions on feminine maternal behaviour, which prevent her from expressing her sexuality and having a meaningful relationship with her baby daughter. Bertha reflects to herself: 'Why be given a body if you have to keep it shut up in a case like a rare, rare fiddle?'(Mansfield 1920). Mansfield's poignant image of the maternal body, shut up in a case, echoes Mamma's denial of her own corporeality in Sinclair's *Harriett Frean*. Later in 'Bliss', Bertha rephrases her earlier rhetorical question, this time asking: 'How absurd it was. Why have a baby if it has to be kept – not in a case like a rare, rare fiddle – but in another woman's arms?' (Mansfield 1920). This episode in Mansfield's story is similar to the passage in *Harriett Frean* when young Harriett puts her beloved doll Ida away in a box or pretend coffin, rather than let her friend Connie Hancock hold her. The recurring imagery in modernist women's writing of maternal abjection and physical denial articulates the resistance to the idealisation of motherhood in the Victorian era, and the continued restrictions placed on mothers in the early twentieth century. Sinclair looks back at this Victorian 'exaggerated selflessness' of the mother and erasure of the maternal body and its complex subjectivity, in order to examine it, interrogate it, and revise it.

Harriett Frean's interventions against the Victorian values associated with mothers and the maternal can be seen in its intertextual references. Coventry Patmore's poem 'The Angel in the House' functions as an important intertext in *Harriett Frean*, as can be seen through the novel's allusions to feminine virtue and domesticity, and the erasure of female assertion and maternal corporeality. Harriett's idealised view of her mother reflects that of her culture: 'Being good was being beautiful like Mamma. She wanted to be like her mother' (Sinclair 1995: 15). In the character of Mamma, Sinclair's novel implicitly and explicitly references Patmore's poem. This point has also been made by Phillips, who suggests that Harriett's mother strives to embody the ideal of the Angel in the House (Phillips 1996: 129). Sinclair's implicit references to Patmore's poem demonstrate the self-conscious literariness of *Harriett Frean*, through which the modernist novel maintains a complicated connection with the past and its traditions. At the same time, Sinclair's novel also echoes other modernist women writers' critiques of idealised femininity. Virginia Woolf's novel *To the Lighthouse* similarly articulates a critical analysis of the domestic feminine 'angel', through the figure of Mrs Ramsay. Ana Parejo Vadillo calls Mrs Ramsey an embodiment of 'nurturing femininity' (Vadillo 2015: 124), suggesting that she 'embodies the modernist idea of mid-Victorian, not early twentieth century, family life' (Vadillo 2015: 124). Through its critical examination of the repressive and damaging aspects of Victorian femininity and motherhood, *Harriett Frean* suggests that Harriett's unmarried and non-maternal life can be seen, not so much as a tragic inability to mature, but as a deliberate choice which enables her to evade the strictures of marriage and maternity. In this regard, Sinclair's novel breaks with conventional plot structures and narrative patterns, and attempts to forge new possibilities.

The serene appearance and self-sacrifice of Harriett's mother represents a form of what Shrock calls 'maternal mystique' (Todd 1993: 346),[10] and she is frequently depicted as radiating an elusive knowledge or mysterious happiness. Harriett is unable to emulate her mother's air of supreme serenity or become like her, argues Raitt: '[Harriett's] story reveals the intense frustration of identifications between mothers and daughters' (Raitt 2000: 249). Even when Harriett's father is dying, Harriett's mother's peaceful demeanour does not change; instead Harriett senses that, 'Her mother was looking at her with a serene comprehension and compassion' (Sinclair 1995: 91). However, Mamma's serenity is a mask for her self-sacrifice and bodily denial, as we see when later, after Papa's death, her own illness and self-sacrifice become part of her maternal mystique. Harriett perceives that her mother is concealing something from her: 'Her mother had some secret that she couldn't share. She was wonderful in her pure, high serenity' (Sinclair 1995: 93). Harriett is unable to 'read' the subtext of her mother's body language, and puzzles over her feeling that: 'Her mother had some secret: some happy sense of God that she gave to you and you took from her as you took food and clothing, but not quite knowing what it was, feeling that there was something more in it, some hidden gladness, some perfection that you missed' (1995: 40–1). Harriett's mother's 'maternal mystique' belies maternal corporeality, just as Fregni Nagler's photos of disappearing Victorian mothers expose the erasure of maternal bodies from pictures of their children.

Harriett Frean scrutinises the denial of the realities of motherhood presented by the 'maternal mystique' through its descriptions of the corporeal ageing process and the changing appearance of Harriett's mother's body. The portrayal of Mamma's physical changes echoes historical changes, through the depiction of different fashions and customs for women, and it is registered with resentment by Harriett, who observes how: 'One day her mother smoothed out her long, hanging curls and tucked them away under a net. Harriett had a little shock of dismay and resentment, hating change' (Sinclair 1995: 40). Harriett's response suggests fear of her mother's ageing, as she sees her idealised Mamma with her pretty hair replaced by a sterner appearance of sexual denunciation, signalled by the severe tying up of hair under a net and concealing its beauty. Later, as her mother ages further, Harriett's unease about the change in her mother's physical appearance is reawakened: 'Her mother parted her hair into two sleek wings; she wore a rosette and lappets of black velvet and lace on a glistening beetle-backed chignon. And Harriett felt again her shock of resentment. She hated to think of her mother subject to change and time' (Sinclair 1995: 49–50). The mother's changing and ageing body is circumscribed and erased by traditional social and cultural definitions of femininity and sexuality.

The image of the nurturing mother plays a highly significant role in Victorian imagery of idealised maternity. It is therefore not surprising that modernist women writers have examined this image, in their efforts to scrutinise and critique feminine sexuality. *Harriett Frean* confronts the association of 'nurturing femininity' with motherhood, through its thematic preoccupation with nurturing, feeding and starving, offering glimpses of more complex maternal identities through the cracks in the narrative fabric. The scenes involving food and eating in *Harriett Frean* illustrate the significance of the association between idealised maternity and nurturing, in which the elevated maternal figure was also the source of food, as Craton states: 'the middle-class idealization of female domesticity elevated the moral status of women and conferred great honor on the work of motherhood: successful performance of nurturance was a woman's finest achievement' (2008: 292). This 'nurturing' maternal position can be seen in the representation of Mamma in *Harriett Frean*. Feeding is a central activity in *Harriett Frean* which involves maternal agency and provides a symbolic space for the mother-daughter relationship, albeit an ambivalent space. Attending a children's party while quite young, Harriett is subjected to the conflicting demands of femininity in relation to nurturance. Her role is to help her mother serve party food to the younger children, thereby being educated into a feminine model of subservience and self-sacrifice. 'Helping' or 'serving' for a woman presents a means of positioning herself within a community, in a way that enables agency and control, a preparation for idealised motherhood, tending to the needs of others, while at the same time being required to deny her own needs. In *Harriett Frean,* this self-denial is particularly apparent around consumption and desire, illustrated through the text's problematisation of food and sexuality. Harriett is taught to adhere to expectations of self-denial and feminine modesty, by controlling her body, ensuring that her appearance is fixed in a pose deemed acceptable, echoing the image of the doll. Harriett's self-conscious reflection on these expectations demonstrates her expert command of her body and facial expression: 'She kept her face very still, so as not to look greedy, and tried not to stare at the Madeira cake in case people should see she was thinking of it' (Sinclair 1995: 12–13). This scene also highlights the contradictions of Victorian motherhood, illustrated by Harriett's mother's actions and behaviour. She sees Harriett with an empty, crumb-filled plate and assumes she has had some cake already. Harriett's attempt to acquire her first slice, therefore, is seen as an unladylike and greedy grab for seconds, and her mother tells her off and unwittingly makes her go without. However, on their return home, and on learning the truth, Mamma offers her cake and fresh creamy milk as an act of nurturance, love and reward. In private, Harriett's mother is able to loosen her prohibition on her daughter's food, demonstrating her obvious pleasure at feeding Harriett: 'Mamma's soft eyes kissed her as they watched her eating her cake with short crumbly bites, like a little cat. Mamma's eyes made her feel so good, so good' (Sinclair 1995: 14). The scene is reminiscent of the mother-baby gaze familiar from breastfeeding imagery, underlining the centrality of the physical bond and mental connection that Mamma and Harriett share. The repetition of the phrase 'so good' underlines the symbolic status of this transaction between the two females, emphasising its importance and illustrating Sinclair's use of linguistic effect to convey the emotional depth of the mother-daughter bond depicted in the scene. At the same time, Mamma's difficulty in negotiating the prohibition on female desire and appetite is seen to have a damaging impact on her daughter. Through its examination of denial and invisibility for Victorian women, this particular scene in *Harriett Frean* furthermore alludes to the physical invisibility of mothers and female bodies suggested by Fregni Nagler's photographs. The motifs of feeding and the withholding of food are further foregrounded by the novel's distressing baby-farming plotline later on in the narrative.

Harriett's response to her mother's demonstration of love and nurturance in the scene is to challenge patriarchal and religious order by asserting her mother's singular importance. Harriett suggests that her mother's goodness exceeds that of God and Jesus, but to question masculine and divine authority in this way is too daunting for Harriett's mother, as Harriett observes: 'Mamma's frightened face spoiled it. What did she think' (Sinclair 1995: 16). Fearing patriarchal retribution, Sinclair's female characters in *Harriett Frean* are left in peace only when living 'under cover', in subservience and conformity. Commenting on modernist women's writing and its capacity for portraying 'the hidden narrative of the passionate attachment between mother and daughter' (Hirsch 1989: 97), Hirsch suggests that 'modernist writing strategies, characterised by increased room for subjective representations of consciousness, allow this previously hidden narrative to come to the surface of women's fiction' (Hirsch 1989: 97). Circumscribed by patriarchal constrictions on female conduct, physicality and appetite, it is only in the private sphere, behind closed doors, that mother and daughter are able to interact without restraint. Through its complex representations of dolls and mothers, *Harriett Frean* exposes the hypocrisy embodied in the 'Angel in the House', using an experimental and contemporary modernist narrative form to engage critically with cultural and social legacies and confront stereotypical images of maternity.

Dead Babies: Baby-Farming and Working-Class Motherhood

The distressing image of a dead baby is the dark counterpart to the 'doll' motif in *Harriett Frean*, and forms another recurrent theme in Sinclair's work.[11] *Harriett Frean*'s portrayal of the controversial Victorian practice of baby-farming is one of the most haunting aspects of her portrayal of motherhood. Recent years have seen increased critical and scholarly attention given to investigations of the practice of baby-farming in Victorian Britain and elsewhere in the world.[12] However, baby-farming remains a repressed aspect of Victorian society. As Cossins argues, 'Baby-farming was an invisible crime, largely committed by women, which occurred within the home of a nurse or midwife' (Cossins 2015: 94). As an 'invisible', private practice, baby-farming has been relatively forgotten, or rather repressed, in contemporary times, as Cossins goes on to explain. She states:

> Many people have never heard the term 'baby-farming', and cannot understand how a mother could sell her child to a stranger who, after pocketing the money, sometimes killed the child or neglectfully allowed it to die a slow, lingering death from starvation. (Cossins 2015: 1)

In *Harriett Frean*, baby-farming is implicitly referred to in the portrayal of Harriett's maid, Maggie, and the fate of her baby son born outside wedlock. Sinclair's preoccupation with this theme reflects a more general concern in modernist literature with using experimental textual modes to explore hidden or silenced dimensions of existence and subjective psychology, in its investigations of the traumas and repressions within.[13] Sinclair's portrayal of Maggie and her baby specifically reflects Cossins' discussion of the social condemnation exerted upon women who failed to adhere to standards of feminine virtue (Cossins 2015: 62). Thus, through its retrospective historical narrative, *Harriett Frean* examines the other side of the 'exaggerated and stylised' Victorian idea of maternal perfection discussed by Craton (2008: 293). In Sinclair's depiction, Harriett's individual psyche and its repression emerges as a critique of the wider social amnesia in Sinclair's own modernist era with regard to Victorian social mores and the way these continued to haunt early twentieth-century culture. *Harriett Frean*'s representation of infant death and the allusion to baby-farming occurs in Chapter XI. In this chapter, Maggie leaves Harriett's service to have a baby, but is allowed to come back into service after the birth:

> Her new servant, Maggie, had had a baby. After the first shock and three months' loss of Maggie, it occurred to Harriett that the beautiful thing would be to take Maggie back and let her have the baby with her, since she couldn't leave it. (Sinclair 1995: 136)

However, unable to bear the sight of Maggie mothering and breastfeeding her baby due to unacknowledged jealousy and longing to be a mother herself, Harriett fires Maggie and asks her to leave. Three months later Maggie returns to ask for her job back, explaining that her baby died while in the care of 'a woman in the country', a baby-farmer: 'Maggie turned up again in a black hat and gown for best, red-eyed and humble. "I came to see, ma'am, whether you'd take me back, as I 'aven't got baby now"' (Sinclair 1995: 139). Maggie explains the death of her baby: '"'e died, ma'am, last month. I'd put him with a woman in the country"' (Sinclair 1995: 139). The arrangement described in *Harriett Frean* was a commonplace solution for working-class and servant women unable to afford to keep their babies, or who had had their babies out of wedlock. Cossins discusses how such baby-farming arrangements worked:

> It was common for working-class women to nurse babies for a weekly fee or to adopt unwanted babies in exchange for a lump sum called a 'premium' [...] Baby-farmers either sold children to childless couples for a profit, or sold children on to poorer baby-farmers for a smaller fee and pocketed the difference. Others kept their adopted babies in 'farming' conditions until they died from disease, neglect, starvation or murder. (Cossins 2005: 68)

The financial aspect of baby-farming – the payment for baby 'care' – is also explicitly referred to in *Harriett Frean*. Maggie explains to Harriett that the 'woman in the country' had been highly recommended, and that she had 'paid her six shillings a week' (Sinclair 1995: 139). In the novel, although tragic, Maggie's shocking and sad story is portrayed as an isolated incident. However, as we have seen, recent research shows that baby-farming was rife in Victorian Britain, and that this practice was an implicit but accepted part of a social order which condemned unmarried working-class and servant mothers to misery, social isolation and poverty.[14] Shanley explains that baby-farming practice entailed:

> the practice of placing infants in the care of women or couples who often took in many such children at one time. Baby farmers did not serve as wet nurses, but fed the babies bottles or pap [...] many of them knew that they were expected to let the infants in their care die. (Shanley 1993: 88)[15]

This awful predicament would also appear to have applied to Maggie's baby. Indeed, Maggie's heartbreaking report indicates this. She explains to Harriett that, on seeing her dead baby, she noticed that he: '"was that wasted you wouldn't have known him"' (Sinclair 1995: 139). This distressing report suggests that Maggie's baby received inadequate food and attention, and that this neglect and mistreatment led to his death. Through the baby-farming storyline, *Harriett Frean* thus depicts how Maggie's own maternity is negated and erased, although paradoxically, because of her class status and employment, Maggie eventually comes to function instead as a mother figure for Harriett in her old age and illness. With her terse, minimal description of maternal grief and affect, Sinclair employs an understated modernist narrative form to throw light on baby-farming as the dark reality behind the idealised image of Victorian motherhood.

The depiction of baby-farming and the exposure of the plight of working-class unmarried mothers are central to *Harriett Frean*'s examination of the contradictions of Victorian maternity. Maggie's situation was typical for servant women at the time according to Cossins, who pinpoints factors such as 'the lack of a welfare state, the fragility of employment without minimum working standards, significantly lower wages for women and the burdens of childbearing without reliable contraception' (Cossins 2015: 66–7), all of which were responsible for creating this social scourge. At the same time, baby-farming also provided a financial incentive for those working-class women taking in the unwanted babies (Cossins 2015: 67). However, moral and religious taboo was equally significant. To have a baby outside wedlock in Victorian times was seen as evidence of immorality in women, as Ginger Frost explains: 'The mother of an illegitimate child had already transgressed Victorian ideals of womanliness through lack of chastity' (2008: 145). Cossins also makes this point, linking social class with perceptions of virtue and chastity. She highlights how: 'underage girls and working-class women who gave birth outside marriage were doubly vulnerable, disadvantaged by poverty and stigmatised by their "lax" moral standards, since conceptions of immorality were class-based' (Cossins 2015: 73).

Maggie's plight serves to highlight the social and political distinctions made between middle- and upper-class motherhood and working-class maternal experience. Such gender-political social perceptions also illustrate why Harriett felt unable to act on her attraction to Robin, and why Harriett's mother felt that virtuous femininity and 'beautiful behaviour' were the only values that would ensure her and her daughter patriarchal acceptance. Sinclair's historical novel enables her to portray such female-orientated and feminist topics as part of her modernist critique of a hypocritical and repressive culture. With Harriett's ambivalent response, first to Maggie feeding her baby, then later to hearing of his death and remembering him, Sinclair's novel illustrates the parallel between repression of shame in the individual, and the wider social amnesia in relation to the phenomenon of baby-farming. These representations of feelings of guilt, shame and repression and their long-term effects furthermore reflect Sinclair's interest in psychoanalysis and the psychological dimensions of existence, as discussed by Elizabeth Mosimann (Mosimann 2015: 199). Through her portrayal of Maggie and her baby, Sinclair's treatment of the topic of baby-farming illustrates her determination to explore taboo and controversial questions and ideas which were out of the public eye, restricted to the private and domestic sphere, and related to women's conditions.

The plight of Maggie and her baby, and the reality of unmarried working-class motherhood, are portrayed through Harriett's perspective. However, by including conversations between Harriett and Maggie, and depictions of Harriett's impressions and memories, the narrative conveys a more complex picture than mere middle-class condemnation of motherhood out of wedlock. Some of Harriett's strongest emotional and physical responses in the novel are reported in the chapter concerning Maggie's baby. Harriett's ambivalent responses towards seeing the physicality of the baby are described closely: 'The baby lay in his cradle in the kitchen, black-eyed and rosy, doubling up his fat, naked knees, smiling his crooked smile, and saying things to himself' (Sinclair 1995: 136). This detailed depiction of the contented, thriving baby is disarmingly lovely – too lovely for her to bear: 'Harriett had to see him every time she came into the kitchen' (Sinclair 1995: 136). Couched by the understated narration, the text reveals the tension in Harriett and her responses to seeing Maggie's bond with her baby. The episode is highly charged with emotional, physical and sexual ambivalence towards working-class women's sexuality and motherhood. Harriett tries to do the right thing, what she considers to be the morally and ethically superior act, by taking Maggie back into her employment and permitting her to keep the baby with her (Sinclair 1995: 136). However, Harriett discovers that she is unable to sustain this moral high ground, due to psychological barriers of her own. The reason why the arrangement becomes unsustainable is not so much because of social scandal or condemnation – that aspect of it is never really mentioned; it is because Harriett cannot bear to see Maggie with her baby, and cannot deal with being confronted with the physicality of motherhood. When Harriett sees Maggie breastfeed her baby, she is overwhelmed by a mixture of emotions. Her yearning to mother and be mothered is palpable, yet she simultaneously recoils from the physical and emotional intimacy it represents. The sight of Maggie's breast and the sound of the baby's cry leave Harriett feeling raw and agitated: 'Sometimes she heard him cry, an intolerable cry, tearing the nerves and heart. And sometimes she saw Maggie unbutton her black gown in a hurry and put out her white, rose-pointed breast to still his cry' (Sinclair 1995: 136–7). Sinclair's vocabulary is all the more powerful because of its minimalism, in this powerful description of the blurring of boundaries between self and other elicited by the sound of the baby's cry. This visual image of mother and baby united in a breastfeeding scene, a tableau reminiscent of the madonna and child, is striking in its physicality but is experienced as a torturous insult by Harriett: 'Harriett couldn't bear it. She could not bear it' (Sinclair 1995: 137). Brown comments that this 'emphatic repetition [of the phrase] brings home forcefully the extent of her distress' (Brown 1992: 45). Tragically, later on, after Harriett has sent Maggie and her baby away, no one will hear or take heed of the baby, and no one will respond to his cries of anguish. This episode illustrates how the stark exposure to the physicality of maternity triggers too many of Harriett's own most traumatic memories; thoughts she had attempted to suppress, but with only partial success.

Unsurprisingly, Harriett's own response to her collusion in the baby's fate is to repress the part that she played in condemning Maggie's baby to his untimely death: 'She had forgotten. The image of Maggie's baby was dead, hidden, buried deep down in her mind' (Sinclair 1995: 164). However, Harriett's recurring references to and memories of Maggie's dead baby are evidence of Alison Pease's insightful assessment of Sinclair's modernist narrative technique. She has it that: 'as the stream-of-consciousness technique Sinclair championed demonstrates, the mind is never at rest, certitudes are never accepted' (Pease 2006: 189). This analysis of Sinclair's technique and its reliance on memory and stream of consciousness illustrates the internalised and subjective way in which Sinclair's novel revisions Victorian history through the prism of individual female characters and their subjective and imaginative engagement with maternity. Rather than condemning Maggie for her pregnancy, loss of employment and subsequent action of leaving her baby with a baby-farmer, *Harriett Frean* suggests that the death of Maggie's baby was not caused by her bad or inadequate mothering; rather, it was the result of an unequal and exploitative patriarchal society in which working-class women had little agency or choice. References to infanticide are implied in Maggie's ambiguous question to Harriett: '"I should think she'd a done something, shouldn't you, ma'am?"' (Sinclair 1995: 140). This could be disbelief that the women had not 'done something' to stop the baby dying once she could see that it was weak, or could be a recognition that the death was deliberate: the woman had 'done something'. However, privately Harriett blames herself for the baby's death: '"No. No. It was I who did it when I sent him away"' (Sinclair 1995: 140). Attempting to make herself feel better about what's happened and absolve herself from responsibility, Harriett muses: 'She could see that Maggie didn't hold her responsible. After all, why should she? If Maggie had made bad arrangements for her baby, Maggie was responsible' (Sinclair 1995: 141). Both of the women's responses reflect an unequal Victorian society where women's problems were individualised, rather than regarded as indicative of wider gender-political and social issues. This tendency to individualise problems – 'If Maggie had made bad arrangements [. . .], Maggie was responsible' (Sinclair 1995: 141) – serves to minimise social responsibility and solidarity among women from different class backgrounds, leading to young working-class women becoming victims of exploitation by unscrupulous baby-farmers. Emma Liggins also makes this point: 'The associations between single or working mothers, and the deaths of children were strengthened by the continuing concern with baby-farming, as discourses on bad motherhood obscured the need to address state provision of child care facilities' (2000: 23). This episode in the novel illustrates Sinclair's engagement with the social and gender-political issues of her time, and her challenge to the concept of maternal perfection. The chapter in *Harriett Frean* on Maggie's baby is central to the novel, and provides a harsh contrast to the studied serenity and sheltered existence of Harriett's idealised mother.

By examining representations of the maternal in *Harriett Frean*, and paying particular attention to the hidden and silenced social and cultural aspects of it, the novel opens up a wider analysis of Victorian motherhood and the way in which it continued to affect women in modernism and haunt women's writing in that period. Although published in 1922, Sinclair's *Harriett Frean* is a historical fiction, set in the latter half of the nineteenth century, and this temporal distance draws attention to the unresolved nature of these questions. Harriett's ambivalence regarding mothering and the maternal, especially the visual presence of the maternal body and the affective dimensions of nurturing, draws attention to the taboo of transgressive femininity in Victorian culture. Sinclair's incorporation of the baby-farming storyline emphatically strengthens her novel's critique of the traditional and idealised Victorian construction of motherhood, and instead exposes the complex and grim realities behind that image. *Harriett Frean* employs a lean modernist narrative form which foregrounds the emotional complexity of motherhood through its very sparsity, reminiscent of Imagist textual strategies: 'Use no superfluous word, no adjective which does not reveal something' (Pound 1968: 4).[16] The starkly transgressive, heartbreaking description of the emaciated body of Maggie's dead baby is harshly contrasted with Harriett's memory of the baby when she last saw him, leaving her house, 'She remembered. She remembered. Fat and round in his white shawl and knitted cap when Maggie carried him down the garden path' (Sinclair 1995: 141). The repetition of the phrase 'she remembered' emphasises the compulsive nature of repressed memory and its repetitive return to haunt Harriett through its evocation of powerful or significant moments. The simplicity with which Sinclair conveys Harriett's emotional and affective response makes it all the more poignant when, in the scenes around Maggie's baby and its death, we do get a sense of Harriett's emotional range and intensity. This strategy, in turn, serves to draw the reader's attention to the portrayal, ensuring that the reader remembers even when (or especially when) Harriett attempts to forget. The effect that Sinclair creates can be likened to a crack opening in a curtain, allowing the reader to glimpse another dimension behind it which contradicts the portrayal they are witnessing. This crack or glimpse is comparable to the glimpse Harriett catches of Maggie breastfeeding her baby in the kitchen. Through Harriett's guilt-ridden memories of Maggie's baby and her unsuccessful attempt to banish those memories, the book condemns the practices that tainted Victorian society, and presented a sharp contrast with the sanctioned narrative of Britishness and religious observance of that time. As Dennis Grube notes in his discussion of the construction of Britishness in the Victorian era:

> In Victorian Britain [. . .] successive governments identified a series of religious or moral 'others' who displayed a set of characteristics or behaviours incompatible with 'Britishness'. In doing so they reinforced the identity of the majority of British people as morally upright and religiously acceptable citizens. (Grube 2013: 2)

Harriett Frean gave its contemporary readers a sharp reminder of the repressive and problematic previous historical eras, reminding readers of the many explicit and implicit remnants of those times still present during the modernist era, and warning them of the precarious nature of the freedoms won for women.

Conclusion: Sinclair's Modernist Reassessment of Victorian Maternity

Sinclair's complex textual and thematic engagement with the gender politics of both the Victorian period and her contemporary modernist time centres on the pervasive and insidious nature of patriarchal definitions of maternity and women's sexuality. Stark comments on this aspect of the author's work, stating that:

> In her feminist writings May Sinclair tried to fight these theories which resulted in the widespread attitude of Victorian society that woman was biologically determined and that all her energy should go into bearing and rearing children rather than into any mental activity outside the closely defined domestic limits. (Stark 1992: 278)

Sinclair herself knew the extent to which Victorian values and ideas continued to influence social and cultural constructions of femininity and motherhood into the modernist period. Raitt explains how Sinclair: 'had spent the first four decades of her life struggling with the values of that Victorian world as they were embodied in her mother' (Raitt 2000: 243). In *Harriett Frean* Sinclair offers a creative and critical reassessment of those Victorian values, and critiques the continued impact of those values on her contemporary times. Commenting on Sinclair's portrayal of motherhood, Phillips suggests:

> Harriett's desire for maternity is the only form which her repressed sexuality is allowed to take. The source of her desire for motherhood is clearly her relationship to her own mother, for whom likewise maternity is the only acceptable expression of sexuality. (Phillips 1996: 135)

Harriett Frean suggests that to be a mother is to become a victim. In the context of the Victorian norms Sinclair describes, for a woman to be a mother is to subject herself to submissive silence, erasure of her own needs and desires, and a life spent serving her family. Her examination of the social and cultural conception of motherhood and its literary depiction in *Harriett Frean* confronts us with complex questions and cultural taboos in relation to the maternal, exposing the ways in which mothers were and are circumscribed by patriarchal restrictions on their identity and agency.

In stark contrast to its portrayal of Harriett's and Mamma's secure and privileged well-to-do lives, *Harriett Frean* illustrates to the reader the difficulties of working-class unmarried motherhood, and the awful consequences of baby-farming. Sinclair's choice to incorporate the baby-farming storyline focusing on the death of Maggie's baby illustrates her determination to utilise her writing not simply to experiment technically, but also to draw attention to social and cultural questions through the portrayal of controversial content. *Harriett Frean* reflects Klaver and Rosenman's point that motherhood during this time was far from one-dimensional: 'The Victorian maternal ideal was at once more complex, less stable, less coherent, and less universal than the iconic simplicity it connoted' (Klaver and Rosenman 2008: 12). In her portrayal of motherhood and maternal practices, Sinclair's novel treats the subject of baby-farms in a complex manner that exposes the hypocrisies at the heart of Victorian ideals of femininity and motherhood, and illustrates the problems around representing the maternal body and presence in Victorian and modernist literature. These were controversial questions but Sinclair did not shy away from tackling them, presenting a powerful criticism of the way in which literary narratives perpetuate particular constructions of feminine identity and motherhood, and thereby contribute to the circumscription of women and mothers by patriarchal restrictions on their identity and agency. Sinclair's pursuit of these creative and thematic issues thus resulted in the terse and affective narrative of *Harriett Frean*, which opens up a powerful and deeply unsettling critique of Victorian maternity and its representation in modernism.

Notes

1. From this point onwards the title of the novel is referred to as *Harriett Frean*.
2. I also discuss the question of idealised Victorian maternity in Beyer 2015: 107.
3. An early version of this chapter was presented as a conference paper at the May Sinclair Symposium, 18 July 2014. The paper was entitled: 'Dolls and Dead Babies: May Sinclair's Social Critique of Constructions of Motherhood in *Life and Death of Harriett Frean*'.
4. I have examined the portrayal of baby-farming in contemporary true crime writing, through the prism of 'true crime' narratives; see Beyer 2015. May Sinclair does not use the term 'baby farming' in *Life and Death of Harriett Frean* to describe the plight of Maggie's baby. The events reported in the novel lead me to regard this as a case of baby farming. Penny Brown also refers in passing to the 'woman in the country' as a 'baby-farmer' (Brown 1992: 45). The topic of baby-farming is also addressed by George Egerton

in her turn-of-the-century writing, as Emma Liggins explains; see Liggins 2000.
5. Her treatment of this topic in the novel has received critical attention from Sinclair scholars since the 1990s, notably Suzanne Raitt's 2000 book *May Sinclair: A Modern Victorian* and Terry Phillips's 1996 essay 'Battling with the Angel: May Sinclair's Powerful Mothers'.
6. The focus on mother figures and the maternal in *Life and Death of Harriett Frean* is also reflected in Elizabeth Mosimann's discussion of the novel as 'an anti-Freudian text' (Mosimann 2015: 199) that 'calls attention to the place that will later become essential to analysts' evolving awareness of the mother' (ibid.).
7. See *Mary Olivier: A Life*, in which the motif is used repeatedly to explore maternal corporeality and mother-baby relationship.
8. Pound's phrase is also cited in Raitt 2000: 195.
9. In an article in the *Guardian*, Bella Bathurst discusses the portrayal of 'disappearing mothers' in Victorian photography referring to Linda Fregni Nagler's work: 'To a twenty-first-century viewer, the images look bizarre – all these unsmiling children strangled by smocking and framed by what appears to be a black-draped Grim Reaper, or by an endless succession of figures in carpets and chintz burqas' (Bathurst 2013).
10. Shrock, cited in Todd 1993: 346, n. 21. Specific page reference omitted in Todd's discussion of Shrock's work.
11. See Sinclair's use of the motif of the dead baby in her short story 'The Intercessor' (1911), from *Uncanny Stories*, in which a character, Mrs Falshaw, gives birth to a stillborn baby (214). Claire Drewery discusses this story and its depiction of the dead baby (Drewery 2011: 73).
12. See Beyer 2015; Cossins 2015.
13. I also mention *Harriett Frean* and modernist textual and thematic experimentation in Beyer 2016: 76.
14. See Cossins 2015.
15. Shanley cites J. Brandon Curgenven, *On Baby-Farming and the Registration of Nurses* (London, 1869), p. 3.
16. For a discussion of Sinclair and Imagism, see Raitt 2000: 193–5; Mosimann describes *Harriett Frean* as an 'imagist text' (Mosimann 2015: 197).

Works Cited

Bathurst, Bella (2013), 'The lady vanishes: Victorian photography's hidden mothers', *The Guardian,* 2 December 2013, http://www.theguardian.com/artanddesign/2013/dec/02/hidden-mothers-victorian-photography (last accessed 22 June 2016).
Beyer, Charlotte (2014), 'Dolls and Dead Babies: May Sinclair's Social Critique of Constructions of Motherhood in *Life and Death in Harriett Frean*', paper given at May Sinclair Symposium, 18 July 2014.
Beyer, Charlotte (2015), 'True Crime and Baby Farming: Representing Amelia Dyer', *The Human* 5 (4 August 2015), 101–14, http://human

journal.org/issue-5-crime-writing-special-issue/ (last accessed 22 June 2016).
Beyer, Charlotte (2016), '"With Practised Eyes": Feminine Identity in *The Mysterious Mr Quin*', in J. C. Bernthal (ed.), *The Ageless Agatha Christie: Essays in the Mystery and the Legacy*, Jefferson, NC: McFarland, pp. 61–80.
Brown, Penny (1992), *The Poison at the Source*, Basingstoke: Macmillan.
Childs, Peter (2007), *Modernism and the Post-Colonial: Literature and Empire 1885–1930*, London: Continuum.
Cossins, Annie (2015), *Female Criminality: Infanticide, Moral Panics and the Female Body*, Basingstoke: Palgrave.
Craton, Lillian E. (2008), 'The Widest Lap: Fatness, Fasting, and Nurturance in Nineteenth-Century Fiction', in Ellen Bayuk Rosenman and Claudia C. Klaver (eds), *Other Mothers: Beyond the Maternal Ideal*, Columbus: Ohio State University Press, pp. 291–312.
Drewery, Claire (2011), *Modernist Short Fiction by Women: The Liminal in Katherine Mansfield, Dorothy Richardson, May Sinclair and Virginia Woolf*, Burlington, VT and Farnham: Ashgate.
Eliot, T. S. (1922), *The Waste Land*, http://www.bartleby.com/201/1.html (last accessed 22 June 2016).
'Evangeline: A Tale of Acadie' (n.d.), http://www.hwlongfellow.org/works_evangeline.shtml (last accessed 22 June 2016).
Frost, Ginger (2008), 'Motherhood on Trial: Violence and Unwed Mothers in Victorian England', in Ellen Bayuk Rosenman and Claudia C. Klaver (eds), *Other Mothers: Beyond the Maternal Ideal*, Columbus: Ohio State University Press, pp. 145–62.
Grube, Dennis (2013), *At the Margins of Victorian Britain: Politics, Immorality and Britishness in the Nineteenth Century*, London: I. B. Tauris.
Haydock, James (2008), *On a Darkling Plain: Victorian Poetry and Thought*, Bloomington: AuthorHouse.
Hirsch, Marianne (1989), *The Mother/Daughter Plot: Narrative, Psychoanalysis, Feminism*, Bloomington: Indiana University Press.
Klaver, Claudia C., and Ellen Bayuk Rosenman (2008), 'Introduction,' in Ellen Bayuk Rosenman and Claudia C. Klaver (eds), *Other Mothers: Beyond the Maternal Ideal*, Columbus: Ohio State University Press, pp. 1–22.
Lawrence, D. H. (1930), 'The Virgin and the Gypsy', http://gutenberg.net.au/ebooks03/0301101h.html (last accessed 22 June 2016).
Liggins, Emma (2000), '"With a Dead Child in her Lap": Bad Mothers and Infant Mortality in George Egerton's Discords', *Literature & History* 9:2, 17–36.
Mansfield, Katherine (1920a), 'Bliss', http://www.gutenberg.org/files/44385/44385-h/44385-h.htm. (last accessed 22 June 2016).
Mansfield, Katherine (1920b), 'Miss Brill', http://digital.library.upenn.edu/women/mansfield/garden/brill.html (last accessed 22 June 2016).
Mosimann, Elizabeth A. (2015), 'Postwar New Feminisms: May Sinclair and Colette', in J.-M. Rabaté (ed.), *1922: Literature, Culture, Politics*, New York: Cambridge University Press, pp. 196–208.
Nagler, Linda Fregni (2013), *The Hidden Mother*, London: MACK; Monaco: Nouveau Musée National de Monaco: MACK, http://www.mackbooks.co.uk/books/1006-The-Hidden-Mother.html (last accessed 22 June 2016).

Patmore, Coventry (1854), 'The Angel in the House', http://www.gutenberg.org/ebooks/4099 (last accessed 22 June 2016).
Pease, Allison (2006), 'May Sinclair, Feminism, and Boredom: "A Dying to Live"', *English Literature in Transition, 1880–1920* 49:2, 168–93.
Pound, Ezra (1913), 'A Few Don'ts by an Imagiste', *Poetry* 1 (March 1913), 200–1.
Pound, Ezra [1918] (1954), *Literary Essays of Ezra Pound*, ed. T. S. Eliot, London: Faber and Faber.
Phillips, Terry (1996), 'Battling with the Angel: May Sinclair's Powerful Mothers', in Sarah Sceats and Gail Cunningham (eds), *Image and Power: Women in Fiction in the Twentieth Century*, New York: Longman, pp. 128–38.
Raitt, Suzanne (2000), *May Sinclair: A Modern Victorian*, Oxford: Oxford University Press.
Rosenman, Ellen Bayuk, and Claudia C. Klaver, eds (2008), *Other Mothers: Beyond the Maternal Ideal*, Columbus: Ohio State University Press.
Shanley, Mary Lyndon [1989] (1993), *Feminism, Marriage, and the Law in Victorian England*, Princeton: Princeton University Press.
Shrock, Alice Almond (1974), 'Feminists, Flappers, and the Maternal Mystique: Changing Conceptions of Women and Their Roles in the 1920s', PhD dissertation, University of North Carolina at Chapel Hill.
Sinclair, May [1919] (2002), *Mary Olivier: A Life*, London: Virago Press.
Sinclair, May [1922] (1995), *Life and Death of Harriett Frean*, London: Virago.
Sinclair, May [1923] (2006), 'The Intercessor', in Sinclair, *Uncanny Stories*, London: Wordsworth Editions.
Stark, Susanne (1992), 'Overcoming Butlerian Obstacles: May Sinclair and the Problem of Biological Determinism,' *Women's Studies* vol. 21, 265–83.
Todd, Ellen Wiley (1993), *The 'New Woman' Revised: Painting and Gender Politics on Fourteenth Street*, Berkeley: University of California Press.
Vadillo, Ana Parejo (2015), 'Generational Difference in *To the Lighthouse*', in A. Pease (ed.), *The Cambridge Companion to* To the Lighthouse, New York: Cambridge University Press, pp. 122–35.
Woolf, Virginia (1925), *Mrs Dalloway*, https://ebooks.adelaide.edu.au/w/woolf/virginia/w91md/ (last accessed 22 June 2016).
Woolf, Virginia (1927), *To the Lighthouse*, https://ebooks.adelaide.edu.au/w/woolf/virginia/w91t/ (last accessed 22 June 2016).
Woolf, Virginia (1928), *Orlando*, https://ebooks.adelaide.edu.au/w/woolf/virginia/w91o/ (last accessed 22 June 2016).

Chapter 9

Why British Society Had to 'Get a Young Virgin Sacrificed': Sacrificial Destiny in *The Tree of Heaven*
Sanna Melin Schyllert

Sacrifice is a key concept for May Sinclair, running through many of her fictional, philosophical and political works.[1] The preoccupation with sacrifice in Sinclair's pre-war fiction is particularly noticeable with regard to female characters, and is often related to what was popularly known as the woman question: issues concerning women's role in and outside of the home. This chapter looks at a significant shift in Sinclair's attempts to use and understand sacrifice at the time of the war, and how it is represented in her writing.

Compared to her pre-war writing, Sinclair's conception of sacrifice became increasingly complex in the works composed during and after the First World War. A greater concern with the community on a national level is noticeable in her writings at this time. *The Tree of Heaven* (1917) combines the two issues and is for that reason of particular interest here. The novel primarily centres on the varying effects of war on the different members of the Harrison family, and in this focus, exemplifies Sinclair's increasing tendency to problematise the will of the community versus that of the individual, not only in the context of British society at war, but also within the project of first-wave feminism. In this chapter, I look at Sinclair's treatment of sacrifice in *The Tree of Heaven* as well as in a small selection of her works that precede its publication – *Audrey Craven* (1897), *The Divine Fire* (1904) and 'The Flaw in the Crystal' (1912) – to illustrate and evidence her conflicted stance towards sacrifice.

In an article written in 1912, 'Defence of Men', Sinclair reflects on the notion that women are forced to sacrifice more of themselves than men, and that women for that reason are nearer to spiritual concerns: 'Spirituality, so difficult for [man] to come by, has been positively thrust upon woman. Born of her sacrificial destiny, it has been expected of her, nourished in her, guarded by all the sanctions of her life. She has had time for it, all the time of all the ages' (Sinclair 1912a: 414). This shows that Sinclair had a distinct idea that women are sacrificed, or make sacrifices, on account of their sex, and furthermore that sacrifice is a crucial and unavoidable element of a woman's spirituality; it is her 'destiny.'

Closely tied to the notion of women as more prone to self-sacrifice is Sinclair's understanding and fictional representation of the sublimation of the libido, which was, to her, a fundamental aspect of psychology. To be required to sacrifice one's sexual desire, or in other words to sublimate one's libido, is a fundamental aspect of being a Sinclair heroine. Sublimation is a central psychoanalytical concept that recurs in several of Sinclair's texts, both fictional and otherwise. In 'The Way of Sublimation', an essay on psychoanalysis that was never published, she uses Jung as a stepping stone to outline four possible channels for sublimating the libido, or for dealing with desire – religion, art, science and 'Concrete Activity' – and argues that liberation from one's desires is key for mental health. The term libido is equated here with sexual desire, and even though Sinclair appears to recognise that libido as a concept comes with other connotations, she continues to use it and explains that she 'must adopt it for the present to avoid confusion' (Sinclair c. 1915: 8). One must convert feelings of desire, especially for that which one cannot have, into healthier channels of output; to do otherwise would be savagery, Sinclair implies, writing that '[c]ivilization is one vast system of sublimations' (Sinclair c. 1915: 22).

It would seem then that if one could channel desire into art, the libido would no longer be a problem, but this is not exactly Sinclair's contention; these channels are none of them seen as a definitive solution to the problem of the libido. For Sinclair, the libido is what psychoanalytic theory, and human nature, consists of: '[i]t is the stuff our dreams, our visions and waking, un-directed phantasies are made of' (Sinclair c. 1915: 8). Many of Sinclair's novels deal with the trouble of unsublimated libido, and the clashes that occur when characters submit to their desires. Predictably, however, most of the characters who get into trouble due to libidinous thoughts and acts are women.

Although Sinclair's writing makes it clear that she believed women should have the same rights as men, it is also separatist in its claims that women and men are fundamentally different beings. Sinclair contends in 'Defence of Men' that women are more virtuous than men due to biological circumstances, such as bearing children. These conditions 'demand from [women] an endurance, a devotion, a capacity for self-immolation, which, for the ends of nature and the race, would be not only a superfluous but a suicidal tax upon [man]. [. . .] Primordially and fundamentally the virtue of a woman is not man's, but nature's, care' (Sinclair 1912a: 412–13). In a pamphlet entitled *Feminism* (1912), Sinclair similarly states that women are predominantly in possession of the 'Life-Force' and are thereby more likely than men to attain spiritual enlightenment, but also more likely to become hysterical and neurotic should their flow of Life-Force be obstructed, as is frequently the case. She connects the Life-Force with desire, which in turn is related to sacrifice: '[T]here is voluptuousness in a man's chivalry and in a woman's tenderness, in her very rapture and self-immolation for her lover, her husband, or her child' (Sinclair 1912b: 32). Sinclair goes on to say that the same function that allows one to make sacrifices for a beloved other is at work both in artists and in those who fight for votes for women: '[T]he sublime enthusiasm and self-devotion and self-sacrifice of the suffragists spring from the same root. They will join with the lovers, the musicians, and the saints [...] in praising God for the wonderful root, deep-hidden, that bears the mystic flower' (Sinclair 1912b: 32). This is an echo of the abovementioned 'sacrificial destiny' of women; Sinclair undoubtedly thought not only that women are disposed to make sacrifices, but that there is a beautiful, mysterious and even transcendent quality in those immolating acts.

In *Audrey Craven*, Katherine Haviland is the archetype of a woman who sacrifices herself for her family. She is a promising artist who leaves her more important works unfinished so as to produce 'pot-boilers', that is, commercially viable works of art, in order for her brother to develop his own art. She is portrayed as inherently good and unselfish, and illustrates the message that if only women were not altruistic first and foremost, they could be just as developed in their respective fields as men. In this case, visual art is the occupation and the sacrificial relationship is between two siblings, but one can easily see how this story has similarities with *Mary Olivier*, in which a woman sacrifices her writing and intellectual work for her mother. *Audrey Craven*, then, is an early version of a story that Sinclair would write again and again, albeit in a variety of guises.

This first book also points to the importance of the purity of intention for Sinclair; if a sacrifice is to have a positive outcome, the one who makes it must be fully committed to the act of immolation. Towards the end of the novel, Katherine again sacrifices her work for a man she loves, but this time for romantic reasons. However, she is not described as bitter or regretful of her choice: '[S]he was giving up, not time alone, and thought, and labour, but love – love that could have no certain reward but pain. And she was still content' (Sinclair 1897: 310). Audrey Craven, the vain and self-centred title character who refuses to give up an ounce of her own comfort for the well-being of others, is much less content with her life than Katherine, who seems to gain a sense of self-worth from her sacrifices. Though the novel does not glorify or romanticise her actions, it does justify them by pointing to Katherine's purity of mind and contentment with her lot. They stand out in contrast to Audrey's thoughts, which express self-interest rather than self-immolation: 'She revolted against the cruelty of her lot. [. . .] If she had only been a man, she could have taken her life into her own hands, and shaped it according to her will. But woman, even modern woman, is the slave of circumstances and the fool of fate' (Sinclair 1897: 317). Due to her unwillingness to sacrifice, Audrey is described as a hollow shell of a person, discovering 'bit by bit [. . .] the nothingness that was [the] being [of her character]' (Sinclair 1897: 316).

Sacrifice and purity go hand in hand in several of Sinclair's novels. In 'The Way of Sublimation', Sinclair discusses the concept of ritual sacrifice in relation to purity. She quotes a passage from Jung, in which he in turn quotes an unidentified 'song of triumph of the ascending soul', which unequivocally connects sacrifice to the conception of purity as well as to unity with God. The text describes an impure soul that is washed clean of its sins in the pools 'in which is purified the sacrifice of mankind for the great God who abideth there' (Sinclair c. 1915: 50). Sinclair goes on to regret that Jung is unable to see the spiritual value of this passage and instead chooses to interpret it clinically, declaring the soul ridden with megalomania for wanting to be as one with God. She further states that Jane Harrison explains the origins of sacrificial rite in her work *Prolegomena to Greek Religion*, and elucidates its connection with purity, both spiritual and physical, claiming that the physical need to be purified preceding sacrificial rites came before the idea of spiritual purification (Sinclair c. 1915: 58). Harrison devotes a section of *Prolegomena* to the topic of the Dian fleece, outlining the circumstances of purification rituals and suggesting that the Dian fleece has inherent powers of purification 'in the ancient sense, not to cleanse physically or to purge morally, but to rid of evil influences, of ghostly infection' (Harrison 1908: 27). It seems that Sinclair would, in 'The Flaw in the Crystal' and *The Tree of Heaven* at least, fuse two meanings of purification that Harrison wishes to separate here: the cleansing of moral and ghostly pollution.

As in *Audrey Craven*, *The Divine Fire* also connects purity and sacrifice by demonstrating purification *through* sacrifice, most noticeably in the main plotline that figures the continual self-abnegations of Keith Rickman for the benefit of his beloved Lucia Harden.[2] Rickman is adamant, almost pathologically so, that his actions towards Lucia must remain pure and untainted by any ulterior motives. He expects nothing from her in return for embarking on the quest to repay a debt incurred by her father, despite ruining both his own life and his father's in the process. To other characters in the novel, not to mention to the modern reader, Rickman's chivalry borders on insanity. To him, however, his love for Lucia is something akin to an otherworldly, religious experience: 'In her presence he drifted into a sort of mysticism peculiar to lovers, seeing the hand of a holy destiny in the chance that had seated him beside her' (Sinclair 1904: 363). It is worth sacrificing anything and everything for this kind of love, just as it is worth making sacrifices for the 'divine fire,' Rickman's appellation of his own creative genius. As opposed to Sinclair's heroines, Rickman does not have to choose between love and art. In the end, Rickman comes to the realisation that his talent for writing and his love for Lucia are of the same origin: 'Yes, love too was the wind of the divine spirit blowing where it listeth, the kindling of the divine fire' (Sinclair 1904: 575). The love Rickman feels becomes sacred, as does Lucia herself, to the point where he venerates things that she has touched almost as relics. Faced with a dinner table that Lucia has laid with her own hands, Rickman imagines that '[t]hese things, in her hands and his eyes, became sacramental, symbolic of Lucia's soul with its pure thoughts and beautiful beliefs, its inspired and burning charities' (Sinclair 1904: 608). Lucia, idolised and sanctified, can turn an ordinary and rather humble dinner into something suggestive of the last supper.

In order to be worthy of the object of his affections, Rickman believes that he has to make himself pure of mind and soul. Therefore he sets out to sacrifice everything – his reputation, livelihood, family, friends and even his genius – for Lucia. Here, the total annihilation of the self for a loved one is treated as more of an unhealthy obsession than in previous novels. Rickman's sacrifice is not demanded by society, but by himself; it is the result of his personal adoration and consecration of Lucia.

In the short story 'The Flaw in the Crystal' – first published in 1912 as a novella and subsequently in the collection *Uncanny Stories* (1923) – self-sacrifice is connected with purity of mind, but here it is more overtly connected to ridding oneself of the libido. Agatha, an unmarried woman who possesses healing powers that can be worked telepathically, has to sacrifice her sexual desire for the man she loves, Rodney, in order to keep her spiritual skill 'clean'. Her acceptance of the demand to give up her love is caused by a fear of impurity of mind, which she believes will cause her to go insane as well as lose her psychical command over others. Here, it seems, is an early instance of sacrifice of the self for a community, however small.

As in many of Sinclair's narratives, sacrifice, purity and communal spirit are strongly linked in 'The Flaw in the Crystal'. In order to be a productive member of society, it is necessary to redirect or sacrifice the libido, through which action purification will be achieved. Desire needs to be sublimated if it is not to interfere with both the freedom of the individual, and the place of that individual within a community, as Agatha comes to realise towards the end of the story.

Sexual desire is a significant factor in the story, and it is clearly tied to the notions of sacrifice and purity. Rodney and Agatha never consummate their liaison physically, although there is a strong attachment between them. At the beginning of the story they have yet to declare their romantic attraction outright to one another, although it is shown through their discussion of the arrival of two friends of Agatha's, the Powells. Rodney is anxious about the possibility that their secret meetings be 'found out' by the Powells. Agatha responds that even if they were to be discovered together, they have nothing to hide. She goes on to reflect on her own, enforced, purity of mind: 'She had always met him, and would always have to meet him, with the idea that there was nothing in it; for, if she once admitted that there was anything, then they *were* done for. She couldn't (how could she?) let him keep on coming with that thought in him, acknowledged by them both' (Sinclair 1923: 72, emphasis original). Not only does Agatha feel the need to curb her own feelings, but she puts it upon herself to control Rodney's thoughts on this point.

Agatha's sacrifice of the libido is prompted by a fear of impurity. When she decides to try to heal Harding Powell of his mental illness through her telepathy, her mind is revealed as tainted, presumably by her sexual desire for Rodney, since that is what she is asked to renounce. The madness from which Harding previously suffered now begins to afflict Agatha. She starts to show the same symptoms that he had before his healing: paranoia, anxiety and feelings of unreality: '[S]he was afraid of being afraid. Harding was the object of a boundless and indestructible compassion, and her fear of him was hateful to her and unholy. She knew that it would be terrible to let it follow her into that darkness where she would presently go down with him alone' (Sinclair 1923: 113). Agatha experiences a total loss of control, both over herself and over the spiritual powers that work through her. She is unable to sleep, as her nights are given over to a never-ending spiritual power struggle between her and Harding. She tries to let go of the telepathic hold on him, but he has come into a spiritual power of his own and leeches on to her, tainting Agatha's mind with his illness: 'It was terrible; for he clung. [. . .] He hung on desperately; he refused to yield an inch of the ground he had taken from her. He was no longer a passive thing in that world where she had brought him' (Sinclair 1923: 123–4). Knowing that Agatha is responsible for the maintenance of his health, Harding clings to her telepathically and forces her to sever her psychic ties to Rodney, which leads to the rapid decline in health of the latter.

Agatha believes that she has been made susceptible to Harding's takeover due to an impurity that has crept into her system, the flaw in the crystal: her desire for Rodney. Her only hope of getting out is to cleanse herself, to make her spirit, the crystal, pure again.[3] Harding has poisoned her from the inside, but he was only able to do so because of her initial, libidinous relationship with Rodney, which is the flaw in the crystal: 'It was the strain of mortality in her love for Rodney [. . .] It had been there all the time, undermining her secret, sacred places' (Sinclair 1923: 136). Agatha realises that her desire is weakening her psychic power and, as a result, she is made susceptible to the spiritual abuse perpetrated by Harding.

This violation shows that the significance of sex in the story is not limited to the need for Agatha to sacrifice her libido. The description of the spiritual invasion, and Agatha's need to cleanse herself after these nightly hauntings, is heavily suggestive of sexual violence. Agatha's feelings of horror are suggestive of a violation similar to rape: 'The awful thing was that she knew she could not get away from him. She had only to close her eyes and she would find the visible image of him hanging before her on the wall of darkness' (Sinclair 1923: 113). Although the two are not physically in bed together, the articulation of Agatha's experiences does imply that she feels as though they were: 'In the morning she woke with a sense, which was almost a memory, of Harding having been in the room with her all night' (Sinclair 1923: 113). Words like 'broken in' (Sinclair 1923: 122), 'enter' (Sinclair 1923: 125) and 'penetrated' (Sinclair 1923: 123) are used to describe what Harding does to Agatha: '*He* was in her' (Sinclair 1923: 117, emphasis original).

The nightly scenes with Harding implicitly criticise sexual morals and the paradoxes underlying them, as Agatha is spiritually infiltrated against her will because her purity is not intact, which makes her even more impure; her desire for Rodney has left her open to invasion by another man. Despite never having acted on her desire, Agatha is still punished for experiencing the emotion and even entertaining the thought of an affair with the married Rodney. It is not enough, then, for her to renounce an illicit sexual relationship; her purity of mind must also be immaculate. Agatha is tempted to give in to Rodney's wishes and live with him even though she feels hesitant about the decision. That is where she, according to the morals that seem to be propounded by the text, goes wrong: she cannot let herself even entertain the thought of being Rodney's mistress if she is to remain entirely pure. She has to be absolutely irreprehensible in spirit, mind and body. Otherwise, she will have to endure the loss of her grip on Rodney's health and remain susceptible to another man's madness and spiritual imprisonment, due to her loss of purity. Therefore Agatha has to give up her feelings for Rodney entirely in order to regain herself from the clutches of Harding.

Sinclair deploys a supernatural force to effect the sacrifice and solve Agatha's problem. When struggling to take back control of her psychic world, Agatha has a vision of a 'Something' that speaks to her, a messenger of an unspecified 'high and holy Power' (Sinclair 1923: 125). The voice explains to her that she has overstepped a boundary in trying to work her healing power as she wishes, by choosing to heal Rodney before others.

Given that Agatha's desire has clouded her judgement as regards the usage of her psychic power, the story can be read as proposing to place the importance of the community above the individual. A free libido wreaks havoc in a community because it causes one individual to desire another individual, which creates conflict.[4] The purpose of the sacrifice is, then, not only to sublimate the libido for its own sake, but presumably also so that Agatha can put her powers to use for everyone equally.

In order for Agatha to retain her power to help others by way of her telepathy, she has to sacrifice her own needs. It is regarded as a necessity that the thing sacrificed is Agatha's desire. As the mysterious voice clarifies, she cannot give up her self instead of giving up her desire of Rodney: 'It is not enough to give yourself for Rodney Lanyon, for he is more to you than you are yourself. Besides, any substitution of self for self would be useless, for there is no more self there' (Sinclair 1923: 125). Sinclair suggests that giving up the self is easier than, or at the very least equal to, the renunciation of one's desires. This concern with the self and its affinity with desire is reminiscent of idealist philosophy, a topic on which Sinclair was well versed.

As with psychoanalytic theory, Sinclair frequently used the standpoint of idealist thought in both her fiction and other work. The tenets of idealism are somewhat ambiguous on the subject of individual freedom versus the common good. While it is maintained that the individual consciousness has the right to exercise complete freedom, it is also stated that the subjective will ought to coincide with the communal will. In other words, individual freedom ought to be exercised by those wills that are compliant with what is good for the society of which they are part.[5] Idealist morality builds on the principle that the common good must decide what is good for the individual and what it should want.

Sinclair uses this assumption in, for instance, *Feminism*, where she justifies the political activism of suffragists by arguing that their methods are legitimised by the virtue of their purpose: to secure women's equal rights, which Sinclair regarded as contributing to the communal good.

Sinclair's interest in idealism, and especially the work of T. H. Green, laid the foundations for her own treatise on the subject, *A Defence of Idealism* (1917). Self-sacrifice and self-realisation are two basic concepts that are intertwined in both Green and Sinclair's respective idealisms. It is argued both by George M. Johnson (2005: 17–18) and Hrisey D. Zegger (1976: 19–22) that Sinclair drew on Green's work when maintaining that the road to self-realisation is through self-sacrifice. Green posits in his *Prolegomena to Ethics* that 'a perfecting of *man*' can only be achieved in 'a life determined by [. . .] a will of all which is the will of each' (Green 2003: 342), that is, a surrender of the individual will to the communal good. Sinclair stresses the importance of selfhood, but also of individuality as 'only one stage, and that not the highest and the most important stage, in the real life-process of the self'. She continues: 'It may be that a self can only become a perfect self in proportion as it takes on the experiences of other selves. [. . .] The individual [. . .] may have to die that the self may live' (Sinclair 1917a: 375). Sinclair considers individuality to be lesser than the selfhood that comes out of sharing 'the experiences of other selves'. However, any and all sacrifice does not perfect the self; it has to bring the self into an intersubjective or 'spiritual' union with other consciousnesses, with a world-consciousness, or world-spirit. A sacrifice that does not is not beneficial to the self-realisation of the one that makes the sacrifice. In this view, then, self-sacrifice is not just made for the sake of a cause that is bigger than oneself, but also in order to achieve the realisation of one's own self.

The connection between self-sacrifice and self-realisation is explored in *The Tree of Heaven*, a novel that is deeply concerned with the issue of the benefit of the community versus that of the individual. It also displays a curious connection between religion and feminism, as the consequences of being involved with the women's suffrage movement bring about a moment of spiritual revelation for one of the main characters, Dorothea Harrison, or Dorothy as she is sometimes called, who finds herself locked up in prison for having taken part in a rally organised by the Women's Franchise Union. In her cell, she feels that she knows what it must be to live like nuns do, 'when they've given up everything and shut themselves up with God' (Sinclair 1917b: 192). Dorothy not only has the feeling of being in a convent cell rather than a prison cell, but she is happy to be in it. Her need to find both solitude and self-sacrifice in order to come close to the ultimate reality of existence has briefly been met, and she now feels that she is part of something great, much greater than the Women's Franchise Union. This culminates in her vision of 'the redeemed of the Lord' (Sinclair 1917b: 193).

Sacrificing herself for the cause of universal suffrage means forsaking her personal freedom and the comforts of her home, but this is no hardship for Dorothy. Instead, it instils in her a sense of fulfilment and peace. The experience gives her a sense of spiritual exultation, a 'deep-down unexcited happiness' that stays with her even after she is released (Sinclair 1917b: 192). It is, however, crucial that she gets to be alone in her prison cell: '[A]fter the crowds of women [. . .] that cell was like heaven. Thank God, it's always solitary confinement' (Sinclair 1917b: 191). Being locked up with fellow suffrage activists would clearly be a far greater punishment in Dorothy's eyes and could possibly have prevented her moment of spiritual insight.

As several critics have previously pointed out, Dorothy's prison revelation marks the beginning of her movement away from the collective feminist project and towards an individualistic spirituality.[6] At a women's suffrage banquet, where most of the other participants behave as though they are at a revival meeting, Dorothy is 'fascinated and horrified' (Sinclair 1917b: 196) at the communal display of enchantment with and dedication to their cause. It is only in the stillness of her cell that Dorothy can find that same feeling of true exultation. At the banquet, which is a milieu that is diametrically opposed to that of a prison or a convent cell, the mood of rapture is so far removed from her that she is almost disgusted with the displays of emotion around her. In the cell, self-sacrifice is prompted by her enforced situation and surroundings and thereby inescapable. Dorothy needs to be engaged in self-sacrifice in order to be spiritually aware. This can be seen in other works by Sinclair, for example the two aforementioned works *The Divine Fire* and 'The Flaw in the Crystal,' as well as in *Mary Olivier*, in which the eponymous heroine finds her spiritual awakening through giving up romantic love.

An additional indication of this is that she has another epiphany, several years later, when her fiancé Captain Drayton comes to tell her that he has been ordered to ship out to war on the very day that they are to be married. Realising that she will have to renounce the man she loves for the sake of the country, Dorothy has a strong experience of what she calls 'reality': '[. . .] suddenly her soul swung round [. . .] There was something [. . .] tremendous. It came to her with the power and sweetness of first passion; but without its fear [. . .] Her swinging soul was steady; it vibrated to an intenser rhythm. [. . .] It was Reality itself' (Sinclair 1917b: 273). This lasts for only an instant, but the memory of it stays with her, like the memory of her vision in prison.

The prison experience also highlights a newfound enjoyment of life's smaller things, such as one would expect of a person who has grown up in a comfortable way, never being deprived of anything and never having to fear deprivation, and who has then lived through a month in prison. Her wish upon release is not to see her fiancé or to go home, but primarily for a cup of coffee and a bun; when Captain Drayton tells her that he 'want[s] to talk [. . .] seriously', she responds: 'I don't mind how seriously you talk if I may go on eating' (Sinclair 1917b: 186). Grounding herself in the physical, Dorothy finds a new outlet for spiritual euphoria in seeking out individual pleasure: 'Did you ever smell anything like this lane? [. . .] If epicures had any imagination they'd go out and obstruct policemen and get put in prison for the sake of the sensations they'd have afterwards' (Sinclair 1917b: 186). The enjoyment of such a basic, sensory experience – consuming food in a beautiful green lane – outweighs anything that Drayton could have to say about their relationship, to the point where Dorothy hardly listens to him at all. His petty, mundane concerns are trifles next to what she has experienced while in prison. The thing that Dorothy has 'got hold of', which is 'bigger than' Frank not being able or even wanting to marry her, is universal freedom. In what seems to be a prophetic vision inspired by her reading of the Bible, Dorothy has seen 'the redeemed of the Lord [. . .] men, as well as women [. . .] [a]nd they were all free' (Sinclair 1917b: 193).

Dorothy's ideas echo those expressed by Sinclair on this point; feminism is a cause worth fighting for, as it is part of the higher purpose of freedom for all. Sinclair assumes the position that the common good must decide what is best for the individual and what the individual should want in her pamphlet *Feminism*. Justifying the political activism of suffragists, she argues that their methods are legitimised by virtue of their purpose: to secure equality for women on all counts. Sinclair regarded this as a purpose that would benefit the community, because, as she writes, '*equal rights for women will mean equal rights for all*' (Sinclair 1912b: 36, emphasis original).[7] Dorothy is apparently at a stage of individualism during her time in prison, but she is also prepared to sacrifice her own well-being for the sake of a higher cause: freedom for all.

The reader is exposed to another angle of sacrifice through Veronica, Dorothy's cousin and later sister-in-law, who is described as a sacrificial victim on several occasions by other characters in the text. During the suffragist procession that takes place after her sojourn in prison, Dorothy remarks that Veronica 'was slender and beautiful and pure, like some sacrificial virgin. [. . .] She would carry a thin, tall pole, with a round olive wreath on the top of it, and a white dove sitting in the ring of the olive wreath' (Sinclair 1917b: 198). Veronica is already here seen as a harbinger of the peace that is eventually to come, as is heralded by her regalia of a white dove and an olive branch. Her own point of view of the procession, however, intimates her status as a perceiving, inviolable subject:

> She was not afraid of the procession, or of the soul of the procession. [...] Her soul was by itself. Like Dorothea's soul it went apart from the soul of the crowd and the soul of the procession. [...] And with the first beat of the drum Veronica's soul came down from its place, and took part in the procession. As long as they played the Marseillaise she felt that she could march with the procession to the ends of the world. [...] And Veronica, marching in front of them by herself, sang another song. She sang the Marseillaise of Heine and of Schubert. (Sinclair 1917b: 200–2)[8]

The very same quality that lets Veronica stand apart from the crowd, just as Dorothy chooses to do, also enables her to lend herself and her soul to the feminist cause and its procession. In later editions the word 'procession' is written with a capital 'P', which suggests that it is to be observed as an entity in itself: a Procession that, while consisting of a number of individuals, nevertheless has a life of its own. While the gaze of others identifies Veronica as a representation of the bloom of British youth, she claims her own subjective space in the communal singing by swapping the Marseillaise for Schumann's *Die Beiden Grenadiere*, emitting a curious omen of what is to come. It is only because she is able to rise up above the masses and her soul goes 'alone in utter freedom' (Sinclair 1917b: 199) that she can be objectified by onlookers as the peace-bringing sacrificial virgin.

Veronica is continually described as having supernatural powers. She is able to portend the future, see ghosts and accurately perceive other people's thoughts and feelings in a way that prompts all those around her to stand in awe of her 'mysterious quality' (Sinclair 1917b: 229). She also appears to have healing powers, which are materialised in the sudden health and well-being of her elderly great-aunts, as perceived by her aunt Frances, who comments that 'It's wonderful what Veronica does to them' (Sinclair 1917b: 231). Veronica's cousin Michael, however, is less inclined to view it as a good thing, and refers to it rather as a sort of leeching of her youth: 'It's horrible. [...] You mustn't let them get hold of you. [...] They feed on you, Ronny. I can see it by the way they look at you. You'll die of them if you don't give it up. [...] They're vampires. They'll suck your life out of you' (Sinclair 1917b: 232–3). His warnings to Veronica are unheeded, however, as the girl herself is entirely unperturbed by the effect she has on the older women. In fact, she enjoys being able to be of service to them and delights in thinking that she can give some pleasure to those who are termed '[g]hosts among living people'. She tells Michael: 'Can't you see how awful it must be for them to be ghosts? [. . .] Everybody afraid of them – not wanting them' (Sinclair 1917b: 234). If Veronica indeed does see herself as a victim of spongers draining her of her life force, then she is apparently happy to be of use to them. She feels sorry for them, lamenting their decrepitude and obsolescence, and does not seem to be bothered by any concern for herself. She gives up her vitality for them, and does not display any bitterness or resentment, only a willingness to sacrifice.

Michael states explicitly that Veronica is a sacrificial object here. In doing so, he evokes a sense of ritual sacrifice: 'They were all old, horribly old and done for, ages ago. [. . .] But they know that if they can get a young virgin sacrificed to them they'll go on. You're the young virgin. You're making them go on' (Sinclair 1917b: 233). Veronica's sacrifice extends far beyond the welfare of the haggard great-aunts; it is emblematic of a much larger event, one which at the time when Sinclair was writing this was already under way, but in the story is just about to start: the First World War.

In November 1914, Sinclair addressed the tension between the war and the women's movement in the article 'Women's Sacrifices for the War', first published in *Collier's Magazine*. She points to work done by organisations previously engaged in the fight for women's votes, stressing their promptness in giving up their original work in order to devote their time and efforts to the more pressing needs of the nation. She also discusses the consequences of women holding men's jobs during wartime, noting the inevitable implication that it is now impossible to claim that women are unable or unfit to do these jobs. However, Sinclair does not perceive this as an immediate benefit to the women's movement:

> It may be that, when it comes to women's sacrifices, the sacrifice required of them may be just this: to withdraw from any field where their competition will be disastrous to men. [. . .] During and immediately after the war, women, in spite of all their services, will have, as a sex, to take a comparatively humble place in popular estimation. The 'woman's movement' will receive a temporary check, though women's work is becoming more valuable every day. As for women's claims, they will be nowhere. In war time there is a general disposition to rate woman, who is not a fighting unit, low. (Sinclair 1914: 25)

Sinclair still asserts that the timing of the war is fortunate, both for the nation and for women, as it has provisionally solved the problem of militant activists fighting for suffrage, as well as placed women in a position to demonstrate their ability in the workforce. As in *The Tree of Heaven*,

Sinclair voices ambivalent thoughts about the coinciding conflicts within and outside of the nation here.

'Women's Sacrifices for the War' reiterates Sinclair's essentialist notions of the difference between sacrifice made by women versus men, previously expressed in *Feminism* and 'Defence of Men', but with a significant change as a consequence of the war context; sacrifices made by women are no longer valued as they were before. In the final paragraphs of the article, Sinclair maintains that women's efforts in wartime are as important as those of men, although they may be different. Women may be forbidden from spilling their blood in the trenches, but they 'are taking part in it as far as they can'. She wishes, however, to renounce the word 'sacrifice' when speaking of women's war work and to replace it with 'service'. Her reason for this is that '[s]acrifice is what is always expected of women' (Sinclair 1914: 25). Service, as opposed to sacrifice, is a concept that has no connotations of spirituality or morality, and should therefore imply a less deep and meaningful investment on the part of the individual. Sinclair, however, does not see it that way; here, the idea is that if one is merely making a sacrifice because it is in one's nature, then that is a less honourable offering than actively choosing to do service.

Sinclair's discussion of these terms displays a crucial turning point in her view of sacrifice. The inference here is that service suggests a purpose, whereas sacrifice has a conceivable meaning of being unintentional and simply habitual. Sinclair argues that service is primarily associated with the duty of men and is therefore taken more seriously, whereas sacrifice is mainly linked to women and is thus not as highly valued. Also, service implies an active stance, while sacrifice is connected to passivity. As Sinclair points out, sacrifice can be both voluntary and involuntary, but for women it is *expected*. It is further implied that voluntary sacrifice is admirable, whereas involuntary sacrifice is merely part of what it is to be a woman.

The presentation of sacrifice as opposed to service in this article, published at the very beginning of the war, is a far cry from the image of women's sacrifice given in *Feminism* and 'Defence of Men', where Sinclair presupposes women's innate tendency to make sacrifices as something positive, not only for women as individuals who may attain a high level of spiritual fulfilment, but also for the community that benefits from these sacrifices. The war has brought a change in perspective on this issue, a change that is illustrated in the way that the characters in *The Tree of Heaven* struggle with the conceptions of sacrifice and service.

The Tree of Heaven, as an illustration of both first-wave feminist activism and wartime losses, exemplifies the expectation that people who are part of a community are to make sacrifices for their cause or their country. Dorothy's involvement in and subsequent disgust with political activism makes the novel a prime example of Sinclair's ambivalent attitude towards sacrifice, and particularly sacrifice for ideological purposes. The simultaneous understanding and condemnation of Michael's reluctance to fight in the war is also a good illustration of this. The author's personal attitude towards both suffragism and the war was alternately positive and negative; she regarded violence on both the intranational and the international level as a necessary evil, and a provisional solution to the problems with which British society was faced in the early twentieth century. Just as Veronica feels the need to heal the old great-aunts, and indeed redeem the whole Harrison family by way of sacrificing herself, so too had the citizens of Britain to go into war service in order to save their country. Even Dorothy, whose disdain for the communal has been well established, wishes that she could go and fight in the trenches: 'Her hidden self was unsatisfied; it had a monstrous longing. It wanted to go where the guns sounded and the shells burst [. . .]' (Sinclair 1917b: 263). But Dorothy does not get to sacrifice herself in the trenches, since the struggle for equality between the sexes was destined to last a lot longer than the First World War.

The change in Sinclair's understanding of sacrifice at the time of the war is, as I have shown, displayed in her writing, both fictional and otherwise. Sinclair's texts written around the time of the war exhibit the opposition between the needs of the community and that of the individual, which is an issue that comes to the fore in times of national crisis. The concept of sacrifice, then, is not only central to Sinclair's work, but evolves with it through the early decades of the twentieth century.

Notes

1. Jean Radford points out in the final paragraph of her 1980 preface to *Mary Olivier: A Life* (1919) that the concept is central throughout Sinclair's oeuvre, and aptly exemplifies this with an excerpt from the poem 'Helen:' '[. . .] for I know|That love is not the whole of woman's life|Nor yet of man's, but there are higher things – |Devotion – honour – faith – self-sacrifice' (unpaginated).
2. Keith Rickman is not the only male self-sacrificial character in Sinclair's oeuvre. *The Combined Maze* (1913) exemplifies another male sacrifice, in which Ranny gives up his life, love and health for the sake of propriety.
3. Crystals are commonly used by Sinclair as symbols for the consciousness,

mind or soul. The clarity, brilliance and translucence of crystals reflect the same qualities inherent in an enlightened mind or soul in such texts as *Mary Olivier* (211; 254; 314; 339–40) and *The Dark Night* (16–17).
4. René Girard's theory of scapegoating proposes that scapegoats are needed to control the constant build-up of violence in society due to mimetic desire, the inclination to want what others have. Girard builds on Hegel in considering desire to be a fundamental drive that feeds into the dialectic of power relations: one individual wants what the other has and vice versa, thereby creating tension and ultimately conflict. See Girard 1977: 169 and Girard 2003: 7–29.
5. See for instance Hegel 2003: 301–2; 351–2.
6. See for example Stempel Mumford 1989 or Ouditt 1994 for a discussion of Dorothy's movement away from feminism in favour of the 'vortex' of war; and Forster 2000 or Law 1997 for discussions of her individualistic spirituality. Law argues that the description of Dorothy's experience can be read as influenced by mysticism (126).
7. Sinclair is primarily referring to economic equality in this passage, but argues throughout the pamphlet that feminism does not only stand to benefit women but men as well, to just as high a degree.
8. The composer of the piece is in fact Schumann, not Schubert. This mistake is amended in later editions.

Works Cited

Drewery, Claire (2011a), '"The failure of this now so independently assertive reality": Mysticism, idealism and the reality aesthetic', *Pilgrimages: A Journal of Dorothy Richardson Studies* 4, 112–36.

Drewery, Claire (2011b), *Modernist Short Fiction by Women: The Liminal in Katherine Mansfield, Dorothy Richardson, May Sinclair and Virginia Woolf*, Burlington, VT and Farnham: Ashgate.

Forster, Laurel (2000), 'The Life of the Mind: Psychic Explorations in the Work of May Sinclair', PhD dissertation, University of Sussex.

Girard, René (1977), *Violence and the Sacred*, trans. Patrick Gregory, Baltimore and London: Johns Hopkins University Press.

Girard, René (2003), *Things Hidden Since the Foundation of the World*, trans. Stephen Bann and Michael Metteer, London: Continuum.

Green, T. H. [1883] (2003), *Prolegomena to Ethics*, ed. David O. Brink, Oxford: Clarendon Press.

Harrison, Jane (1908), *Prolegomena to the Study of Greek Religion*, Cambridge: Cambridge University Press.

Hegel, G. W. F. (2003), *The Phenomenology of Mind*, trans. J. B. Baille, Mineola, NY: Dover Publications.

Johnson, George M. (2005), *Dynamic Psychology in Modern British Fiction*, Basingstoke: Palgrave Macmillan.

Law, S. A. J. (1997), 'Ecriture Spirituelle: the Mysticism of Evelyn Underhill, May Sinclair and Dorothy Richardson,' PhD dissertation, Queen Mary, University of London.

Ouditt, Sharon (1994), *Fighting Forces, Writing Women*, London: Routledge.
Pippin, Robert B. (1997), *Idealism as Modernism: Hegelian Variations*, Cambridge: Cambridge University Press.
Radford, Jean (1994), 'Introduction' in May Sinclair, *Mary Olivier: A Life*, London: Virago.
Sinclair, May (1897), *Audrey Craven*, Edinburgh and London: William Blackwood and Sons.
Sinclair, May (1904), *The Divine Fire*, London: Archibald Constable and Co.
Sinclair, May (1912a), 'A Defence of Men', *The Forum* 48 (October 1912), 409–20.
Sinclair, May (1912b), *Feminism*, London: The Women Writers' Suffrage League.
Sinclair, May (1914), 'Women's sacrifices for the war', *Collier's*, 21 November 1914, http://catalog.hathitrust.org/Record/009038258 (last accessed 22 June 2016).
Sinclair, May (1915), *Journal of Impressions in Belgium*, London: Hutchinson & Co.
Sinclair, May (c. 1915), 'The Way of Sublimation', May Sinclair Collection, Rare Book and Manuscript Library, University of Pennsylvania, Box 23, Folders 436–8.
Sinclair, May (1917a), *A Defence of Idealism*, London: Macmillan & Co.
Sinclair, May (1917b), *The Tree of Heaven*, London: Cassell & Co.
Sinclair, May [1919] (2002), *Mary Olivier: A Life*, London: Virago Press.
Sinclair, May (1923), 'The Flaw in the Crystal', in Sinclair, *Uncanny Stories*, London: Hutchinson & Co.
Sinclair, May (1924), *The Dark Night*, London: Cape.
Stempel Mumford, Laura (1989), 'May Sinclair's *The Tree of Heaven*: The vortex of feminism, the community of war', in Helen Margaret Cooper, Adrienne Auslander Munich and Susan Merrill (eds), *Arms and the Woman: War, Gender, and Literary Representation*, Chapel Hill and London: University of North Carolina Press, pp. 168–83.
Troy, Michele K. (2006), 'A very "Un-English" English writer: May Sinclair's early reception in Europe', in Andrew J. Kunka and Michele K. Troy (eds), *May Sinclair: Moving Towards the Modern*, Aldershot: Ashgate, pp. 23–48.
Zegger, Hrisey D. (1976), *May Sinclair*, Boston: Twayne.

Chapter 10

'Odd How the War Changes Us': May Sinclair and Women's War Work

Emma Liggins

On arrival in Belgium in 1914, May Sinclair waited expectantly to hear what kinds of work would be assigned to the five women and nine men of Hector Munro's Ambulance Corps, whether it be managing the wards, stretcher-bearing or other 'suitable feminine tasks' (Sinclair 1915a: 23) in the hospital. In her autobiographical account of her war experience, *A Journal of Impressions in Belgium* (1915), she described herself as 'utterly submissive' to the 'Power' of the male Commandant, who might well think, 'what the devil are [five women] doing in a field ambulance?' (Sinclair 1915a: 23) and send them back to England. This was her chance to take her place alongside brothers, uncles and nephews who had performed military service, an escape from her 'irrelevant former self' (Sinclair 1915a: 24) as spinster novelist.

Although middle-class women had been entering the labour force in much larger numbers since the end of the nineteenth century, the opportunities available to them to take on jobs left vacant by men, or to work alongside men on the Front, were unprecedented. Women therefore became increasingly scornful of work seen as suitably feminine: 'Odd how the War changes us', concludes Sinclair in her new role as war correspondent (Sinclair 1915a: 23). According to historian Janet S. K. Watson, attitudes to war work between 1914 and 1918 need to be positioned 'along a spectrum of ideas about work and service' (Watson 2004: 5), in order to consider the contribution made by women. She argues that 'women could only be equal-but-different, and their efforts were always perceived as those of women in particular, not just citizens' (Watson 2004: 7). In 'Women's Sacrifices for the War', an article commissioned for the magazine *Woman at Home* in 1915, Sinclair emphasised the new value of women's work in the context of the suffrage movement, and shifted the emphasis from the notion of sacrifice, 'what is always expected of women', to service, aligning 'woman at her best' with the British soldier (Sinclair 1915b: 11, 7). In Virginia Woolf's radically pacifist essay *Three Guineas* (1938), women's participation in the war is denounced as a misguided and dangerous acceptance of militarism, brought about by the British woman's 'loathing' for the confinement of the private home: the rush to volunteer for service abroad; 'that amazing outburst in 1914', showed that 'unconsciously [women] desired our splendid war' (Barrett 1993: 160–1). Usurping men's roles in the public arena was dangerous not only because it threatened gender hierarchies, but because it posed uncomfortable questions about women's patriotism and citizenship, their potential 'desire' for war.

Agnes Cardinal, Dorothy Goldman and Judith Hattaway have written of 'the complexity and moral ambiguity of women's responses to war', noting the diverse ways in which 'women experienced the war, created their own cultural myths, and, during and after the conflict, assumed new roles in the national culture' (Cardinal et al. 2004: 6). These new roles occupied by women included the figure of the ambulance driver, who became as necessary as the nurse in her contribution to ministering to the wounded. This chapter considers May Sinclair's representations of the female ambulance driver in the light of contemporary debates around women's war work, arguing that scenes which depict the driving of ambulances, and collecting the wounded, are used to stage conflicts over gendered notions of service and power. The uniformed woman ambulance driver, both a new type of female masculinity and an erotic object, threatens conceptualisations of female sexuality. Developing critical discussions of Sinclair as a writer of spinster fiction, I address the ways in which unmarried heroines negotiate their non-combatant outsider position in *The Tree of Heaven* (1917) and *The Romantic* (1920). Whilst both texts reproduce the propagandist rhetoric of 'the glamour of the Front' (Sinclair 1917: 187), the lesser-known later novel, set primarily in Belgium, allows its ambulance-driver heroine to show her ability to fill men's places without returning her to domesticity. The inability of the woman war worker to return to obsolete ideologies of femininity comes to symbolise the dangerous political repercussions of broadening the field of women's work.

Women's War Work and Patriotism

In non-fiction writing of the 1910s and 1920s, women's war work has connotations of adventure, liberation and danger, as well as mercy, patriotism and citizenship. Doing 'man's work' is a sign that woman 'has won her place in the State', according to the editor of *Women War Workers* (1917), proving that 'this is not a "men's war" [. . .] but one in which both sexes throughout the Empire must share the burden and responsibilities' (Stone 1917: 11, 5). Nurses, munitions workers, ambulance-drivers and the 'splendid' women in the Voluntary Aid Detachment (VADs) are to be celebrated for their unselfish demonstration of their fitness to work, with both men and women addressed through the rhetoric of 'slacking': 'the discipline which the war has brought to so many of us ought to leave the world with fewer slackers' (Stone 1917: 201). In the opening pages of her memoir *A VAD in France* (1917), Olive Dent recorded her enthusiasm for 'foreign service' after seeing the 'battered bodies' of 'our boys' coming back from the war: 'England had taken and broken them, and still there were so many of us women doing nothing of value, nothing that counted' (Dent 1917: 5). The new responsibilities of war service include a denial of the fripperies of conventional femininity: on arrival in France her group of VADs 'shop-gazed' at a 'delectable blouse' before 'we scolded ourselves, – for this was only our second day in uniform, – and whipped the offending Eve out of us' (Dent 1917: 10). In her famous war memoir *Testament of Youth* (1933), Vera Brittain described the necessary transition from knitting socks and 'twenty years of sheltered gentility' to 'the finest work any girl can do now' (Brittain 1933: 213) as a VAD nurse in a British hospital. She added, 'not being a man and able to go to the front, I wanted to do the next best thing [. . .] really the work is not too hard' (Brittain 1933: 214), a sentiment linked to her medical training to dress amputated limbs 'unaided and without emotion' (Brittain 1933: 216). Interwar feminist accounts of women's entry into the professions often traced the links between women's occupation of men's roles during the war and the movement towards 'complete occupational freedom' (Holtby 1934: 71) offered by the Sex Disqualification (Removal) Act of 1919. The rewards of war service easily outweighed the nothingness of conventional femininity in such accounts, with the role of volunteer nurse offering 'the ultimate gendered expression of patriotism, honor and sacrifice in wartime' (Watson 2004: 300).

Critics such as Andrew Kunka, Sharon Ouditt and Claire Tylee have examined gender roles in Sinclair's war novels in relation to patriotism, psychological trauma, cowardice and shell shock (Kunka 2006: 237–54; Tylee 1990: 131–3), tending to privilege the male experience of war over the non-combatant experience. The patriotic agenda of Sinclair's *The Tree of Heaven* certainly focuses on the experiences of the British soldier and the conscientious objector, but Ouditt's verdict that it reinforces 'women's active but deferential part in [the conflict]' via 'cliché[s] of wartime propaganda' (Ouditt 1997: 103, 107) needs qualifying. Women's eager participation in the 'immense vortex of the War' (Sinclair 1917: 188), explored through the experiences of female family members, is shown to supersede their embracing of the suffrage movement, and is represented as an exchange of one vortex for another. The release from imprisonment in Holloway into a frenzied involvement in war work appears to be a more socially acceptable form of pushing at gender boundaries for the heroine Dorothy Harrison, who drives ambulances for the Women's Service Corps in London in the anticipation of being sent to Belgium. The limitations of women's usefulness as war workers are, however, highlighted by the trio of bored spinster aunts, whose hopes of being sent to the Front after their bungled attempts at bandaging in the Red Cross ambulance classes are satirically shown up by Sinclair to be an 'absurdity'; an 'extraordinary illusion' (Sinclair 1917: 187). The absurdity of women's contribution to the war effort is also figured through Grannie's 'conspicuous' knitting of socks for Kitchener's army, 'as a protest against bandage practice' (Sinclair 1917: 188); knitting which has to be unravelled each night in order to save wool. The advice given to British women in the early stages of the war to concentrate on rearing children, looking good and knitting socks was very much anchored in 'the reassertion of separate spheres with its implied dichotomies of private and public, of different natures of women and men, of home and front' (Kingsley Kent 1993: 15).

British women's exchanges with Belgian women refugees are used in Sinclair's writing to negotiate their sense of participation, often via the trope of mothering and childbirth. Ouditt has rightly categorised Dorothea's thinking as 'anti-suffragist': although she thinks that 'it is a war that makes it detestable to be a woman' and laments her inability to fight, she accepts her relatively passive war role as a necessary and natural consequence of her gender (Ouditt 1997: 107). This is to downplay Dorothea's contribution to the war effort, and the complicated exchanges with the Belgian women refugees she collects from Cannon Street station.

> Her mind was like Cannon Street Station – a dreadful twilit terminus into which all the horror and misery of Belgium poured and was congested [...] for the first few weeks the War meant to Dorothea, not bleeding wounds and death, but just these train-loads of refugees – just this one incredible spectacle of Belgium pouring itself into Cannon Street station [...] This morning they were here, brave and gay, smiling at Dorothea as she carried their sick on her stretcher and their small children in her arms. (Sinclair 1917: 189)

This passage typically describes the effects on psychic life of the trauma not of wounding, but of the break-up of the family occasioned by war. In the ghastly Gothic station, in which huge, 'triumphant' engines disgorge human bodies, the maternal qualities of the heroine, whose importance is signalled by the elision of any other stretcher-bearers, mitigate against the homelessness of the women and children, who proudly cling to what they have salvaged from the wreckage. It is significant that the 'terrible things' Sinclair includes to balance this over-sanitised account include 'the ring screening the agony of a woman giving birth to her child on the platform' (Sinclair 1917: 189), typically focusing on the maternal body as a site of envy amidst the trauma. This scene recalls the moment of exchange with 'the very image of disaster', a Belgian mother breast-feeding in a London taxi recorded (or imagined?) in 'Women's Sacrifices for the War' (Sinclair 1915b: 8). As Sinclair meets the woman's eyes, the maternal breast is not 'screened' but resonates with the other images in her fiction of the maternal body as both grotesque and ardently desired; the exposure of her servant's 'white, rose-pointed breast' for her baby is a traumatic moment of longing for Harriett Frean in her later novel, 'She could not bear it' (Sinclair 1980: 137). Sinclair's investment in the maternal body as a potent signifier of the 'disaster' of war plays to the sympathies of the woman reader: in *A Journal of Impressions* her imagining of the 'horrors upon horrors' she will find in Ostend includes not only mutilated bodies but the 'unspeakable' state of the refugees' homes and the fear of bearing witness to 'children [. . .] being born in the streets' (Sinclair 1915a: 4). She records, 'I imagined the streets of Ostend crowded with refugee women bearing children' (Sinclair 1915a: 4). Rewriting propagandist reports of German atrocities against Belgian women and children in the British press (Kingsley Kent 1993: 24–6), Sinclair uses these images of childbirth and the maternal body to give a non-military version of the woman war worker's engagement with other women involved in the conflict.

An agonised awareness of the boundary between home and front comes to haunt sexual relationships after 1914 in both fictional and non-fictional accounts, as the enforced separation of soldiers from their lovers shifted the ground in relation to marriage and motherhood. Brittain characterised the division between home and front as 'that terrible barrier of knowledge by which War cut off the men who possessed it from the women who, in spite of the love that they gave and received, remained in ignorance', 'the inevitable barrier – the almost physical barrier of horror and dreadful experience' (Brittain 1930: 215). According to Susan Kingsley Kent, 'the disconnection between home and front [. . .] caused great anguish to women at home', with those successful in 'making the transition from home to front' undergoing an initiation into 'a wholly different existence' (Kingsley Kent 1993: 52, 53).

In *The Tree of Heaven*, the heroine's suffering from the enforcement of this terrible barrier of knowledge is inseparable from her gradual withdrawal from the 'vortex' of the suffrage movement. Frank's criticisms of her involvement in a violent suffrage demonstration, and her brothers' hatred for the Suffrage Banquet, reflect contemporary male attitudes to female militancy, against which Dorothy has to be positioned. A term of imprisonment in a 'convent cell' in Holloway, where she felt 'absolutely happy' (Sinclair 1917: 139) and her awareness of her lover's disapproval of her campaigning, hardens her resolve not to marry. But it is her own fear that by embracing the movement she takes on the hysterical behaviour of her aunt Emmeline, who ruins the Banquet with her 'frightful', 'lacerating screams', that encourages her to 'settle down' out of the 'whirlwind' (Sinclair 1917: 142, 148) in the quiet offices of the Social Reform Union, writing articles on economics and the new marriage laws. War work, like suffrage activity, is to be policed by men in the text. Instead of a marriage ceremony, Frank's last request is for Dorothy to give up 'the hardest and most dangerous job' of volunteering for service abroad: 'you can't expect us to fight so comfy, and to be killed so comfy, if we knew our womenkind are being pounded to bits in the ground we've just cleared' (Sinclair 1917: 197). Not consoled by the reminder of her brother going out to fight, Dorothy responds that she's thinking of England, 'so disgustingly safe' (Sinclair 1917: 197). Her 'anti-suffragist' regret for not sleeping with him, 'all those years – like a fool – over that silly suffrage' (Sinclair 1917: 199), is not simply a denouncing of political action for women, however, but a marker of the ways in which war produces shifts in female sexual identity and attitudes to motherhood. Veronica's reiteration of the need to honour the promise to Frank not to go to Flanders shows the reification of the home front in the early stages of the war and the patriotic imperative to bolster the domestic roles which keep men 'comfy'. The uncrossed boundary between home and front also signals the middle-class heroine's frustration at non-participation, her sense of exclusion despite the gains promised to women by the suffrage movement.

Angela K. Smith has considered the concept of participation in women's war testimonies, arguing that 'women are able to contribute alternative literary constructions of [front-line] experience despite, or perhaps because of their alien status' (Smith 2000: 7). This alien and ambiguous status of the woman at the front is explored in modernist narratives that deconstruct traditional notions of heroism and the 'romance' of the danger zones in Europe. Female ambulance drivers were closer to the centre of the conflict than other women war workers, yet in the mixed ambulance corps their power was defined in relation to, and sometimes by, men, who usually occupied the position of commandant. In Sinclair's *The Romantic*, whose title mocks the popularisation of war service as a 'romantic' adventure, gendered roles are reversed, as it is John who voices the view that going out to Belgium was 'the most romantic thing that ever happened' (Sinclair 1920: 67), a propagandist notion associated with women's supposed admiration for men in uniform in the early days of the conflict. John's lover, the more powerful Charlotte, constructed as the masculinised Jeanne d'Arc, is to be admired for revising such deluded perceptions. Her gradual realisation of his cowardice, which coexists with his 'delight in danger', produces a 'queer, baffled sense of surprise and incompleteness' (Sinclair 1920: 160), as if the woman war worker cannot fully achieve her desired subjectivity in the knowledge of male deficiency. In a discussion about danger and involvement in the 'big, dangerous thing', Charlotte corrects his 'enjoyment' of participation by remarking, 'I don't care as much as I did about what you call the romance of it; and I do care more about the solid work' (Sinclair 1920: 136). Sutton tells her that her impulsive decision to risk 'enemy fire' in order to 'save' the guns of the wounded 'would have been splendid if you'd been a combatant' (Sinclair 1920: 105) but actually contravened the Hague Convention rules about entering a danger zone. This reinforces her position as a non-combatant who has to be reminded of the rules by men. Sinclair's examination of women's feelings of exclusion and the difficulties of participating in what she refers to in her *Journal* as 'the game of war', played by women with men's permission, only 'if they're fit enough, up to a certain point' (Sinclair 1915a: 105), reflects and responds to contemporary reservations about women's fitness for war work.

Wasting Khaki? Women in the Ambulance Corps

In *The Tree of Heaven* Grannie, figurehead of outdated Victorianism, protests against bandage practice as catering to 'a set of silly women, getting in Kitchener's way and wasting khaki' (Sinclair 1917: 188). This speaks to the fetishisation of uniform in this period, when looking like a soldier was a transgressive way of '"aping" men' (Kingsley Kent 1993: 37), as well as a visible badge of patriotism and participation. Laura Doan has noted the diversity of responses to 'the impact of a uniformed woman in the public sphere' (Doan 2001: 65) in relation to the signifying of female masculinity through fashion in the interwar period. Writing of the new uniforms for the Women Police Service created in 1914, Doan identifies 'the dangerous, radical potential symbolically invested in the uniform to upset normative gender roles and the interrelationship between masculine women and sexuality' (Doan 2001: 71). Sharon Ouditt has argued that the 'mystique' of uniform works against its signifying of standardisation and defeminisation: 'Femininity in all its undisciplined plurality was more durable as a cultural formation than anything uniform could do to it' (Ouditt 1994: 20). Khaki or a nurse's uniform could also signify a woman's class credentials, marking out those deemed fit to represent England, as well as guaranteeing greater freedom of movement (uniformed women could travel for free on public transport for the duration), though its 'symbolic power' could signal sexual availability as well as service (Watson 2004: 34–5, 55). An examination of 'the effect of uniform on subject-position' (Ouditt 1994: 18) is revealing when analysing the figure of the woman war worker, not least because fictional representations of the uniformed female body are often used to dramatise gender conflict, with the 'odd' or 'masculine' appearance of the ambulance worker offering women a gender-neutral form of power whilst inviting both contempt and desire from male onlookers.

In *A Journal of Impressions* wearing khaki is no guarantee of service; women in the correct gear do not always achieve authenticity, and the odd attire of the others tallies with their failure to participate in rescuing the wounded. Sinclair's outsider status in Belgium relates to her age and abilities as well as her strange costume; as a wealthy fifty-four-year-old woman with no medical training and no driving licence, the 'war correspondent' was excluded from the role she wished to play, forced to spectate rather than serve. The 'funny' spectacle of the newly arrived Ambulance Corps is contrasted with the trained nurses in their Red Cross overalls and the men in military uniforms, 'we had never agreed as to our uniform, and some of us had had no time to get it, if we had agreed [. . .] we look more like a party of refugees, or the cast of a Barrie play, than a field ambulance corps' (Sinclair 1915a: 17). Whereas some of the men are in 'complete khaki', making them 'indistinguishable from any Tommy', the women's khaki tunics and putties make them look as if they were about to sail on an Arctic expedition: 'I was told to wear dark blue serge, and I wear it accordingly; Ursula Dearmer and Mrs Lambert are in normal clothes' (Sinclair 1915a: 17). The angelic Belgian ladies who serve them tea and cake behave as if 'there was nothing in the least odd about our appearance' (Sinclair 1915a: 18), both denying and reinforcing the connections between oddity and service.

Another example of women being 'left behind' when there are 'not enough ambulance cars to go round' appears later in the text when Sinclair contrasts her own 'fraudulent' situation with that of the frustrated Janet McNeill, who appears 'wounded in her honour [. . .]

conscious of the rottenness of putting on a khaki tunic, and winding khaki putties round and round her legs to hang about the Hospital doing nothing' (Sinclair 1915a: 65, 64). Being left behind is equivalent to being wounded, incapacitated, denied agency. The embarrassment of non-participation is also symbolised in the tunic and breeches hidden in Sinclair's hold-all which she 'dare not own to having brought' (Sinclair 1915a: 65), as if daring to 'own' and wear khaki would too obviously display her fraudulent appropriation of a masculine role. This is juxtaposed in the next sentence with an encounter with 'Mrs Torrence in khaki. Mrs Torrence yearning for her wounded. Mrs Torrence determined to get to her wounded at any cost' (Sinclair 1915a: 65), where the uniform validates the determined woman war worker's yearnings for action and participation. As both 'a trained nurse' and 'an expert motorist', who can exchange technical remarks with the men about the ambulances (Sinclair 1915a: 13), the younger woman has a right to her uniform and is better fitted to minister to 'her wounded' than Sinclair, who feels like an impostor, 'doing nothing for the Belgians, doing nothing for anybody' (Sinclair 1915a: 64). If uniform 'offered the enticing illusion of a coherent identity' (Ouditt 1994: 17), then it was an identity only made available to women with the requisite skills; class credentials and the desire to participate were not enough.

The woman in khaki also produced a visual shock of the new, reinforcing the incongruity between the old domestic self and the modern type of female masculinity. In *The Tree of Heaven* 'this grown-Dorothy in khaki breeches, with her talk about white frocks and blue frocks, made Frances want to cry' (Sinclair 1917: 194–5), whilst the mother mourns the disjunction between khaki and dresses signalling her only daughter's (un)availability as a wife. This is complicated by the comparisons with the suffragette's modified dress: when Dorothy emerges from her 'convent cell' in Holloway with her torn clothes and 'no hat on', Frank's evident dismay at her appearance, as she is no longer 'perfectly ladylike and perfectly dignified' (Sinclair 1917: 138), chimes with his disapproval for 'that silly suffrage'. In contrast, when she comes in with her hands black with oil and dirt from the car:

> He looked at her, taking it all in: the khaki uniform (it was the first time he had seen her in it), the tunic, breeches and puttees, the loose felt hat turned up at one side, its funny, boyish chin-strap, the dust and dirt of her; and he smiled. His smile had none of the cynical derision which had once greeted her appearances as a militant suffragist.
> 'And yet,' she thought, 'if he's consistent, he ought to loathe me now.' (Sinclair 1917: 190)

This patriotic admiration for uniform is less inconsistent than it seems; there is still a sense that a woman dressed in this way looks 'funny' or wrong, even if her boyishness attracts him more than her pose as an undignified suffragette. Significantly, his complaints that the boyish chin-strap gets in the way when he tries to kiss her are met with her laughter and throwing it onto the floor, as if to discard her female masculinity, which might interfere with heterosexual desire. His final comment that she can wear anything as long as she marries him is dismissive of her futile attempts to throw off her true gender. The uniform acts as a negotiating point for whether she will be able to make the transition from home to front, as he comments 'You look like business. Do you really mean it? Are you really going to Flanders?' (Sinclair 1917: 191), though her confident retort 'do you suppose any woman would go and get herself up like this if she wasn't going *some*where?' (Sinclair 1917: 191) sours when she is trapped by her promise and never leaves England. In *A Journal of Impressions in Belgium*, the Red Cross uniform which guarantees that women have crossed the boundary between home and front is linked to 'swanking' about (Sinclair 1915a: 65), a word often used in the novels to denote the women's departure from submissive femininity, a kind of 'showing off' of their new freedoms. As Doan contends, 'there is nothing uniform about the spectatorial effects generated by women in uniform' (Doan 2001: 82).

In *The Romantic*, the shortness of the skirts worn by ambulance drivers is interpreted as evidence of women's uncontrolled sexuality. John's self-confessed loathing for female ambulance drivers in general is linked to both the ways in which he sees Alice 'making eyes at Sutton over a spouting artery' and the visibility of the women's knees in uniform: 'Gwinnie hangs her beastly legs about all over the place. So do you' (Sinclair 1920: 167). When they travel across to Belgium, Charlotte wears a 'fawn-coloured overcoat belted close round to hide her knees', and asks John if her knees 'show awfully' (Sinclair 1920: 63, 66) when she walks, reflecting the fear that the drivers' uniforms were too revealing, yet this urge towards the ladylike seems to be abandoned after arrival on the front. Sutton tries to shield them from 'the batteries of amused and interested eyes' (Sinclair 1920: 73) in the Hotel-Hospital, looking at their breeches and puttees. The women's involvement in the war is only guaranteed by Gwinnie 'parad[ing]' their ambulance-car 'all round the blessed town' (Sinclair 1920: 88) and showing off the tyres, electric lights and stretchers with wheels to an excited Colonel, who invites her into the hotel for tea; another example of the ways in which women have to trade on their sexual attractions in wartime (evoking the attacks on 'vile' women 'preying' on soldiers discussed by Kingsley Kent [1993: 39–40]). Andrew Kunka's argument that the war has a 'penitential effect' on Charlotte, washing away 'the moral taint' of the affair with her married employer described in the opening chapters (Kunka 2006: 247), inadvertently reproduces some of the assumptions about female sexuality that taint women in the public sphere; what is more important is that the progression from office work to foreign service does not prevent women from being sexually appraised within the workplace (it is Charlotte's employer who initiates the affair). Katherine Mansfield drew attention to both John's preference for a celibate relationship and 'Charlotte's obsession by her sexual experience' in her *Athenaeum* review of the novel (Mansfield 1920: 522), remarking that the heroine's compulsion to 'tell' others about her affair was as interesting in psychoanalytic terms as John's cowardice. Sinclair's development of the sexually active heroine, which aligns her with contemporaries like D. H. Lawrence, intersects with her commitment to representing women's wartime experiences without trapping them in sexual stereotypes.

All-female ambulance units imagined by other modernist women writers, including Radclyffe Hall and Helen Zenna Smith, also showed women war workers as 'liberated from notions of ladylike behaviour or sexual sluttishness [...] (gender-free) comrades' (Tylee 1990: 183), but this liberation was still tempered by trauma and alienation. The relations between women within such units show the spectrum from camaraderie to competition, with lesbian desire seen as a threat to notions of women's service. The 'author's note' preceding Hall's *The Well of Loneliness* (1928) attributes the representation of the Breakspeare unit to the 'very fine service' done by a motor ambulance unit of British women (Hall 1982: 6), generally taken to be a reference to her friend Toupie Lowther's all-women unit, which consisted of twenty cars and twenty-five women drivers (Tylee 1990: 179). As critics have noted, Hall's writing validates the position of the lesbian heroine at the Front: Stephen's governess remarks, 'this war may give your sort of woman her chance. I think you may find that they'll need you' (Hall 1982: 271). Despite being told that 'England did not send women to the front-line trenches' (Hall 1982: 274), on the same page Stephen identifies in the crowded station 'unmistakable figures' like herself, waiting for the wounded, who gained courage from the wartime relaxation of gender roles:

> England had taken [the invert], asking no questions – she was strong and efficient, she could fill a man's place [...] England had said, 'Thank you very much. You're just what we happen to want [...] at the moment.' (Hall 1982: 274)

Women's war work assumes national importance, with the masculinised strength and efficiency of the ambulance worker putting her on a level with the soldiers England valued, though the caveat 'at the moment' suggests the filling of men's places will be short-lived. In her reading of Hall's novel, Laura Doan argues that 'this uniformed, happy breed of female inverts were not passing as men but passing as women who desired women – the uniform was their lesbianism made visible, satisfying a desire to wear less stereotypically feminine garb and perhaps to signal to others within a small circle of inverts' (Doan 2001: 76). Certainly, the war facilitates lesbian romance, with ambulance duty allowing Stephen to shield the childlike Mary from the maimed men, and to protect her from death by ensuring that they always drive together. The camaraderie of the all-female group is, however, fractured by antagonism towards this intimacy; the maternal leader, with her ample bosom, discourages 'anything in the nature of an emotional friendship' which 'might lead to ridicule in the Unit' (Hall 1982: 291). Lesbian attachments are also policed in Helen Zenna Smith's shocking, anti-war novel *Not So Quiet . . .* (1930), in which the acerbic heroine, ironically hailed as 'one of England's splendid daughters, proud to do their bit for the dear old flag', willingly exchanges her 'sheltered life' as a middle-class daughter for the 'filthy smells of gangrenous wounds' (Smith 1989: 13, 33). Transformed from Helen into the masculinised 'Smithy', she is used to deflate and critique patriotic whitewashing of the realities of women's war work, as the text registers her fright, her exhaustion and her revulsion at the wounds, the vomit and the filthy ambulances. A typical scene shows her spirited friend Tosh, 'the brave, the splendid', dying in her arms after a bombing raid, whilst she laughs hysterically, 'the funniest joke I ever heard' (Smith 1989: 160, 161). On her return to the war after leave, Smithy takes a vicious pleasure in choosing to be an 'immoral' domestic worker, a lower kind of war work popularly associated with 'mixing with dreadful people out of the slums' (Smith 1989: 211). This is the only way to drown out her mother's 'ladylike voice' boasting to neighbours about 'my eldest daughter, Helen, an ambulance driver in France; oh, a most exclusive class of girl, most exclusive, all ladies – they stipulate that, you know' (Smith 1989: 211). The privileged class position of the female ambulance driver partially explains her attractions to the middle-class modernist woman writer, who could use such a figure to deconstruct patriotic notions of women war workers as 'England's splendid daughters'.

Narratives about the hierarchical structures of the new ambulance corps always focus on the activity of driving as a test case for women's fitness for war service, even in depictions of all-female units. Although it is John who teaches Charlotte 'to steer and handle the heavy ambulance-car' (Sinclair 1920: 60), on arrival in France, she proves herself to be the better driver, taking the seat in the vehicle that will shield him from the possibility of enemy fire. Negotiations over who is in the driver's seat in the face of danger always signify negotiations about gender and power:

> She thought again of John on his exposed seat. If only he had let her drive – but that was absurd. Of course he wouldn't let her. If you were to keep on thinking of the things that might happen to John – Meanwhile nothing could take from them the delight of this dangerous run across the open. She had to remind herself that the adventure, the romance of it was not what mattered most [. . .] when they came to the wounded, when they came to the wounded, then it would begin. (Sinclair 1920: 98)

The woman's desire to be behind the wheel – 'you know I like driving' (Sinclair 1920: 92) – is reiterated in a number of key scenes in this text, with John's inability to cope with wounded men tallying with his inferior driving skills; he is repeatedly 'exposed' as unfit for his role. The function of the ambulance to collect the wounded is here in tension with the modernist fascination with the 'delight' and speed of motoring (Thacker 2005: 45), where a 'dangerous run' in the dark is at once a difficult duty and a thrilling 'adventure'. Suzanne Raitt has discussed Sinclair's 'desperate desire to be under fire rescuing the wounded' and her 'fascination with danger' in her *Journal*, as more characteristic of men's writings about the war: 'For a woman to express such greed for adventure and for sensation was unusual' (Raitt 2000: 158). By putting her heroine in the driving seat, Sinclair registered women's desires to prove themselves as rightful and worthy occupants of the danger zone, though, as this passage implies, the presence of horrifically wounded men in the ambulance will mark a traumatic 'beginning' of a new level of participation.

In a consideration of the shared interest in the injured or dead male body in soldiers' and nurses' narratives, Trudi Tate has argued that 'the war alters bodies in disturbing new ways; the difference between someone who is wounded and someone who is not is far more profound and psychically disturbing than the distinctions of sexual difference' (Tate 1998: 84). But the contention that 'sexual difference disappears in the face of modern weaponry' (Tate 1998: 85) is not borne out in Sinclair's writing, which always insists on the inescapably gendered gaze of the female war worker, even if the psychic identities of male and female non-combatants do not always tally with expectations about cowardice and slacking. In *The Romantic*, the disappearance of Charlotte's sexual interest in John is anchored in her growing awareness of his fear of danger: 'Do I hate him because he doesn't care about me? Or because he doesn't care about the wounded?' (Sinclair 1920: 199). After he leaves her to drive thirteen wounded men home by herself across dangerous terrain, she is supported on her return and praised for her courage by the three other female members of the ambulance corps: she is 'the pluckiest little blighter in the world', in their opinion, whereas he is a 'damned coward', a 'beastly humbug' (Sinclair 1920: 193). Sinclair's privileging of the woman's 'plucky' heroism over the man's desire for safety reinforces women's investment in their roles as war workers, despite their fear ('shelling's all in the day's work' [Sinclair 1920: 196]). Kunka's argument that in *The Romantic* 'the female characters are imbued with an innate sense of duty towards saving the lives of wounded men which seems to be an intrinsic part of their femininity, rather than the result of some occupational discipline' (Kunka 2006: 248) ignores the necessary seven weeks' training and 'the long evenings in the ambulance classes', the driving practice and the 'endless preparation' that guarantee their 'intolerable longing to be out there' (Sinclair 1920: 60, 61). John's dismissal of Charlotte's participation as merely an attempt 'to cut Mrs Rankin out', as a form of competition between women, has to be corrected because of its denial of this commitment: 'I never thought of such a rotten thing' (Sinclair 1920: 196). McClane's proviso, 'I can't have anyone in my corps who isn't fit' (Sinclair 1920: 243), underlines women's fitness for the demands of war service, even if this has to be achieved by emphasising male cowardice. John is later shot in the back by a Belgian servant for running away from a 'horribly wounded' captain (Sinclair 1920: 229), an apt punishment for turning his back on his obligations. For Sinclair, ways of dealing with the wounded became a means of transcending sexual difference and, to some extent, erotic attraction. In both her memoir and her novel, the mixed ambulance corps remains hierarchical with the weakest being excluded.

Women's Ability to Fill Men's Places?

The longer-term effects on society of the shift in gender roles accelerated by women's war work proved to be a cause of cultural anxiety during the war, and this anxiety is addressed but not diffused in the final chapters of Sinclair's novels; a strategy typical of women's war fiction. In 'Women's Sacrifices for the War', she predicted that this breakdown of gender distinctions would be questioned after the war, when it might be recognised that:

women's ability to fill men's places [...] constitutes a very serious problem and a danger [...] it may well be that there will not be enough men to fill civilian places for another generation, and that the more than ever surplus women will be imperatively called upon to fill them and keep the civil machine going. (Sinclair 1915b: 10, 11)

These ideological contradictions mobilised fears around the future of gender roles and the 'emptiness' to which women were expected to return. The 'problem of woman's competition with man', according to Gilbert Stone, was manifested in the 'problem of the [returning] war worker' (Stone 1917: 319) who struggled to return to the more conventional position occupied by British women before 1914. In *The Well of Loneliness*, the armistice brings the fear of the return to traditional gender roles: 'none could know what the future might hold of trivial days filled with trivial actions' (Hall 1982: 298). At a time when the lost generation of eligible bachelors left many 'surplus' women stranded without a role, the dissatisfaction of the returning war workers, no longer 'content to live within the bounds of their old life' (Stone 1917: 311), became a problem to be addressed by the modernist woman writer.

It could be argued that Sinclair's 'splendid' wartime heroines are offered the compensatory roles of mourning war widows repositioned in the safety of the home, though their stories still seem less important than those of the cowardice or heroism of their soldier lovers and brothers. In his essay 'Mourning and Melancholia' (1917), Sigmund Freud characterised the 'work of mourning' in terms of the withdrawal of libido, the severing of the attachment to the 'lost object' (Strachey 1959: 255–6). Many of the female characters in *The Tree of Heaven* are left stranded with this process incomplete, risking the pathologised disorder of melancholia; Veronica becomes the silent recipient of Michael's letters, in which her work in Hampstead Hospital is assumed to make her 'happier' (Sinclair 1917: 247). It is significant that as a war worker Dorothy carries small children to ambulances but the loss of her *fiancé* leaves her childless by the end of the novel; she does not transfer her libidinal drive to another man in order to complete what Freud assumed to be the 'normal' process of mourning (Strachey 1959: 245). Still bound by her promise to Frank not to go out to the Front, she almost vanishes from the narrative after he is killed during a retreat. Her mother mourns the two sons lost in conflict, taking pride in Nicky's 'personal daring and impetus' (Sinclair 1917: 238) memorialised in the final letter, and in Michael's poetry sent back from France. Frances recalls how she had never understood Michael's stance as a conscientious objector, talking to him 'as though he had been a shirker and a coward', ' bully[ing] him till he went' (Sinclair 1917: 253). This appears to reiterate women's importance in the shaping of notions of cowardice, as it is often the female characters who have the harshest views on male non-participation or avoidance of danger, linking back to their investment in 'the glamour of the Front'. This delusionary investment in the thrills and romance of war is questioned by the pointless deaths of many of the male characters in the third section of the novel, ironically titled 'Victory'. In contrast, women's suspension in the process of mourning acts as a potential liberation from the libidinal economy, even though this can only be achieved at the cost of their silencing.

Significantly, both heroines remain unmarried in the concluding chapters, showing their antipathy to marriage to be consolidated by their experiences of war. Critical complaints about the 'sheer romancing' of *The Tree of Heaven*, such as Claire Tylee's view that 'by 1917 the sordidness of trench warfare was common knowledge, yet Sinclair continued to preach the Victorian message of the spiritual values of war' (Tylee 1990: 132, 133), have not taken account of its commentary on the women mourning their dead, nor the shift in sensibility this produced. Frances may suffer from the loss of the bodies of her sons, 'the price we pay for being mothers' (Sinclair 1917: 255), but the lesser mourning for a *fiancé* or brother of the lost generation indicates that Dorothy's inconclusive marginality in the final chapter may offer possibilities as well as restrictions. Whilst the heroine might seem to be reprising the familiar role in Sinclair's oeuvre of embittered daughter caring for a querulous mother who preferred her lost sons, she adds a significant condition to this domestic arrangement: 'I wouldn't leave you for the world, Mummy, ducky. Only you must let me work always and all the time' (Sinclair 1917: 255). In *The Romantic*, Charlotte's rejection of an offer of marriage from Sutton is also a valuing of service over desire, as she prefers to appropriate John's role: 'I must pay his debt to Belgium. To all those wounded men' (Sinclair 1920: 233). The eradication of her libidinal drive, her belief that she 'can't see any afterwards' (Sinclair 1920: 239) is left hanging, a reminder of the ways in which war's irreversible transformation of gender roles impacted on sexual identities. Whilst Freud argued that 'people never willingly abandon a libidinal position' (Strachey 1959: 244), the heroine's refusal to transfer her affections again suggests that the incomplete 'work of severance' from the lost object (Strachey 1959: 245) is potentially liberating for women. McClane, the psychotherapist who offers the detailed 'explanation' of John's failed masculinity to Charlotte, claims that:

> he jumped at the war because the thrill he got out of it gave him the sense of power. He sucked manhood out of you. He sucked it out of everything – out of blood and wounds [. . .] the war upset him. (Sinclair 1920: 245–6)

This final commentary on cowardice is also an indication of the 'plucky' woman war worker's 'manhood'; rather than being upset by the war, it is implied, Charlotte is liberated from the trauma of sexuality on men's terms. The final contrast between John's 'adventurous' excitement of going out to war and 'the long lines of beaten men' (Sinclair 1920: 249) in the final chapter may appear to exclude the female experience, but its refusal to register female fears about resuming the triviality of civilian life could be interpreted in a more positive light. The woman war worker never completes her 'return' in this elliptical modernist conclusion, but remains stranded between home and the Front. The return never begins in *Not So Quiet* . . ., which concludes by lamenting the alienation of the woman war worker, with her 'emotionless eyes' at the side of a 'blood-spattered trench', surrounded by the 'mangled women' (Smith 1989: 238–9) of her ambulance unit. Both of Sinclair's open-ended texts then leave the problem of the returning war worker unresolved, whilst stopping short of the angry attacks on war work for reducing women to automatons in later interwar fiction.

In Ray Strachey's *The Cause* (1928), which chronicled women's progress from domestic subordination to the achievement of the vote, 'the great success of women's war work, and the great publicity which attended it' (Strachey 1980: 101) is one of the contributory factors towards suffrage victory. The double-edged publicity surrounding the woman in uniform, both a splendid citizen doing her bit and a threatening usurper of men's roles, suggests the ideological contradictions surrounding this new type of femininity. Masculinised, middle-class heroines jolted out of domestic triviality by the new working opportunities available after 1914 are used in *The Tree of Heaven* and *The Romantic* to signal the gendering of notions of patriotism and participation, as shown in negotiations about fitness, power and the maternal involved in women's ambulance work. Rather than returning the woman war worker to the 'trivial actions' expected of her gender, Sinclair capitalises on the open-endedness of the modernist text to leave her heroines in the process of mourning, temporarily liberated from the libidinal drive and sexuality on men's terms, and still firmly positioned in the world of work. This questioning of the links between female sexuality and women's potential unfitness to participate in 'the game of war' is indicative of a broader need to question historical understandings of service as always reiterating gendered notions of citizenship.

Works Cited

Brittain, Vera [1933] (1978), *Testament of Youth*, London: Virago.
Cardinal, Agnes, Dorothy Goldman and Judith Hattaway, eds (1999), *Women's Writing on the First World War*, Oxford: Oxford University Press.
Dent, Olive (1917), *A VAD in France*, London: Grant Richards.
Doan, Laura (2001), *Fashioning Sapphism: The Origins of a Modern English Lesbian Culture*, London and New York: Routledge.
Freud, Sigmund [1917] (1957), 'Mourning and Melancholia', in *The Standard Edition of the Complete Psychological Works of Sigmund Freud*, vol. 14, trans. James Strachey, London: The Hogarth Press and Institute of Psychoanalysis, pp. 243–58.
Hall, Radclyffe [1928] (1982), *The Well of Loneliness*, ed. Alison Hennegan, London: Virago.
Holtby, Winifred [1934] (1978), *Women and a Changing Civilization*, Chicago: Academy Press.
Kent, Susan Kingsley (1993), *Making Peace: The Reconstruction of Gender in Post-War Britain*, Princeton: Princeton University Press.
Kunka, Andrew J. (2006), '"He isn't quite an ordinary coward": Gender, Cowardice, and Shell Shock in *The Romantic* and *Anne Severn and the Fieldings*', in Andrew J. Kunka and Michele K. Troy (eds), *May Sinclair: Moving Towards the Modern*, Aldershot: Ashgate, pp. 237–54.
Kunka, Andrew J., and Michele K. Troy, eds (2006), *May Sinclair: Moving Towards the Modern*, Aldershot: Ashgate.
Mansfield, Katherine (1920), 'Ask no Questions' (review of *The Romantic*), *Athenaeum*, 22 October 1920, pp. 552–3.
Ouditt, Sharon (1994), *Fighting Forces, Writing Women: Identity and Ideology in the First World War*, London: Routledge.
Raitt, Suzanne (2000), *May Sinclair: A Modern Victorian*, Oxford: Clarendon Press.
Sinclair, May (1915a), *A Journal of Impressions in Belgium*, London: Hutchinson.
Sinclair, May (1915b), 'Women's Sacrifices for the War', *Woman at Home*, 67, 7–11.
Sinclair, May (1917), *The Tree of Heaven*, London: Cassell.
Sinclair, May (1920), *The Romantic*, London: Collins.
Sinclair, May [1922] (1978), *Life and Death of Harriett Frean*, London: Virago.
Smith, Angela K. (2000), *The Second Battlefield: Women, Modernism and the First World War*, Manchester: Manchester University Press.
Smith, Helen Zenna [1930] (1989), *Not so Quiet . . . Stepdaughters of War*, New York: Feminist Press.
Stone, Gilbert (ed.) (1917), *Women War Workers: Accounts Contributed by Representative Workers of the Work Done by Women in the More Important Branches of War Employment*, London: Harrap & Co.
Strachey, Ray [1928] (1980), *The Cause*, London: Virago.
Tate, Trudi (1988), *Modernism, History and the First World War*, Manchester: Manchester University Press.

Thacker, Andrew (2003), *Moving through Modernity: Space and Geography in Modernism*, Manchester: Manchester University Press.
Tylee, Claire (1990), *The Great War and Women's Consciousness: Images of Militarism and Womanhood in Women's Writings, 1914–1964*, Basingstoke: Macmillan.
Watson, Janet S. K. (2004), *Fighting Different Wars: Experience, Memory, and the First World War in Britain*, Cambridge: Cambridge University Press.
Woolf, Virginia, *Three Guineas* [1938] (1993), in Michèle Barrett (ed.), *A Room of One's Own/Three Guineas*, London: Penguin.

Chapter 11

Transgressing Boundaries; Transcending Bodies: Sublimation and the Abject Corpus in *Uncanny Stories* and *Tales Told by Simpson*

Claire Drewery

The short fiction of May Sinclair reveals a sustained fascination with the transgressive power residing within physical, intellectual and cultural boundaries. A noteworthy feature of two of her short-story collections in particular, *Uncanny Stories* (1923) and *Tales Told by Simpson* (1930), is the repeated violation and disruption of border-states; conveyed through striking and frequently voyeuristic representations of gratuitous violence perpetrated against physical and aesthetic bodies. Visual and textual artefacts are typically depicted as disjointed, incomplete or imperfect and are consistently juxtaposed with disfigured, grotesque or discorporated physical forms. These representations, this chapter will argue, are underscored by a continual aesthetic tension between the spiritual form of subjective consciousness frequently associated with the modernist epiphany – in Sinclair's writing represented as spiritual and pure – and physical, corporeal sexuality, which, conversely, she depicts as repellent, distorted and grotesque. For Sinclair, this tension resides within cultural and subjective border-sites which are threatening; liminal; abject. All are evocative of the revulsion which Julia Kristeva, in her much later essay *Powers of Horror*, identifies as arising from the corporeal boundaries of the human subject: for her the locus of 'what disturbs identity, system, order. What does not respect borders, positions, rules. The in-between, the ambiguous, the composite' (1982: 4).

This chapter will suggest a close affinity between Sinclair's representations of the abject borders of the physical and textual corpus and her aesthetic of sublimation, which connects sexuality to art through the channelling of the libido into artistic creation. This seeming paradox is informed by Sinclair's interest in Freudian theories of sublimation as elucidated in '"Civilised" Sexual Morality and Modern Nervousness', in which he claims that sexual instinctual forces are deflected 'away from their sexual aim to higher cultural aims' (1959: 193). Significantly, in this essay Freud locates sublimation's end result within the sphere of artistic creation; the locus Sinclair privileges in her claim that 'the striving of the Libido towards manifestation in higher and higher forms' is realised within 'innumerable religious and artistic texts' (1916a: 119). Through these cultural and aesthetic means is declared 'the unity of all things in the Absolute'; a term she uses interchangeably with the idea of the 'ultimate reality' she believed existed behind and beyond material surfaces (1917: 272; 1916b: 144).[1] Her *Uncanny Stories* – probably indebted for its title to Freud's 1919 essay *The Uncanny* – contains numerous examples of sublimation as a cerebral, quasi-mystical state which is continually undercut by the corporeal abject. In *Tales Told by Simpson*, however, any aspiration towards such unity is corrupted through a series of satirical depictions of distorted, incomplete textual and aesthetic bodies which might ultimately be interpreted as ironic commentaries on the literary marketplace and on modernism itself.

In the stories I discuss in this chapter, the motif of the physical and textual corpus encompasses a conflict between the cleanliness and purity Sinclair associates with transcendental, spiritual reality and the filth and defilement which, in her world, do violence to artistic genius. For Sinclair, '[t]he perfect individual is the person perfectly adapted to reality through the successive sublimations of his will'; a reality achieved through what she defines as a 'metaphysical quest' culminating in a pure, cerebral form of spiritual ecstasy (1917: 81; 272). The purpose of this sublimation, Sinclair claims, is that, like the Christian mysteries, it leads 'the useless, regressive, incestuous libido' into rational activity and thus transforms 'the obscure compulsion of the libido working up from the unconscious into social communion and higher moral endeavour' (1916a: 120).

A fuller discussion of Sinclair's complex philosophical and psychoanalytic conceptualisation of sublimation is beyond the scope of the present chapter, but this brief summary nonetheless reveals that this has a marked similarity with the modernist epiphany; long recognised not only as a conspicuous aesthetic of literary modernism but as a structuring principle of the short story in particular.[2] The modernist moment of intense, spiritual illumination first receives the name 'epiphany' in James Joyce's draft novel *Stephen Hero*, an early version of *A Portrait of the Artist as a Young Man*, when the protagonist Stephen Dedalus defines it as a 'sudden spiritual manifestation'; a unity of form capable of revealing transcendent, universal truths (1944: 216). It is, moreover, the *Künstlerroman* genre through which the revelatory moment and sublimation are most closely linked in Joyce and Sinclair. In their respective novels *A Portrait* (1916) and *Mary Olivier: A Life* (1919), both Joyce's Dedalus and Sinclair's eponymous protagonist perfect their sublimative aesthetics through similar experiences of spiritual ecstasy which are ultimately realised through learning to channel their physical desires into poetry.

As Joshua Jacobs has observed, however, as opposed to revealing momentary glimpses of a transcendental, ultimate reality, the epiphany may also be read as an intrinsically sexual experience constructed through corporeal, material language. Observing that the dynamic of the Joycean epiphany is one of 'body, speech, and sexuality', Jacobs argues that '[i]ts language, despite Stephen's intellectual pretensions, is 'insistently grounded in the corporeal'. Moreover, it is staged within the context of his sexual crises (2000: 21, 32). Similar sexual crises, I shall argue, underpin Sinclair's representations of artistic revelation and sublimation in her short fiction. In contrast with the *Künstlerroman*, however, her stories do not depict the pure ecstasy of Mary Olivier or echo Stephen Dedalus's battles with sublimation, which culminate in his artistic freedom. Their representations of mystical states comprise no spiritual interludes of heightened experience or glimpses of transcendent reality; they are, conversely, base, corporeal and intensely sexual.

Throughout Sinclair's novels and short stories, numerous descriptions of the sublimation of sexual energy are written in openly and explicitly sexual language. In *The Three Sisters*, for example, Alice Carteret's piano-playing is equated with a 'great climax of the soul', the build-up to which her 'excitement gathered; it swung in more and more vehement vibrations; it went warm and flooding through her brain like wine' (13). A passage in the short story 'If the Dead Knew' conveys piano-playing in similar sensual language: '[t]he climax had come. The voluntary fell from its height and died in a long cadence, thinned out, a trickling, trembling diminuendo [. . .] The young girl released her breath in a long, trembling sigh' (p. 163).

It is noteworthy, however, that despite the explicit sexual frankness conveyed within these climactic passages, the experiences they depict are almost exclusively cerebral rather than physical. A consistent feature of Sinclair's writing, Faye Pickrem argues in Chapter 6, is that the body is constantly rejected in disgust as a site of non-sublimated sexuality. This is conceivably why, in Sinclair's short fiction, a consistent emphasis on sublimation is also marked by a 'revolt' of being which Kristeva locates in bodily orifices and their emissions. Abjection arises from 'fluids, [. . .] defilement, [. . .] shit'; 'what goes out of the body, out of its pores and openings' and 'points to the infinitude of the body proper' (1982: 3). For Kristeva, this revulsion is permanent and thus inescapable, emanating not from 'an exorbitant outside' but from within 'the boundaries of the 'clean and proper body' (1982: 101; 113). For Sinclair, also, this is the locus in which subjective identity is at its most fluid, threatened and precarious.

Such border-sites are a prominent focus in *Uncanny Stories*: a collection of fictional representations of sublimation which, invariably, culminate in abjection. In the third story of the volume, 'The Flaw in the Crystal', the tension between 'pure', cerebral sublimation and abject forms of physical desire is particularly marked. The faith-healing capacity of the protagonist, Agatha Verrall, is realised through a sensual exaltation where she is able to exist 'poised in the ultimate unspeakable stillness, beyond death, beyond birth, beyond the movement, the vehemence, the agitations of the world' (87). Sinclair's fictional language is here markedly similar to that of her philosophical theories. 'On the threshold of 'Ultimate Reality', she suggests in *A Defence of Idealism*, 'there is no doubt as to the meaning of the words "New Birth" and "Union with God"' (1917: 276).

In the earlier stages of 'The Flaw in the Crystal', Agatha's mystical abilities are described on numerous occasions in quasi-religious language as 'clean'; 'pure'; 'a holy thing'; a 'flawless crystal' (87). The purity of Agatha's mind is a necessary condition 'to ensure the blessed working of the gift' and equally, 'it was by the blessed working of the gift' that she is able to retain this purity (74). Moreover, Agatha's initial realisation of her 'uncanny, unaccountable Gift' (62) is described as primal and virginal; a condition necessary to her ability to control the secret of its working and reduce it 'to an almost intelligible method. You could think of it as a current of transcendent power, hitherto mysteriously inhibited' (85).

This passage is reminiscent of the Joycean epiphany in terms both of the spiritual ecstasy Agatha experiences and its connection with the sublimation of the libido by means of the 'divine will'. The essence of Agatha's faith-healing capacity is her restraint, which she is able to refine to the extent that 'she could shut out, and by shutting out destroy, any feeling, any thought that did violence to any other' (63). When Agatha works her gift 'that was ecstasy; when every leaf and every blade of grass shone with a divine translucence; when every nerve in her thrilled, and her whole being rang with the joy which is immanent in the life of things' (119). The language here bears a strong similarity to that of Stephen Dedalus's major epiphanic moment in Joyce's *A Portrait*, when he experiences a profoundly sexual vision of a girl on a beach which passes into his soul 'for ever' and inspires him '[t]o live, to err, to fall, to triumph, to recreate life out of life!' (131–2).

As Sinclair's story progresses, however, the process of sublimation becomes corrupted by Agatha's involvement in a love triangle comprising her own physical desire for her married lover, Rodney Lanyon, and the desire of Harding Powell, her married friend, for her. Subsequently, increasingly sickening scenes of violence are perpetrated by Harding against Agatha's gift and, the text implies, to her subjective boundaries, both conscious and physical. Vampiric and terrifying incursions into the realm of abjection occur when Agatha attempts to effect a cure upon Harding's 'madness' – implicitly his physical desire – and his insanity leaches through to her (122). As Paul March-Russell has noted, these interludes are depicted in a language that is consistently evocative of violation and rape: '*He* was in her. Hitherto it had been in the darkness that she felt him most [. . .] In the flesh, as in the spirit, he was pursuing her' (March-Russell 2006: 19; Sinclair 1923: 117–18).

The language in this passage is powerfully corporeal, material and physical, and Harding's encroachment into Agatha's psychic and physical boundaries conceivably amounts to a dark underside of the epiphanic ecstasy she experiences earlier in the narrative. Her new-found horror 'of the evil which was Life' is antithetical to Stephen Dedalus's desire to 'recreate life out of life', or her own earlier joy in 'the life of things' (Joyce 2000: 131–2; Sinclair 1923: 119). It manifests in the 'invisible things unborn, driven towards birth' she perceives in 'that gross green hot-bed, the earth teemed with the abomination; and the river, livid, white, a monstrous thing, crawled, dragging with it the very slime' (119). Moreover, the references to fluid and slime are not dissimilar to the language of Stephen's later confession in which 'his sins trickled from his lips, one by one, trickled in shameful drops from his soul, festering and oozing like a sore, a squalid stream of vice' (2000: 144).

Significantly, the notion of the modernist epiphany as encompassing a revealing, transformative power has more recently been reconceptualised in terms of its capacity to obscure rather than afford transcendent insight. This form of anti-epiphany has been referred to by Dominic Head as a 'non-epiphany principle', and in a more general context, José María Díaz has noted that canonical modernism 'abounds in failed, missed or truncated epiphanies' (1992: 37–8; 2012: 47–8). In a similar vein, Joshua Jacobs suggests that Stephen's confession is located 'within the epiphanic mode' and is thus articulated through 'an utterly foul emission of physicalised language' (2000: 27).

This form of language-specific abjection, according to Kristeva, is threatening because it resides within the preserve of 'a speaking being who is innerly divided and, precisely through speech, does not cease purging himself of it' (1982: 113). In 'The Flaw in the Crystal', Agatha's efforts at purging herself of her abject sexuality follow her realisation that her healing 'crystal' has a flaw. Its form is 'the strain of mortality in her love for Rodney; the hidden thing, unforeseen and unacknowledged, working its work in the darkness. It had been there all the time, undermining her secret, sacred places' (186). This description is again overtly sexual and revealingly casts Agatha's own desire for Rodney in similar invasive language to that of Harding's metaphoric rape. For Kristeva, a similar distinction applies to the revulsion ensuing from the language of abjection, which is 'the symptom of an ego that, overtaxed by a "bad object", turns away from it, cleanses itself of it, and vomits it' (1982: 45).

Agatha's ultimate desire to regain her 'gift' entails a similar retreat from physical desire into silence and isolation and a rupturing of the bonds between herself, Rodney and Harding. As Jacobs notes in Joyce's work, however, 'such a vomiting-forth cannot rid one of sexuality, nor can the sin and redemption be reassuringly embodied outside oneself' (2000: 27). In Sinclair's work, likewise, abject forms of sexuality are threatening precisely because of their invasive presence within her characters' own subjective boundaries. Harding, who consistently violates Agatha in her bed at night and keeps her 'afraid of sleep', is conceivably a manifestation of her response to her own reviled sexuality (121). The 'haunting' she experiences, in the 'unlit roads down which, if she slept, the Thing would surely haunt her' and which were 'ten times more terrible than the white-washed, familiar room where it merely watched and waited', emanates from within, not beyond, Agatha's own psyche (121). Significantly, the form of Harding here becomes less distinct – described merely as 'the Thing' – and might thus be read as a metaphor for Agatha's own failure of sublimation.

The realm of the abject here is reminiscent of Freud's notion of the uncanny, which he defines as 'that species of the frightening which goes back to what was once well known and had long been familiar' (2003: 124). For Freud, the uncanny is not an external source of fear, but a return of something in our sexual history which has been repressed and forgotten. In his explanation, *Heimlich* 'becomes increasingly ambivalent, until it finally merges with its antonym *unheimlich*. The uncanny (*das Unheimliche*, "the unhomely") is in some way a species of the familiar (*das Heimliche*, "the homely")' (2003: 134). It thus contains within itself its own opposition, and hence comes to apply to 'everything that was intended to remain secret, hidden away, and has come into the open' (2003: 132).

In Sinclair's *Uncanny Stories*, the abjection inherent within her aesthetic of sublimation frequently takes on the form of the uncanny, the most prevalent forms of which, according to Freud, are a compulsion to repeat, images of the double, and the returned dead (2003: 142, 145). These are all prominent characteristics of the story 'Where Their Fire Is Not Quenched', in which the protagonist, Harriott Leigh, attempts to repress her guilt and disgust over an extramarital affair that had concluded some twenty years prior to her death. In common with many of Sinclair's displaced ghosts, Harriott reaps in the afterlife the psychological consequences of her unacknowledged physical desires in the earlier stages of the story. However, whilst the mystic faith-healer of 'The Flaw in the Crystal' is ultimately able to reclaim her gift by relinquishing her desire for Rodney, Harriott, by contrast, is left wandering around in a timeless, post-death space, denied access to the Absolute and fated to repeat endlessly her dissatisfying union with her married lover, Oscar Wade.

Harriott's fate, the story implies, is the result of her refusal to acknowledge her sexual needs and her determination to possess only the 'clean, beautiful part of it' (20). Her desire for spiritual love leads her to seek 'something just beyond it, some mystic, heavenly rapture, always beginning to come, that never came' (17). The text, whilst reminiscent of aspiration to the kind of spiritual ecstasy experienced by Agatha Verrall, is also strongly suggestive that Harriott craves physical satisfaction which constantly eludes her. She is inclined to view Oscar, who openly acknowledges his sexual desires, as repellent, and berates him that everything high and noble in love 'you dragged down to that, till there's nothing left for us but that' (21). The comment is prophetic, as Harriott's denial of her own physical desires and ultimately of the affair itself – which she omits to confess upon her deathbed – ironically condemns her to repeat it.

Harriott's ultimate confrontation with the abject in this story is depicted in a similar vein to that of Agatha in 'The Flaw in the Crystal'. Her experiences culminate in violent, invasive forms of abject sexuality, psychological rape and a grotesque consummation of the marriage Harriott had dreaded during her life but is ultimately unable to escape. This verdict is pronounced by Oscar, who by this stage in the narrative has come to represent Harriott's own repressed memories:

> We shall lie here together, for ever and ever, joined so fast that even God can't put us asunder. We shall be one flesh and one spirit, one sin repeated for ever, and ever; spirit loathing flesh, flesh loathing spirit; you and I loathing each other. (37)

For Harriott, the utmost of the abject experiences she encounters is the condemnation endlessly to repeat her 'sin'. This compulsion also finds an explanation in Freud's theory of the uncanny, in which he suggests that 'it is only the factor of unintended repetition that transforms what would otherwise seem quite harmless into something uncanny and forces us to entertain the idea of the fateful and the inescapable, when we should normally speak of "chance"' (2003: 144). On encountering Oscar at every turn within her post-death state, Harriott at first mistakenly believes that if she can move back far enough in time to a point in her life before she met him, she will be 'safe, out of Oscar's reach' (30). Yet her increasingly desperate efforts to escape Wade only draw her inexorably back to him. As he gradually usurps her cherished memories of her father and her former two unconsummated love affairs – memories of love she considers to be 'innocent' – she fails to recognise that the memory of Oscar is embedded within her own psyche. As the voice of her consciousness, Oscar tells her: '[y]ou think the past affects the future. Has it never struck you that the future may affect the past? In your innocence there was the beginning of your sin. You *were* what you *were to be*' (35–6).

Harriott is, then, unable to escape Oscar because, like Harding Powell in 'The Flaw in the Crystal', he is within her. Her psychic boundaries are violated by his presence on the borders of her own existence, in a loathsome liminal hinterland from which there can be no escape. Wade ceases to become an other to Harriott's self; he is horrifying because he occupies a space in her own psyche as a manifestation of the guilty sexual affair she spends years trying to repress by unsuccessfully sublimating her desires into religion.

As a manifestation of Harriott's memories, Oscar therefore symbolises the abjection resulting from the failed sublimation of her libido into religion. This failure implicitly arises from the fact that Harriott's religious pretensions are not spiritual but superficial, material and defined only in terms of the outward paraphernalia associated with her religion: 'the uniform of a deaconess, the semi-religious gown, the cloak, the bonnet and veil, the cross and rosary, the holy smile' (22). Her compulsion to hide and repress her desires, to shroud, obscure and disavow the physical corpus – later represented in the narrative through images of corpses – accords with Freud's theory in *Three Essays on the History of Sexuality* that

> The progressive concealment of the body which goes along with civilisation keeps sexual curiosity awake. This curiosity seeks to complete the sexual object by revealing its hidden parts. It can, however, be diverted ('sublimated') in the direction of art, if its interest can be shifted away from the genitals on to the shape of the body as a whole. (1962: 22)

Harriott, however, possesses no sublimative capacity: she is not a faith-healer, a mystic or an artist. As she is unable to channel her libido into 'higher' ends, it becomes corrupted, and condemns her to an eternal repetition of the desire and disgust encompassing her own vacillating response to her sexuality. Such ambivalence is characteristic of abject experience, which according to Kristeva 'beseeches, worries, and fascinates desire, which, nevertheless, does not let itself be seduced' (1982: 1). In a particularly ironic, comedic scene, this form of abjection is symbolised in Harriott's discovery of Oscar's dead body when contemplating the sheeted corpse of her father. As Harriott reveals the hidden body by folding back the sheet, the face revealed becomes that of Oscar Wade, 'stilled and smoothed in the innocence of sleep, the supreme innocence of death' (29). For Harriott, this vision instantly evokes the Hotel Saint Pierre, scene of her tryst with Oscar in Paris:

> The dead face frightened her, and she was about to cover it up again when she was aware of a light heaving, a rhythmical rise and fall. As she drew the sheet up tighter, the hands under it began to struggle convulsively, the broad ends of the fingers appeared above the edge, clutching it to keep it down. The mouth opened; the eyes opened; the whole face stared back at her in a look of agony and horror. (30)

In this passage the image of the corpse is both multifarious and ambiguous, encompassing numerous facets of both the Freudian uncanny and Kristevan abjection. If Oscar is interpreted as metaphor for the return of Harriott's repressed libido, then his physical body, having metamorphosed from the body of her father, is the site of both necrophilic and incestuous horror. The notion of the corpse as a metaphor for the return of the repressed is reiterated in Harriott's contemplation of her own 'sheeted body on the bed', which she is unable to reconcile in any way with herself (24).

In its dual connotations of the father and Wade, as well as the discorporation and separation of the forms of Harriott's 'ghost' and her own dead body, the notion of uncanny 'doubling' is also implicit within the image of the corpse. In Freud's explanation of this element of the uncanny, the double both affirms and denies mortality: 'an insurance against the extinction of the self' which ultimately becomes the harbinger of death (2003: 142). Harriott's ambivalence in the presence of the shrouded, sheeted bodies, as well as their relationship to her sexual past in their form as the return of her repressed libido, again connect her abject experiences with the Freudian uncanny.

Abjection is thus comparable with uncanny doubling because, according to Kristeva, 'like an inescapable boomerang, a vortex of summons and repulsion places the one haunted by it literally beside himself' (1982: 1). For Kristeva, moreover, the image of the corpse is 'the utmost of abjection'; the ultimate form of the bodily waste 'permanently thrust aside in order to live' until 'nothing remains in me and my entire body falls beyond the limit—*cadere*, cadaver' (1982: 3). The corpse is 'something rejected from which one does not part', representing '[i]maginary uncanniness and real threat,' which 'beckons to us and ends up engulfing us' (1982: 4).

In 'Where Their Fire Is Not Quenched', the uncanny, abject double residing within the boundaries of the clean and proper body is, then, both threatening and unpredictable. The story occupies the borderline states that Kristeva defines as abject – 'the place where meaning collapses' – which invokes revulsion but also has a potentially seductive aspect because 'that impetus, that spasm, that leap is drawn toward an elsewhere as tempting as it is condemned' (1982: 1–2). Boundaries are simultaneously seductive and repulsive because they contain within themselves the capacity to challenge the limits of subjective and cultural identity, at the same time encompassing the threat of annihilation.

For Sinclair these border-states of disgust and loathing, in which the divine, spiritual will is defiled and the physical corpus distorted and maligned, are the abject alternative to perfect sublimation. Thus, in both 'The Flaw in the Crystal' and 'Where Their Fire is Not Quenched', sexual desire translates into repulsion, and depictions of repressing and denying the sexual impulse are conveyed in the invasive language of physical violation; implied rape being at the centre of both these stories. The distorted body is, then, a manifestation of aesthetic, intellectual failure. In this sense, there is a clear affinity between Sinclair's trope of sublimation in her stories and her readings of psychoanalysis which, according to Suzanne Raitt, intensified her belief that 'only the chosen few ('geniuses') could benefit from the kind of isolation she herself embraced' (2000: 110).

Sinclair elaborates this idea in the second of her two lectures on 'Symbolism and Sublimation', in which she concludes that 'only the creative, the enlightened and progressive will is holy', and that the creative will becomes 'unholy' when 'directed out of the path of social well-being and of progress' (1916b: 144). Thus arises the 'utterly unholy' sterility of the libido of 'the libertine, the neurotic and the sexual pervert'; the reason, she argues, behind 'all the repressions, and taboos – the primitive, religious, moral and social taboos' (ibid.). Herein lies the abjection within her conceptualisation of sublimation, in which 'all transgression is regression' and the libido 'frustrates the purpose of evolution by sending the individual backward on the path by which he came' (ibid.).

This is precisely the fate which befalls Harriott Leigh, the source of whose revulsion is a fear of being submerged by physicality; the 'unholy libido' as opposed to the 'divine' will.

This tension also characterises the modernist epiphany and is a particularly noteworthy feature of modernist short fiction. In Joyce's short stories, however, rather than transforming experience into truth, the epiphany both obscures and corrupts the characters who experience its ostensibly transformative power. As Zack Bowen has argued, it is in *Dubliners* in particular that the epiphany offers insights into characters' 'own follies and ludicrousness'. Unlike Stephen Dedalus, moreover, most of these characters are 'certainly not artists' (1981: 105). This observation applies equally to the two volumes of Sinclair's short stories discussed in this chapter. The 'ghosts' of *Uncanny Stories* are likewise not artists; nor is Roly Simpson, who narrates the *Tales Told by Simpson* sequence, and nor are his artist-contemporaries. The irony is that they all believe themselves to be proficient painters and writers, and all in their own ways try to achieve literary or artistic immortality. Sinclair's wit is at its most caustic in this volume, as seen through the tragi-comic depictions of the failures of most of these attempts.

Like *Uncanny Stories*, the *Tales Told by Simpson* sequence also centres upon a failure of sublimation. The volume comprises a series of tales about artistic incompetence and lack of vision, focusing primarily on the failure of the 'genius' of art and artists and of the invariably corrupted forms of the corporeal, textual and aesthetic bodies they own or produce. A noteworthy feature of Simpson's artefacts, both organic and inanimate, is that all are distorted, malformed, dismembered or dead. They are depicted as images of hands, eyes, corpses and mutilated and grotesque bodies. Simpson, the narrator, is a voyeur who revels in the abject distorted physical and textual bodies he analyses in his studio, inadvertently revealing much more about himself than his subjects in the process. His form of sublimation actively embraces abjection and a sense of power over the bodies of others. His relentless, voyeuristic gaze is cynical and sardonic, but also selective, as it rarely extends to himself. That Simpson 'collects' people as well as artefacts, for instance, is clear from his observation in 'The Collector' that 'I have known many collectors of celebrities' (49). As the stories unfold, Simpson himself is revealed as just such a collector: a hoarder of a salacious body of texts and visual artefacts which all in some way exploit the human subjects on which they are based.

As Simpson reveals in a rare moment of self-awareness in the story of 'The Pictures', his own artistic productions are mediocre and consistently hampered by his failure of vision. Ironically, however, his stories present fascinating case studies of the subjects he tries unsuccessfully to paint. Simpson's artist's couch is the couch of the psychoanalyst: his visual art is inadequate but he draws highly skilled, insightful textual portraits of his subjects – himself included – within the body of stories itself. The irony of these tales is that their failure of sublimation in the artistic sphere allow for successful textual illustrations.

Like the *Uncanny Stories*, Simpson's tales focus on the disavowal of the physical corpus and the idea that sublimation is cultural as well as the deflection of an individual's physical desires. In this idea of sublimation Sinclair digresses from Freud's assertion that 'primordial sexual desire' is 'the one and only libido', preferring Jung's sense that sexuality is 'only one among many aspects and functions of the libido' (Freud 1959: 193; Sinclair 1916: 120). For Sinclair, '[a]ll religion, all art, all literature, all science are sublimations in various stages of perfection'; in short, 'civilisation is one vast system of sublimations' (1916a: 119). Significantly, Kristeva also identifies abjection as intrinsic to culture and aesthetics, and to avant-garde and modernist literature in particular. As she argues, all literature is located on the fragile border 'where identities (subject/object, etc.) do not exist or only barely so – [. . .] metamorphosed, altered, abject' (1982: 207).

Likewise, for Kristeva the abject and abjection are 'the primers of my culture' (1982: 2) and in *Tales Told by Simpson* the connection between the physical and textual corpus is presented through the cultural, artistic sphere. Conveyed through Simpson's detached, sardonic gaze, these artistic bodies typically displace the 'spiritual' supplanting of physical experience through images of eyes and gazing; images of abjection; images of failed sublimation which are bound up not with the cerebral, spiritual realm of reality but with physical, corporeal disgust. Such images are prevalent in 'The Pictures', which takes the form of Simpson presenting a series of disjointed and distasteful sketches to an unseen listener, to whom he confides that he has 'little use' for his 'insignificant' model, Markham (119). By his own account, the interest of the sketches 'doesn't lie in their cleverness' but in the fact that examining them in sequence will ultimately reveal 'the gradual putting together of a man' (119). The man revealed is primarily Simpson himself. As a painter and a narrator he recreates, reforms and depicts Markham with increasing contempt and disgust, presenting him at first through a series of mutilated body parts as represented in his sketches:

> First of all there are only bits of him – not even that, bits of his clothes, a boot, a sleeve, a trouser leg. Then *he* comes – a hand, a foot, dozens of them. [. . .] Then the figure – every conceivable posture, and all spontaneous. Then his face –

> The faces frighten you, do they? They used to frighten me, some of them. (121)

The narrative is a mimesis of the sketches themselves, anticipating Kristeva's emphasis in *Powers of Horror* upon abjection residing in liminal, border states, '[w]ithin the blanks that separate dislocated themes (like the limbs of a fragmented body)' (1982: 49). Although Simpson's form of abjection differs from Harriott Leigh's failure of sublimation and consequent denial of absolute reality, the broken, elliptical narrative style of this passage is reminiscent of Stephen Dedalus's fragmented, ambiguous anti-epiphanies. Not only does its language frequently reveal a failure of insight rather than an ultimate, transcendental reality, it obscures revelation and is vested in the corporeal rather than the spiritual.

It is noteworthy that in *Stephen Hero*, Dedalus's first definition of the epiphany is inspired by an elliptical, enigmatic passage comprising fragments of conversation between a man and a woman, who concludes by telling him 'O . . . but you're . . . ver . . . ry . . . wick . . . ed . . .' (216). Whilst the full meaning of this fractured exchange remains inaccessible, its mildly flirtatious tone and the status of Dedalus as watcher and listener is suggestive of an element of voyeurism on the part of the protagonist and, by implication, the reader. From its first inception, then, the language of the epiphany is associated with the discourse of sexuality.

The connection between epiphany, voyeurism and abjection is also suggestive in Kristeva's observation that voyeurism 'accompanies the writing of abject' in 'a catharsis of looking', serving as 'a structural necessity in the constitution of object relation, showing up every time the object shifts towards the abject' (1982: 46). It is the nakedness of his subject, Markham, that enables Simpson to reveal what is truly abject in his observations of him: 'I found that his precise type of insignificance was jolly difficult to draw. There was something subtle and elusive, as they say, about his character'; an essence of Markham which, for Simpson, 'could only be revealed in its perfection through his whole body' (122). Through this wholeness, the text implies, Simpson is able to capture the 'the horridness of his horrid little soul' (ibid.).

The form of artistic exploitation Simpson indulges in throughout this series is at its most marked in 'The Pictures' and also 'The Pin-Prick', the story of the suicide of Simpson's fellow-artist, May Blissett, in which the body itself becomes the artefact whose story he supplants with his own narrative. Simpson views May's death-scene as having been beautifully stage-managed and 'quite decent':

> She had set the candles, one on each side, one at the head, and one at the foot.
> No, there's nothing stately and ceremonial about a sulphur candle. [...]
> There's a crimson ooze from it when it burns, as if the thing sweated blood before it began its work. (246)

In its theatricality and funereal appearance, the presentation of the corpse in this story is carefully staged by the artist herself but is represented by Simpson in terms distinctly evocative of abjection: the blood and sweat residing on the borders of the body which surround the corpse as the ultimate manifestation of abject bodily waste and emissions. There is, moreover, a blurring of the boundary between the artist's inanimate body and the painting Simpson presents to his observer at the story's outset, bequeathed to him by May and personified by Simpson as a part of its creator:

> a little sensitive, palpitating shred, torn off from her and flung there – all that was left of her. It stands for her mystery, her queerness, her passionate persistence and her pluck. To anybody who knew her the thing's excruciatingly alive. (237)

The artist's 'mystery' refers to the capacity for sublimation, which Simpson distinctly lacks. He contends that whilst May 'couldn't draw', she did nonetheless possess 'a sense of beauty, [...] a sort of magic queerness that was suggested irresistibly even when the things didn't quite come off' (237). May's artistic insights, and the ironic failure of Simpson's own aesthetic vision, is further emphasised by his continual misreading of his subject, whom he is incapable of fully *seeing*.

Likewise, in 'The Pictures', Markham takes revenge against Simpson's exploitation by capitalising upon his own awareness that Simpson's work is mediocre, whilst Markham himself is an artist who does possess a capacity for sublimation. This quality is revealed when Simpson sees Markham out of doors with his canvas, a look of ecstasy on his face, 'plunged deep; immersed in his dream, his vision. He seemed to float, to drift by me in it. Uncanny' (127). Simpson's resulting sketch of Markham as a visionary – 'the only wonderful thing I ever did' – is still, as Simpson recognises, a pale imitation of Markham's work (ibid.). It is, ironically, within the forms of modernist art described by Ezra Pound as the 'cult of ugliness' wherein Simpson sees Markham's value, commenting that '[t]he more I worked at his face, the more I wanted to see and to draw his body, poisoned, stunted and distorted by his soul' (Pound 1935: 45; Sinclair 1930: 122). The forms of Markham, textual, corporeal, physical and spiritual, are here closely interrelated. Moreover, as in Dedalus's original epiphany, Simpson's narrative makes the reader complicit in his voyeurism. He tells his observer Markham 'wouldn't have liked you to see these studies from the nude; but [...] it's the only way you can get at him. And if he'd known how tender you are – I shouldn't show them to you if you weren't' (121).

The exploitative tendency of Simpson is further revealed in this passage, in which Markham's disjointed body becomes the focus of the objectified gaze of Simpson, the unseen observer in his story, and the reader. His art is the product of others' trauma; the means by which his artefacts and collection of stories originally come into being. In 'The Pictures', within the series of sketches which arguably represent the whole volume in concise form, the abject effect of modernist art is illustrated. According to the art historian Hal Foster, this abjection tends in two directions:

> The first is to identify with the abject, to approach it somehow – to probe the wound of trauma, to touch the obscene object-gaze of the real. The second is to represent the condition of abjection in order to provoke its operation – to catch abjection in the act, to make it reflexive, even repellent in its own right. (1996: 114–15)

The *Tales Told by Simpson*, in which sublimation and abjection are each intrinsic to the other as well as to the sexuality, materiality and fragmented narrative forms associated with the modernist epiphany, accord closely with this definition. Simpson's object-gaze is illustrated in 'The Pictures' through his repeated, almost obsessive representations of disjointed, abject physical forms. The more sketches of Markham he reveals, the more his visions manifest as increasingly sadistic and grotesque. These visions culminate in the last two images he conveys textually through his narration: the first of which is the abject form of Markham's wife in the process of dying from starvation; the face 'livid; the lips drawn up stark from the teeth; the eyes staring' because Markham 'would as soon think of selling his wife's honour or his own' than his art (130). The second image Simpson observes is the 'indescribable' purity in Markham's face: 'the impetus of passion and defiance – defiance of death – and, above all, tenderness' (128; 130).

These visions implicitly relate to the juxtaposition of 'bestselling', presumably unsublimated art forms with the purity of vision only possible through 'perfect' sublimation. At the outset of the story Simpson is aware that Markham hates him because, in employing him as his artist's subject, he 'stood between him and starvation' (122). After the death of Markham's wife, Simpson is only able to respond in the language of commercialism: 'There was nothing you could do for him except to pay the doctor and the undertaker. I believe he hated me for that more than ever' (130). The final irony of the story is Simpson's misconception that '[i]t rubbed it into him, you see, that I could do what he couldn't' (ibid.).

In its propensity towards exploitation, Simpson's narrative may thus be read as a satire of the literary marketplace in which he places a significant value on art on the basis of whether or not it is sellable. In 'The Pin-Prick', he refers to 'the poor art' which 'got itself hung', and thus supported May Blissett financially, as 'tactful. It had no embarrassing pretensions [...] you could look at it without sacrificing your sincerity to your politeness' (243). In 'The Pictures' Simpson is eager to boast to Markham when he sells a picture, but Markham dismisses his work as mass-market, 'the kind of picture that *would* sell ... The Gr-reat Bir-ritish Public!' (124).

By contrast, Markham prefers to 'strip and stand naked' on Simpson's platform rather than 'prostitute his genius' by selling pictures (128). In this passage, the language of exploited, invasive forms of physical sexuality is again evoked. Like the metaphoric rapes that characterise the failure of sublimation in *Uncanny Stories*, Markham's resistance to the commercial exploitation he despises in Simpson amounts to a prostitution of his physical, corporeal body as opposed to a violation of his cerebral, artistic genius. Faced with this choice, Markham perversely opts not only to prostitute his own physical body, but to sacrifice the body of his wife to death through starvation rather than violate his own sublimated artistic corpus.

In 'The Pictures', Sinclair's representations of physical and textual bodies through the eyes of Roly Simpson thus raise pertinent questions surrounding the abject art Kristeva designates as modernist. According to Hal Foster, similar abject forms are adopted by contemporary artists who are discontented 'not only with the refinements of sublimation but with the displacements of desire' (1996: 118). The constant countering of sublimation with abjection throughout both *Uncanny Stories* and *Tales Told by Simpson* tends to suggest that for Sinclair, this is also the case. Moreover, Simpson's voyeurism and propensity to revel in abjection is also significant in relation to the options offered by abject art which Foster goes on to question:

> Is this, then, the option that abject art offers us – Oedipal naughtiness or infantile perversion? To act dirty with the secret wish to be spanked, or to wallow in shit with the secret faith that the most defiled might reverse into the most sacred, the most perverse into the most potent? (1996: 118)

These questions are implicitly raised throughout Sinclair's corpus of modernist short fiction, particularly within the two volumes discussed in this chapter. The trope of the abject physical and aesthetic body constantly undercuts the 'sacred' nature of Sinclair's perfect sublimation, which is countered again and again by abject forms of sexuality, desecration and bodily death. The 'pure'; the holy 'will', to use Sinclair's terms, are sacrificed to physicality and sexuality, revealing a constant, morbid fascination which the critic Sandra Kemp has previously linked to modernist women's short fiction specifically: 'the idea that we are extinguished by, overwhelmed by, our bodies' (1990: 109). Perhaps, as Kemp speculates, pornography of death as well as sex exists because 'the essence of the obscene [is] that we are nothing but bodies' (ibid.).

Sinclair's short fiction, I suggest, reveals just such an anxiety in its consistent representations of sublimation and abjection as encapsulated within the motif of transgressing boundaries and transcending bodies. Suffused with abjection, the stories depict the ugliness, decay and disrupted forms of literary modernism through distinctly modernist elliptical syntax and fragmented narratives. Significantly, for Kristeva it is the language of avant-garde literature specifically which represents 'the ultimate coding of our crises, of our most intimate and most serious apocalypses. Hence its nocturnal power, "the great darkness"' (1982: 208). Thus situating May Sinclair within a modernist context reveals that her abject writings on sublimation offer fresh potential for investigating possible influences on the key modernist aesthetics of mysticism and transcendent insight. Her stories resonate with the pertinent contemporary intellectual discourses of her era, across the rich, interdisciplinary fields of psychoanalysis, philosophy, fiction and modernism, and illustrate the value of her contribution to the radical contemporary shift in literary representations of the textual, corporeal and conscious forms of the modernist subject.

Notes

1. For detailed analyses see Drewery 2011a; Neff 1979, 1983; Pickrem 2016.
2. See O'Connor 1963: 22; Hanson 1985: 55.

Works Cited

Bowen, Zack (1981), 'Joyce and the Epiphany Concept: A New Approach', *Journal of Modern Literature* 9:1, 103–14.

Díaz, José María (2012), 'Allegory and Fragmentation in Lewis's *The Wild Body* and Barnes's "A Book"', in Joge Sacido (ed.), *Modernism, Postmodernism and the Short Story in English*, New York: Rodopi, 47–76.

Drewery, Claire (2011a), '"The Failure of this Now So Independently

Assertive Reality": Mysticism, Idealism and the Reality Aesthetic in Dorothy Richardson's Short Fiction', *Pilgrimages: A Journal of Dorothy Richardson Studies* 4, 112–36.

Drewery, Claire (2011b), *Modernist Short Fiction by Women: The Liminal in Katherine Mansfield, Dorothy Richardson, May Sinclair and Virginia Woolf*, Burlington, VT and Farnham: Ashgate.

Foster, Hal (1996), 'Obscene, Abject, Traumatic', *October* Vol. 78 (Autumn), 106–24.

Freud, Sigmund [1908] (1959), '"Civilised" Sexual Morality and Modern Nervousness', in *The Standard Edition of the Complete Psychological Works of Sigmund Freud*, vol. 9, trans. James Strachey, London: The Hogarth Press, p. 193.

Freud, Sigmund [1919] (2003), *The Uncanny*, trans. David McLintock, London: Penguin.

Freud, Sigmund (1962), *Three Essays on the History of Sexuality*, trans. James Strachey, New York: Basic Books.

Hanson, Clare (1985), *Short Stories and Short Fictions 1880–1980*, New York: St Martin's Press.

Head, Dominic (1992), *The Modernist Short Story: A Study in Theory and Practice*, Cambridge: Cambridge University Press.

Jacobs, Joshua (2000), 'Joyce's Epiphanic Mode: Material Language and the Representation of Sexuality in *Stephen Hero* and *Portrait*', in *Twentieth Century Literature: A Scholarly and Critical Journal* 46.1 (Spring), 20–33.

Joyce, James [1916] (2000), *A Portrait of the Artist as a Young Man*, ed. Seamus Deane, London: Penguin.

Joyce, James (1944), *Stephen Hero: Part of the First Draft of A Portrait of the Artist as a Young Man*, ed. and intro. T. Spencer, London: Cape.

Kemp, Sandra (1990), '"But how describe a world seen without a self?" Feminism, Fiction and Modernism', *Critical Quarterly* 1 (Spring): 99–121.

Kristeva, Julia (1982), *Powers of Horror: An Essay on Abjection*, New York: Columbia University Press.

March-Russell, Paul (2006), 'Introduction', in May Sinclair (1923), *Uncanny Stories*, Ware: Wordsworth Editions.

Neff, Rebeccah Kinnamon (1983), 'May Sinclair's *Uncanny Stories* as Metaphysical Quest', *English Literature in Transition* 26:3 187–91.

O'Connor, Frank (1963), *The Lonely Voice: A Study of the Short Story*, London: Macmillan.

Pickrem, Faye (2016), 'Disembodying Desire: Ontological Fantasy, Libidinal Anxiety, and the Erotics of Renunciation in May Sinclair', in Rebecca Bowler and Claire Drewery (eds), *May Sinclair: Re-Thinking Minds and Bodies*, Edinburgh: Edinburgh University Press.

Pound, Ezra (1935), *Literary Essays of Ezra Pound*, ed. T. S. Eliot, New York: New Directions.

Raitt, Suzanne (2000), *May Sinclair: A Modern Victorian*, Oxford: Oxford University Press.

Sinclair, May (1914), *The Three Sisters*, London: Hutchinson.

Sinclair, May (1916a), 'Clinical Lecture on Symbolism and Sublimation – I', *The Medical Press and Circular* 153, 118–22.

Sinclair, May (1916b), 'Clinical Lecture on Symbolism and Sublimation – II', *The Medical Press and Circular* 153, 142–5.
Sinclair, May (1917), *A Defence of Idealism: Some Questions and Conclusions*, London: Macmillan.
Sinclair, May (1923), *Uncanny Stories*, London: Hutchinson.
Sinclair, May (1930), *Tales Told by Simpson*, New York: Macmillan.

Notes on Contributors

Charlotte Beyer is Senior Lecturer in English Literature at the University of Gloucestershire. She has published on contemporary literature, including a number of articles and book chapters on women's writing and crime and genre fiction. She is on the Steering Committee for the Crime Studies Network, and on the editorial board for the journal *American, British and Canadian Studies*.

Rebecca Bowler is Lecturer in Twentieth-Century English Literature at Keele University. She is the author of *Literary Impressionism: Vision and Memory in Dorothy Richardson, Ford Madox Ford, H.D., and May Sinclair*, published as part of Bloomsbury's 'Historicizing Modernism' series in 2016. She has published on Richardson, Sinclair, Ford and Mansfield.

Leslie de Bont is a *professeure agrégée* who teaches English at the faculty of psychology in the University of Nantes, France. Her PhD dissertation is entitled '"Like anecdotes from a case-book": dialogues entre discours théoriques et représentations du singulier dans les romans de May Sinclair' (Paris 3 University). She has given talks and published articles about May Sinclair, including 'From the Priest to the Therapist: Secrecy, Language and Technique in Ford's *A Call* and May Sinclair's *Anne Severn and the Fieldings*' in *The Edwardian Ford Madox Ford* (Rodopi, 2013) and '"I was the only one who wasn't quite sane": être femme, épouse, mère et artiste dans *The Creators* (1910) de May Sinclair' in *Cahiers victoriens et édouardiens* 79 (2014).

Claire Drewery is a Senior Lecturer at Sheffield Hallam University with research interests in modernism, short fiction and women's writing. Her book *Modernist Short Fiction by Women: The Liminal in Katherine*

Mansfield, Dorothy Richardson, May Sinclair and Virginia Woolf was published in 2011. She has contributed chapters to Jochen Achilles and Ina Bergman (eds), *Liminality and the Short Story* (Routledge 2015) and Dominic Head (ed.), *The Cambridge History of the English Short Story* (2016). She is currently working on a monograph on modernism, performativity and visual cultures.

Emma Liggins is Senior Lecturer in English Literature at Manchester Metropolitan University. She has published broadly on the New Woman and the *fin de siècle* in journals such as *Women's Writing, Literature and History* and *Victorian Periodicals Review*. Recent publications include *George Gissing, the Working Woman and Urban Culture* (Ashgate, 2006) and *Odd Women? Spinsters, Lesbians and Widows in British Women's Fiction, 1850s–1930s* (Manchester University Press, 2014). Her chapter on modernist women's ghost stories appeared in Emma Young (ed.), *British Women Short Story Writers* (Edinburgh University Press, 2015).

Terri Mullholland holds a doctorate in English from the University of Oxford. Her teaching and research interests are in early twentieth-century women's writing, modernism and the intersections of literature and spatial theory. She has published articles on Jean Rhys and Dorothy Richardson, and is currently completing a monograph on literary representations of women living in boarding houses in the interwar period.

Faye Pickrem is currently completing her doctoral dissertation on May Sinclair at York University, Toronto, for which she received a Social Sciences and Humanities Research Council of Canada Doctoral Fellowship. As Lecturer in the Cultural Studies Programme and in the English Department at Trent University, Faye taught twentieth-century literature, cultural theory and drama. Faye was shortlisted for the Best Lecturer in Canada Award in 2006. She is co-editor, with Linda Hutcheon, of two Special Issues of the *University of Toronto Quarterly*: *Cultural Studies in Canada* 64.4 (Fall 1995) and *Cultural Studies: Disciplinarity and Divergence* 65.2 (Spring 1996).

Suzanne Raitt is Professor of English at the College of William & Mary. Her books include *May Sinclair: A Modern Victorian* (Oxford, 2000), *Vita and Virginia: The Work and Friendship of V.Sackville-West and Virginia Woolf* (Oxford, 1993) and *Virginia Woolf's 'To the Lighthouse'* (St Martin's, 1990). She also co-edited a collection of essays with Trudi Tate called *Women's Fiction and the Great War* (Oxford, 1997), and in 1995 she published an edited collection of essays on lesbian criticism, *Volcanoes and Pearl Divers* (Onlywomen Press).

Editions include a Norton Critical Edition of Virginia Woolf's *Jacob's Room* in 2007, Katherine Mansfield's *Something Childish and Other Stories* for Penguin in 1996 and Virginia Woolf's *Night and Day* for Oxford World's Classics in 1992. She has published numerous essays and articles in journals including *Modernism/Modernity* and *History Workshop Journal*, and for twelve years she was on the editorial collective of *Feminist Studies*. She is currently working on a scholarly edition of Virginia Woolf's *Orlando*, co-edited with Ian Blyth, for Cambridge University Press, and completing a book called *Waste and Efficiency in British Culture, 1864–1922*.

Sanna Melin Schyllert is a doctoral researcher at the University of Westminster, currently working on a thesis about sacrifice in modernist women's fiction with a focus on prose works by Mary Butts, H.D. and May Sinclair.

Elise Thornton received her BA from New York University and her MA and PhD from King's College London. She works in the modernist period with particular interest in Virginia Woolf, women's writing, gender and artistry, modernism and empire and the Great War. Her doctoral thesis, '"I'm an artist, sir. And a woman": Representations of the Woman Artist in Modernist Literature', examined the intersection of modernism, gender and creativity in the work of Woolf, Dorothy Richardson, May Sinclair and Vita Sackville-West.

Wendy Truran is an English doctoral student at the University of Illinois Urbana-Champaign (UIUC), specialising in twentieth-century British and Irish literature. She earned her BA in English Literature and MA in Contemporary Literary Studies from the University of Lancaster, England. Wendy had a successful career in academic publishing for ten years at publishers such as Brunner-Routledge and SAGE Publications before returning to graduate study in 2011. Currently she is serving as the Assistant to the Director of Undergraduate Studies at UIUC.

Index

abjection, 13, 213, 215–16, 217, 220–4, 226, 227
Adler, Alfred, 63, 121, 123
Adorno, Theodor, 110
Ahmed, Sara, *The Promise of Happiness*, 81, 82, 94
Aldington, Richard, 24
Anninos, Charalambos, 149
Armstrong, Tim, 4

baby-farming, 12, 165–71
Badmington, Neil, 3
Battersby, Christine, 24, 29, 31, 55
Baudrillard, Jean, 135–6
Beale, Dorothea, 6, 41–2, 43, 44, 55
Bell, Michael, 3, 4
Benjamin, Walter, 99–100
 phantasmagoria, 100
Bergson, Henri, 68
Beyer, Charlotte, 12
BLAST!, 146, 147
Boll, Theophilus, 1, 2, 7, 13, 22, 135
Bollas, Christopher, 129–30, 132, 133, 134
Bont, Leslie de, 7
Bowen, Zack, 223
Bowlby, John
 Attachment and Loss, 64
 'The Nature of the Child's Tie to His Mother', 64
Bowler, Rebecca, 5–6, 11, 23
Brittain, Vera, 198
 Testament of Youth, 196
Brontë, Charlotte, 25, 26, 43, 123
Brontë sisters, 24, 33, 149

Brown, Penny, 31, 169
Browning, Elizabeth Barrett, 25
Browning, Robert, 25
Buck-Morss, Susan, 99
Bynner, Witter, 25
Byron, George Gordon, 48

Cardinal, Agnes, 195
Certeau, Michel de, 59, 109
Cheltenham Ladies' College, 6, 39, 41–2, 43
Cheltenham Ladies' College Magazine, 43
Childs, Peter, 3, 157
Coe, Jonathan, 23
Cossins, Annie, 156, 165, 166, 167
Craton, Lillian, 160, 165

Darwin, Charles Robert, 79–80
 Darwinism, 151
 Origin of Species, 152
Dent, J. M., 24
Dent, Olive, 196
Dial, the, 24, 25
Diaz, José María, 217
Doan, Laura, 200–1, 205
Downey, Georgina, 114
Dowson, Jane, 24
Drewery, Claire, 9, 13, 23, 32, 135

Egoist, the, 11, 24
Eliot, T. S., 24
Engels, Friedrich, 3
English Review, the, 24, 27
epiphany, modernist, 13, 213, 214–15, 216, 217, 223, 225, 226

Euripides, 55, 109
  The Bacchæ, 52, 54
Eysteinsson, Ástráður, 6

feminism, 14
  first-wave, 190
  women's education, 39–42
Finn, Howard, 29, 31, 32
Flint, F. S., 24
Ford, Ford Madox, *Parade's End*, 142
Forster, E. M., 8
Fortnightly Review, the, 24
Foster, Hal, 227, 228
Fowler, Rowena, 49
Freud, Sigmund, 3, 4, 7, 27, 59–60, 67, 68–9, 74, 122, 123, 124
  afterwardsness, 69
  'Analysis Terminable and Interminable', 60, 67
  '"Civilised" Sexual Morality and Modern Nervousness', 213–14
  dreams and symbols, 60, 71, 73
  'Mourning and Melancholia', 208
  Oedipus complex, 64
  Project for a Scientific Psychology, 69
  Three Essays on the History of Sexuality, 220
  The Uncanny, 13, 214, 218–19, 220
  'The Wolf Man', 71

Gardiner, E. Norman, 149–50
Gaskell, Elizabeth, 24
God, religion, 30, 82, 91, 93–4, 179, 214, 220, 224
  the Absolute, 90, 119, 122, 133, 135, 214, 219
  Anglicanism, 66
Goldman, Dorothy, 195
Greek Accidence, 47
Green, T. H., *Prolegomena to Ethics*, 185
Grube, Dennis, 171
Gunn, Simon, 100

Haeckel, Ernst, *History of Evolution*, 152
Hall, Radclyffe, *The Well of Loneliness*, 204, 205, 208
Harraden, Beatrice, 32
Harrison, Jane, *Prolegomena to Greek Religion*, 180
Hattaway, Judith, 195
H.D. (Hilda Doolittle), 24

Head, Dominic, 217
Health and Strength, 141–2, 142–4, 151
Hegel, G. W. F., 11, 120, 136
  The Phenomenology of Spirit, 119
Henrichs, Albert, 52
Hirsch, Marianne, 66, 159–60, 164
Homer, 49
  Iliad, 46
Howarth, Herbert, 10
humanism, 3
Humm, Maggie, 64

Ibsen, Henrik, *A Doll's House*, 159
idealism, philosophical, 14, 184, 185
Imagists, imagism, 24, 52, 53
impressionism, 54

Jacobs, Joshua, 215, 217, 218
James, William, James-Lange theory of emotions, 79–80
Johnson, George, 10, 23, 63, 67, 185
Jones, Charlotte, 23
Jones, Ernest, 134
Joyce, James
  Dubliners, 223
  Finnegans Wake, 121
  A Portrait of the Artist as a Young Man, 214, 216, 217
  Stephen Hero, 214, 225
  Ulysses, 10–11
Jung, Carl G., 59, 64, 67, 122, 123, 124, 180
  Elektra complex, 64
  Psychology of the Unconscious, 72

Kane, Julie, 8
Keats, Gwendoline, 32
Kemp, Sandra, 229
Kent, Susan Kingsley, 198, 204
Klaver, Claudia C., 158, 160, 173
Klein, Melanie, 64, 65, 67
  'Love, Guilt, and Reparation', 67
Kristeva, Julia, 13, 122, 124, 134, 228
  Powers of Horror, 213, 215–16, 217, 218, 221–2, 224–5, 229
Kunka, Andrew, 14, 23, 196, 204, 207

Lacan, Jacques, 119, 120
Lange, Carl, James-Lange theory of emotions, 79–80
Lawrence, D. H., 23, 204
Lewis, Percy Wyndham, 146
  Creation, 147

Lewis, Pericles, 5
Liggins, Emma, 12, 13, 170
Ling, Pehr Henrik, 142
Liska, Vivian, 6
Little Review, the, 24
Lombroso, Cesare, 61
Loy, Mina, 'Feminist Manifesto', 79, 83, 91, 96

Maenads, 51, 52
Maleuvre, Didier, 111
Mansfield, Katherine, 7
   'Ask No Questions' (review of *The Romantic*), 204
   'Bliss', 156, 160–1
March-Russell, Paul, 217
Martindale, Philippa, 23, 24, 63, 64, 67
Marx, Karl, 3, 4
Maudsley, Henry, 40, 61–2
   Body and Mind, 152
   Physiology and Pathology of Mind, 152
   Responsibility in Mental Disease, 152
Meyer, Albert, 149
Miracky, James, 23–4
Moretti, Franco, 119
Mosimann, Elizabeth, 24, 168
Mullholland, Terri, 9
Munro, Hector, 194
mystic; mysticism; mystical ecstasy, 4, 5, 7, 8, 14, 29, 30, 123–4, 133, 219, 229

Nagler, Linda Fregni, 162, 164
   The Hidden Mother, 161

Olympic Games, 149
O'Mahoney, Mike, 149
Orwell, George, 109
Ouditt, Sharon, 196–7, 201

Parkes, Adam, 10
Patmore, Coventry, 'The Angel in the House', 10, 50, 84, 87, 96*n*, 127, 139, 157, 161, 165
Pease, Allison, 135, 149, 169
Phillips, Terry, 157, 161, 172
Pickrem, Faye, 11, 31, 215
Pinch, Adela, 135
Pollitt, Katha, 23, 93
Pope, Alexander, 46
Potter, Rachel, 10
Pound, Ezra, 24, 147, 171
   Vorticism, 146

Proust, Marcel, 110
psychoanalysis; psychoanalytic theory, 7, 29, 60, 64, 74, 86, 178, 184

Radford, Jean, 135
Raikes, Elizabeth, 41
Raitt, Suzanne, 2, 4, 5, 14, 22, 23, 42, 43, 84, 98, 105, 114, 121, 130, 135, 157, 162, 206, 222
Ribot, Théodule, *Heredity*, 152
Richardson, Dorothy, 24
Romantics; Romanticism, 48–9, 53
Rosenman, Ellen Bayuk, 158, 160, 173
Rouse, W. H. D., 44
Russell, Bertrand, 80

Schyllert, Sanna Melin, 12
Sharp, Evelyn, 32
Shelley, Percy Bysshe, 46
Shin, Kuno, 67
Showalter, Elaine, 67
Shrock, Alice Almond, 162
Sinclair, Amelia, 42
Sinclair, May
   Audrey Craven, 120, 177, 179–80
   'Clinical Lectures on Symbolism and Sublimation', 7, 13, 59, 143, 222
   'The Collector', 223
   The Combined Maze, 11, 127–8, 139–51, 154
   'The Cosmopolitan', 124–7
   The Creators: A Comedy, 5, 7, 9, 60, 61, 62–3, 65, 149
   A Defence of Idealism, 5, 7, 22, 29, 59, 66, 67, 80, 82, 95, 185, 216
   'A Defence of Men', 12, 177–8, 190
   The Divine Fire, 5, 7, 9, 98–114, 127, 177, 180, 186
   'Fame', 9
   Feminism, 87, 122–3, 179, 185, 187, 190
   'The Finding of the Absolute', 29, 30
   'The Flaw in the Crystal', 177, 180, 216, 217–18, 222
   'If the Dead Knew', 27, 215
   'The Intercessor', 22–3, 27, 32–3
   A Journal of Impressions in Belgium, 13, 194, 200–2, 206
   Life and Death of Harriett Frean, 5, 12, 22, 32, 66, 79, 82, 94, 123, 135, 149, 156–73
   Mary Olivier: A Life, 5, 6, 7, 8, 11, 21, 22, 23, 30–1, 39, 44, 60, 64,

Sinclair, May (*continued*)
    65–6, 68–70, 79, 82, 85, 89–94, 132–5, 139, 179, 180, 214
  Mr and Mrs Nevill Tyson, 65, 66
  'The Nature of the Evidence', 26
  The New Idealism, 7, 59
  'The Pictures', 223–4, 226
  'The Pin-Prick', 9, 225–6, 228
  'Portrait of My Uncle', 61
  'Psychological Types', 7
  'The Reputation of Ezra Pound', 24
  The Romantic, 63, 195, 200, 203, 206–7, 209, 210
  'Superseded', 63
  Tales Told by Simpson, 9, 213, 214, 223, 224, 227
  The Three Brontës, 24
  The Three Sisters, 22, 79, 82, 84, 93, 123, 128–31, 149, 150, 154, 215
  'The Token', 23, 26, 27, 32, 33
  The Tree of Heaven, 12, 151, 177, 180, 181–7, 189–91, 195, 196, 199, 200, 208, 209, 210
  Uncanny Stories, 8, 22, 26, 27, 213, 214, 216, 218, 221, 223, 225, 228
  'The Victim', 23, 26
  'Villa Désirée', 23
  'The Way of Sublimation', 7, 59, 63, 64, 66, 180
  'Where Their Fire Is Not Quenched', 29, 219–22
  'Women's Sacrifices for the War', 189, 194–5, 198, 207–8
  'The Wrackham Memoirs', 9
Smith, Angela K., 199
Smith, Helen Zenna, 204
  Not So Quiet, 205, 210
Smith, William, *Classical Dictionary*, 47
Spencer, Herbert
  First Principles, 152
  The Principles of Biology, 152
  The Principles of Psychology, 152
Spinoza, Baruch, 8, 95
  Ethics, 91–2
Stark, Susanne, 158, 172
Stein, Gertrude, *Autobiography of Alice B. Toklas*, 121
Stone, Gilbert, 208

Strachey, Ray, *The Cause*, 210
stream of consciousness, 5, 21, 29, 52, 53
sublimation, 3, 4, 11, 13, 14, 66, 88–9, 120, 121, 124, 128, 133, 135, 178, 213, 214–15, 216, 218, 220–4, 226–7, 229
supernatural, 26, 184

Tate, Trudi, 206
Thornton, Elise, 6–7, 152
Thrall, James, 130, 135
Thurston, Luke, 24, 27, 127, 135
Tiersten, Lisa, 113
Troy, Michele, 9, 14, 23
Truran, Wendy, 8
Tylee, Claire, 196, 209

Vadillo, Ana Parejo, 161
vers libre, 47, 52
Vim, 141–2

Wallace, Diana, 110
war, 12–13, 14
  women's war work, 194–212
  World War I, 80, 177
Watson, Janet S. K., 194
Wheeler, Kathleen, 108
Whitman, Walt, 51
Williams, Raymond, 2–3
Wilson, Cheryl A., 49–50
Women War Workers, 196
Woolf, Virginia, 8, 39, 44, 49
  attitude to May Sinclair, 21
  'The Feminine Note in Fiction', 47
  Mrs Dalloway, 156
  'On Not Knowing Greek', 45–6, 51
  'Professions for Women', 9–10
  A Room of One's Own, 40–1
  Three Guineas, 41, 195
  To the Lighthouse, 156, 161
  'Two Women', 40
Wright, Almroth, 87

Zach, Natan, 53
Zegger, Hrisey D., 13, 22
Žižek, Slavov, *The Plague of Fantasies*, 120–1
Zweiniger-Bargielowska, Ina, 141, 144

EU representative:
Easy Access System Europe
Mustamäe tee 50, 10621 Tallinn, Estonia
Gpsr.requests@easproject.com

www.ingramcontent.com/pod-product-compliance
Lightning Source LLC
Chambersburg PA
CBHW070938240426
43667CB00036B/2309